Performance Interventions

Series Editors: **Elaine Aston**, Universi
University of California, Irvine

Performance Interventions is a series o
theatre, performance, and visual cultu
to the radical and political potential of the arts in oui
or give consideration to performance and to visual culture from the past
crucial to a social and political present. *Performance Interventions* moves trans-
versally across artistic and ideological boundaries to publish work that promotes
dialogue between practitioners and academics, and interactions between performance communities, educational institutions, and academic disciplines.

Titles include:

Alan Ackerman and Martin Puchner (*editors*)
AGAINST THEATRE
Creative Destructions on the Modernist Stage

Elaine Aston and Geraldine Harris (*editors*)
FEMINIST FUTURES?
Theatre, Performance, Theory

Maaike Bleeker
VISUALITY IN THE THEATRE
The Locus of Looking

Lynette Goddard
STAGING BLACK FEMINISMS
Identity, Politics, Performance

Leslie Hill and Helen Paris (*editors*)
PERFORMANCE AND PLACE

Amelia Howe Kritzer
POLITICAL THEATRE IN POST-THATCHER BRITAIN
New Writing: 1995–2005

Melissa Sihra (*editor*)
WOMEN IN IRISH DRAMA
A Century of Authorship and Representation

Performance Interventions
Series Standing Order ISBN 978–1–4039–4443–6 Hardback
978–1–4039–4444–3 Paperback
(*outside North America only*)

You can receive future titles in this series as they are published by placing a
standing order. Please contact your bookseller or, in case of difficulty, write to us
at the address below with your name and address, the title of the series and the
ISBN quoted above.

Customer Services Department, Macmillan Distribution Ltd, Houndmills,
Basingstoke, Hampshire RG21 6XS, England

Máire Hastings as Agnes and Stella McCusker as Julie in the 1994 Abbey Theatre production of *The Mai* by Marina Carr. Peacock Stage. Photo: by kind permission of Amelia Stein

Women in Irish Drama

A Century of Authorship and Representation

Edited by

Melissa Sihra

Foreword by

Marina Carr

First published 2007
This paperback edition first published 2009 by
PALGRAVE MACMILLAN

Palgrave Macmillan in the UK is an imprint of Macmillan Publishers Limited,
registered in England, company number 785998, of Houndmills, Basingstoke,
Hampshire RG21 6XS.

Palgrave Macmillan in the US is a division of St Martin's Press LLC,
175 Fifth Avenue, New York, NY 10010.

Palgrave Macmillan is the global academic imprint of the above companies
and has companies and representatives throughout the world.

Palgrave® and Macmillan® are registered trademarks in the United States,
the United Kingdom, Europe and other countries.

ISBN-13: 978-0-230-00647-8 hardback
ISBN-10: 0-230-00647-7 hardback
ISBN-13: 978-0-230-57791-6 paperback
ISBN-10: 0-230-57791-1 paperback

This book is printed on paper suitable for recycling and made from fully
managed and sustained forest sources. Logging, pulping and manufacturing
processes are expected to conform to the environmental regulations of the
country of origin.

A catalogue record for this book is available from the British Library.

Library of Congress Cataloging-in-Publication Data
Women in Irish drama : a century of authorship and representation/edited
    by Melissa Sihra ; foreword by Marina Carr.
        p. cm. — (Performance interventions)
    A collection of essays about Irish women playwrights.
    Includes bibliographical references and index.
    ISBN-13: 978-0-230-00647-8 (cloth) 978-0-230-57791-6 (pbk)
    1. English drama—Irish authors—History and criticism. 2. English
    drama—Women authors—History and criticism. 3. English drama—
    20th century—History and criticism. 4. Women in literature. 5. Women
    and literature—Ireland—History—20th century. 6. Feminism and
    literature—Ireland—History—20th century. I. Sihra, Melissa, 1973–
    PR8789.W58 2007
    822'.91099287—dc22   2006047822

10   9   8   7   6   5   4   3   2   1
18 17 16 15 14 13 12 11 10 09

Printed and bound in Great Britain by
CPI Antony Rowe, Chippenham and Eastbourne

For my Mother, Margaret, and Grandmother, Kathleen

Oh, whatever men may say
Ours is the wide and open way.

Oh, whatever men may dream
We have the blue air and the stream.

Men have got their towers and walls,
We have cliffs and waterfalls.

Oh, whatever men may do
Ours is the gold air and the blue.

Men have got their pomp and pride –
All the green world is on our side.

Women's Rights,
Eva Gore-Booth, 1929

Contents

List of Illustrations

Foreword

Marina Carr

If you asked anyone, who are the women in Irish Theatre for the last one hundred years, I think you would be hard pressed to get a response beyond Lady Gregory and Maud Gonne. Playwrights? A blank. Designers? Another blank. Directors? A complete blank until you wander down to the eighties. One wonders why this is. Yes, there is the gender question. Yes, there is the whole history of the role of women in Irish society. There is all of that but there is also The Theatre itself. Is there something so public about the Theatre that seems to frighten women off, or that seems to be against the nature of women? One only has to look at the list of women poets, short-story writers, novelists in this country and abroad to realise that women do not seem to be drawn *en masse* to the theatre as a viable art form.

Why is this? I think there are several reasons. There is the structure of the Theatre, the collaborative nature of actually getting a play on, all the disparate voices, opinions, inputs that go into the producing of a play. There is the very public exposure of rehearsal and performance which goes against the nature of how women have been traditionally perceived. And sometimes against how women see themselves. There is the domestic factor. If you are child bearing, cooking, cleaning, night-feeding, how much time do you actually have to devote to the theatre regardless of desire to do so. The Theatre is a demanding art form. It sucks up time like no other form. And this factor, as much as anything I believe, has kept women away in their droves.

It is also incredibly difficult to bring a play to completion. I'm talking from the point of view of playwriting now. It will be three years at least. It will be several drafts. It will be warding off the chorus of voices suggesting change. It will be sifting this disparate chorus and taking the necessary advice and discarding the rest. A gift in itself that is not learnt in a day or a year or a decade.

It is also problematic dealing with the messiness of Theatre. If you write a poem, it stands or falls on the page. Or a novel. Or a short story. Not so with a play because plays are rarely read anymore. A play's survival in this day and age depends upon performance, production, design, lighting, direction. All of these disciplines have to come together at the same time in order for your play to work. It is not enough to have written the thing. You must then be prepared to go on the extraordinary and frequently harrowing journey of play-making and all of the sacrifice of ego that jaunt involves. And your play will rise or fall according to how finely tuned your instruments are, your actors, your director, your set designer, your costume designer, your lighting designer, your audience. It is not an enterprise for the faint-hearted and I think one of the achievements of this book *Women in Irish Drama* is that it reminds us that given all the difficulties for women in Theatre traditionally, so many actually managed to work in it.

The joy of this book is the naming of these vanished women. Women we didn't even know existed in Irish Theatre. Who is Margaret O'Leary? Dorothy Macardle? Helen Waddell? Alice Milligan? Teresa Deevy? Patricia O'Connor? Who are these women? Where are their plays? Why have we never heard of them until now? How did they slip through the net? Are their plays any good? This will be the next very important question which follows the retrieval of these women from obscurity.

Does the work stand up? I certainly hope it does. It would provide us with several role models instantly. Irish women who have written for the Theatre long before we started to write. Playwrights whose work we could visit to learn something.

Let us hope the plays themselves will stand the brutal test of time. This will be the next stage of the journey. But for now the naming, the announcing, the retrieval is the thing.

Preface

You are about to read an extraordinary collection of essays about Irish Women playwrights. Perhaps it would be better to say 'a collection of essays about extraordinary Irish Women playwrights'. No matter where the adjective goes, what it registers is a sense of discovery and surprise at the richness and complexity of the writing of Irish women writers in the twentieth century. Most scholars of theatre and avid theatre-goers will have heard of Lady Gregory and associated her with early Irish Nationalism. Others will have encountered contemporary writers such as Marina Carr or Marie Jones whose work is widely produced internationally in this new century. But few will know in any detail many of the women in between. The Appendix lists over 250 playwrights, making a large archival contribution to theatre studies. In addition to expanding the archive, Melissa Sihra gives us rich performance and textual analyses by a range of Irish scholars, and provides contextual 'Interchapters' of cultural and theatrical information to aid her readers' grasp of the roles these plays have had in the unfolding histories of the Republic and Northern Ireland.

This is also a work of feminist scholarship in a moment too often considered post-feminist – not only because the volume is a project of recovery and documentation of the elided contributions of women to Irish arts and letters, but also because the volume disentangles real women from the mythical figures of female-as-nation, as mother, as abject that have populated accounts of the Irish stage. Sometimes these are historical women, such as Lady Gregory, whose co-authorship of *Kathleen ni Houlihan* went unacknowledged until 1988. Sihra writes, 'Yeats's attitude to Lady Gregory throughout the course of their acquaintance and collaborations clearly highlights gendered issues of authorship and authority, as well as the overall disempowerment of women in mainstream channels of artistic expression.' Sometimes these are fictional women who, like Stewart Parker's figure of the Phantom Bride in *Northern* Star, are able to transcend time and point up gender energies and their differences. Moreover, the vibrant work of younger women playwrights challenges patriarchy in ways that make it clear that independent and agential female figures are reconfiguring what it means to be Irish in the twenty-first century.

For me, a US scholar with little direct experience of the Republic and none at all of Northern Ireland, the most exciting essays introduce previously invisible women writing in the early part of the century, taking part in politics and suffrage, (Geraldine Cummins and Susanne Day), or going to prison and participating in the Republican hunger strike (Dorothy Macardle). These essays reminded me of recent work by Maggie Gale on British women writers of the 1920s and 1930s and Christine Gray's work on African American women writers before 1930 – scholarship of recovery, surely, but also of affirmation of an alternative 'tradition' or counter-canons, a concept Sihra develops in her introduction to the volume.

The familiar themes and stereotypes of Irish drama appear in this volume in order to be interrogated, contested and transformed. Many of the plays treat ironically or contest the linkage between women's bodies and the nation, and in Brian Singleton's words, 'de-essentialize the new woman and her position'. If not all characters escape from the confines of the past, the writers shape their dramaturgy to reveal the structures which constrain them. Marina Carr, preferring tragedy and therefore the downward arc leading toward death in *By the Bog of Cats...* also gestures toward apotheosis. Indeed, Melissa Sihra writes about the effects of her plays that 'Carr's conceptual spaces of otherness forge rooms where enactments of alterity are possible and female expressiveness can begin to take place', thereby reminding us that the effect or affect of a particular dramaturgy may be different from its literal trajectory.

Another interesting aspect of *Women in Irish Drama* is the inclusion of selected male writers (such as Stewart Parker) within the volume. Often, feminist scholarship is concerned with bringing forth women's voices about women's writing – and I myself have argued that that is appropriate to a political project of correcting the imbalance of representation of women scholars as well as artists. However, masculinity studies and treatments of gender differentials have contributed to a fuller understanding of the entire nexus of gender and sexualities, and several of the essays in this volume enrich its overall impact by focusing on male writers. Anna McMullan, well-known Beckett scholar, contributes a study of Beckett's early women characters from the 1930s and 1940s in order to argue that gendered embodiment is part and parcel of Beckett's developing form and 'the engine or dynamic of a gendered imaginary'. She also points out that Beckett's deployment of gender can provide a key to understanding the way gender functions in later post-independence male writers such as Brian Friel or Tom Murphy.

Sexuality – gay sexuality – is less represented in the texts and discussions that make up the volume than one might imagine. The Irish main stages have not fully explored the theme of women's sexual love for women. While it might be easy to speculate on the effects of the Catholic Church on the repression of homosexuality and lesbian sexuality in particular, it is also a matter of legality: homosexuality was only decriminalized in 1993. When Frank McGuinness wrote *Innocence* for the Gate theatre in the 1980s, he reportedly received threats. My search for the missing lesbians led me to the slight gesture toward female/female desire in Stella Feehily's *Duck* (in Brian Singleton's essay), and also to Emma Donoghue's plays listed in the appendix. More satisfying was Eamonn Jordan's essay on women characters in plays by Frank McGuinness. Not only is McGuinness a male playwright who dares in his work to figure male homosexuality, he also surpasses his male peers in creating female characters that 'deliberate, perform, accuse and fail in the same way that his male characters do'. Thus examining male writers alongside female writers provides a rich and complex account of gender representation and its intersection with sexuality.

At a recent six-campus teleconference at the University of California, graduate students asked Marina Carr about whether or not she feels a responsibility to counter patriarchy and put forth female themes in her plays. 'Absolutely not!' she responded. 'The writer can't do that, can't carry that. We tell stories and it's up to you critics and scholars to see what they might say or not about women and patriarchy and such things. It's up to you!' Sihra seems to have taken that to heart in this book, which brings together a group of theatre scholars who are able to interrogate representations by/of Irish women and draw some conclusions about what they might collectively achieve.

Janelle Reinelt

Acknowledgments

I would like to extend my gratitude to Anthony Roche, Janelle Reinelt and Brian Singleton, who were immensely supportive in the early stages of this project. I would like to thank Hugh Odling-Smee, curator of the Performing Arts Archive at the Linen Hall Library, for his help with the Appendix, images and manuscript information. I also wish to thank Mairéad Delaney at the Abbey Theatre for her huge efforts in sourcing images and also for her input into the Appendix. Further gratitude goes to Amelia Stein, Tom Lawlor, Chris Hill, Ann Patten, Rob Reid and Colum O'Riordan for their generosity, expertise and advice with images. I would also like to thank Bróna Olwill and Sandra McDermott at the National Photographic Archive of the National Library of Ireland for their efforts in sourcing and providing images for the volume. For her tireless work on compiling the contemporary section of the Appendix, I wish to extend thanks to my Research Assistant Rhona Trench. For their contributions to the Appendix, I wish to thank Patrick Lonergan, Paul Murphy, Elizabeth Mannion, Anthony Roche, Ninian Mellamphy, Ros Dixon, Frances Clarke, Ann M. Butler, Charlotte Headrick, John Hildebidle, Loredana Salis, Patricia Lynch, Joan Dean, Dawn Duncan, Paul Davis, Julie Donovan, Lucy McDiarmid and Maureen Waters. I also wish to thank David Johnston and all of my colleagues at Queen's University Belfast, where I began working on this book.

I wish to extend my gratitude to each writer in this collection, for their knowledge, passion, and commitment to the work and histories of women in Irish drama. I would like to thank my family for their immense encouragement, my father and mother, my friends Sorcha Duggan, Déirdre Carr and Jan Duffy, and Paul Murphy for all his wonderful support, discussions and feedback. I wish to extend immense gratitude to Paula Kennedy, Commissioning Editor of Literature and Performance at Palgrave Macmillan, for publishing the book and for her support and warmth over the last two years. I also wish to thank the Performance Interventions Series Editor Elaine Aston for her insightful feedback and encouragement throughout this enriching experience. I would like to thank Series Editor Bryan Reynolds, and all the staff at Palgrave Macmillan, especially Christabel Scaife, Ruth

Ireland and Helen Craine, for being so helpful during the preparation of the manuscript. Finally, I wish to extend huge thanks to Ann Mulligan and Rhona Greene at Trinity College Dublin and Penny Simmons whose editorial expertise and astute suggestions in the final stages of the volume have enriched the work enormously.

Notes on Contributors

Marina Carr is a playwright. She grew up in County Offaly in the Irish Midlands and graduated from University College Dublin in 1987. She has written 11 plays to date, including *The Mai* (1994), *Portia Coughlan* (1996), *By the Bog of Cats...* (1998), *On Raftery's Hill* (2000), *Ariel* (2002) and *Woman and Scarecrow* (2006). She has been Writer-in-Residence at the Abbey Theatre (1997), Trinity College Dublin (1998) and Dublin City University (1999) and is a member of Aosdána. She received the E. M. Forster Award from the American Academy of Arts and Letters in 2001 and the Irish American Fund Award in 2004. In 2003 Carr held the post of Heimbold Chair of Irish Studies at the University of Villanova. Her plays are published by Faber & Faber and Gallery Press and have been translated into many languages and produced all over the world.

Enrica Cerquoni is Lecturer in Drama Studies at University College, Dublin, where she completed her doctoral dissertation on the plays of Marina Carr and Anne Devlin. Main areas of research include space in the theatrical event, space and gender in theatrical performance, scenography and twentieth-century and contemporary Irish theatre. She has published articles on Augusta Gregory, J. M. Synge, Anne Devlin and Marina Carr.

Lisa Fitzpatrick is Lecturer in Drama Studies at the University of Ulster at Magee and is a graduate of the Drama Centre at the University of Toronto. Her research interests are contemporary Irish theatre, women's writing, intercultural theatre and Canadian theatre.

Olwen Fouéré became an actor 25 years ago and has been based mainly in Ireland. She has performed and toured internationally with many theatre companies in Ireland and the United Kingdom including the Abbey, the Gate, The Royal National Theatre, The Royal Shakespeare Company and the English Stage Company. She has created and performed her own work with Operating Theatre, a music-based theatre company which she co-founded with composer Roger Doyle in 1980.

Velma O'Donoghue Greene is a doctoral candidate in the School of Drama, Trinity College, Dublin. Her thesis explores the dramatic contributions of women in the emergent Irish theatre movement from 1910–25, including the examination of recovered plays by Cork writers Geraldine Cummins, Susanne Day and Hester Travers Smith (nee Dowden). Velma is a drama tutor with Wicklow VEC and also directs and produces theatre.

Eamonn Jordan is Lecturer in Drama Studies at University College, Dublin. He has written extensively on Irish Theatre. His book *The Feast of Famine: The Plays of Frank McGuinness* (Peter Lang, 1997), is the first full-length study on McGuinness's work. In 2000 he edited *Theatre Stuff: Critical Essays on Contemporary Irish Theatre* (Carysfort Press) and in 2001 he co-edited, with Lilian Chambers and Ger Fitzgibbon, *Theatre Talk: Voices of Irish Theatre Practitioners*. He is also co-editor, with Lilian Chambers, of *The Theatre of Martin McDonagh: A World of Savage Stories* (Carysfort Press, 2006).

Cathy Leeney is Subject Leader and Lecturer in Drama Studies at University College Dublin. She is interested in contemporary and twentieth-century Irish theatre, gender in performance and directing for theatre. She is editor of *Seen and Heard: Six New Plays by Irish Women* (Carysfort Press, 2001) and is co-editor, with Anna McMullan, of *The Theatre of Marina Carr; 'before rules was made'* (Carysfort Press, 2003).

Anna McMullan is Chair of Drama at Queen's University Belfast. She is author of *Theatre on Trial: The Later Drama of Samuel Beckett* (Routledge, 1993) and co-editor of *The Theatre of Marina Carr: 'before rules was made'* with Cathy Leeney. She has published many essays on Beckett's theatre and media plays and on contemporary Irish theatre and performance.

Paul Murphy is Lecturer in Drama Studies at Queen's University, Belfast. His research focuses on two main areas: Irish theatrical production during the first half of the twentieth century and post-deconstructionist approaches to critical theory and cultural politics. He is the Chair of the Steering Group of the Irish Society for Theatre Research.

Rachel O'Riordan is Lecturer in Drama Studies at Queen's University, Belfast. She is Artistic Director of Ransom Productions and a freelance theatre director. In 2006 she directed *Miss Julie* for the Peter Hall

Company and was Associate Director to Peter Hall on his production of *Measure for Measure*. She recently directed three new Irish plays; *Hurricane* in the West End, *Protestants* at the Soho Theatre and *The Half* at the Drama Studio at Queen's. She has published articles on Shakespeare and Irish theatre.

Mark Phelan is Lecturer in Drama Studies at Queen's University, Belfast. His research focuses on Irish theatre, specialising in theatre and performance in the North of Ireland. He has published a number of articles on nineteenth and twentieth-century Irish theatre and photography and is a member of the National organizing committee of the Irish Theatrical Diaspora.

Janelle Reinelt is Professor of Theatre and Performance at Warwick University and President of the International Federation for Theatre Research. She has published widely on politics and performance, feminism and performance theory, including editing *The Cambridge Companion to Modern British Women Playwrights* with Elaine Aston.

Anthony Roche is Associate Professor in the School of English and Drama at University College, Dublin. His publications include *Contemporary Irish Drama: From Beckett to McGuinness* (1994) and *The Cambridge Companion to Brian Friel* (2006). From 1997 to 2002 he was editor of *The Irish University Review*. He is Director of the Synge Summer School.

Melissa Sihra is Lecturer in Drama Studies at Trinity College, Dublin. She is a dramaturg and has worked at the Abbey Theatre and in the United States on productions of plays by G. B. Shaw, Brian Friel and Marina Carr. She is co-editor of *Contemporary Irish Theatre* (Colin Smythe) and is currently completing a monograph on the theatre of Marina Carr.

Brian Singleton is Head of the School of Drama, Trinity College, Dublin. He is former Editor of *Theatre Research International* (Cambridge University Press) and currently Vice-President for publications of the International Federation for Theatre Research. He has published two books on the life and work of Antonin Artaud, a monograph on Orientalism and British Musical Comedy, and co-edited collections of essays on contemporary Irish theatre for *Australasian Drama Studies* and *Modern Drama*.

Introduction: Figures at the Window

Melissa Sihra

Throughout the course of the twentieth century, theatre in Ireland has been a highly charged and controversial space of cultural enactment regarding notions of woman and gender. Since Augusta Gregory's and W. B. Yeats's 1902 drama *Kathleen ni Houlihan* it is important to interrogate the signification of 'woman' as idealized trope of nation and to look at the ways in which the work of later Irish dramatists either contests or perpetuates this legacy. The social and cultural position of woman has historically been one of symbolic centrality and subjective disavowal as both colonial ideology and nationalist movements promoted feminized concepts of the nation, while subordinating women in everyday life. Eavan Boland writes of women's iconographic prominence and lack of agency in *Object Lessons*:

> What female figure was there left to identify with? None. The heroine, as such, was utterly passive. She was Ireland or Hibernia. She was stamped, as a rubbed-away mark, on silver or gold; a compromised regal figure on a throne. . . . Her flesh was wood or ink or marble. And she had no speaking part. Her identity was an image. Or was it a fiction?[1]

The governing of gender, sexuality and the female body, in particular, as encoded by both the Catholic Church and the Irish Constitution, has had a huge impact on women's status and rights in the twentieth century and is reflected in many of the plays of this period. The mutually reinforcing ideologies of the Catholic Church and Irish Free State became embedded in Éamon De Valera's *Oireachtas* (government) Bills in 1937. At this time, severely confining roles for women were drawn up in consultation with ultra-conservative Archbishop John Charles McQuaid

1

and became enshrined within the constitution, many of which remain in place today. The monotheistic patriarchal meta-narrative valorized the heterosexual family unit and glorified the role of motherhood while intervening in issues pertaining to sexuality and morality. For precisely the last 70 years the position of women in Ireland has been officially located within the domestic sphere in De Valera's Family Article, the wording of which is only now under revision. In Article 41 'woman' is explicitly defined by the role of 'mother', and the two terms remain interchangeable. Plays by Irish women, in particular, have sought to challenge this limiting constitutional ideology and often display anxiety in relation to motherhood and home through dramatizing disillusionment and employing dramaturgical strategies which challenge conventional realist modes and realms of representation. Maryann Valiulis cites the Catholic publication *The Irish Monthly* from 1925, which promoted typically essentialist associations of woman and motherhood:

> The [vocation] for which nature has admirably suited her is that of wife and mother. The woman's duties in this regard, especially that of bringing up the children, are of such far-reaching importance for the nation and the race, that the need of safeguarding them must outweigh almost every other consideration.[2]

The lack of positive outcomes for many of the female protagonists in plays by women, from all periods of the twentieth century, can be read as a potent response to the false legacy of the new State, and reveal an unresolved disaffection. The promise of equality in Article 3 of the 1922 constitution, which stated that 'every person, without distinction of sex, shall ... enjoy the privileges and be subject to the obligations of such citizenship', was not followed-through in the following decade.[3] Catríona Beaumont points out: 'In 1932 Fianna Fáil came to power under the leadership of Éamon De Valera. The new regime soon revealed its willingness to enact legislation which again differentiated between the citizenship rights of men and women.'[4] From the 1930s on, women's perceived primary social function as wife and mother, and the implementation of the draconian 1932 public service 'marriage bar', which prevented married women from being employed as civil servants and as national schoolteachers, was used to limit their role and potential in public life.[5]

The recurring interior of the home on the Irish stage has come to signify an enduring association and conflation of family and nation. While ideals of family were promoted in the cultural life, 'home' in

Irish drama has remained a precarious space, denoting a lack of security and prone to invasion and penetration. Within this site of instability and violation, women seek agency and subjective accommodation. In Marina Carr's 1994 drama, *The Mai*, the eponymous character describes the house that she has built and her fraught relationship with it:

> This house – these days I think it's the kind of house you'd see in the corner of a dream – dark, formless, strangely inviting. It's the kind of house you build to keep out neuroses, stave off nightmares. But they come in anyway with the frost and the draughts and the air bubbles in the radiators. It's the kind of house you build when you've nowhere left to go.[6]

Gaston Bachelard expresses how, 'All great, simple images reveal a psychic state. The house, even more than the landscape, is a "psychic state".'[7] In Brian Friel's *Dancing at Lughnasa* (1990), this 'psychic state' is apparent as the imminent crises that await the Mundy sisters are foreshadowed through the vivid metaphorical debilitation of the family home. Kate says:

> You work hard at your job. You try to keep the home together. You perform your duties as best you can – because you believe in responsibilities and obligations and good order. And then suddenly, suddenly you realize that hair cracks are appearing everywhere; that control is slipping away; that the whole thing is so fragile it can't be held together much longer. It's all about to collapse.... [8]

Potent threshold spaces such as windows and doorways emphasize issues of containment and transformation in performance, reinforcing the place of the body within history and culture. The *limen* of the window powerfully frames the emptiness that it outlines on stage. The Mai is continually seen passing by, or framed within, the 'huge bay window', while the five Mundy sisters fleetingly glance at modernity, hope and possibility through the small kitchen window in 1930s rural Ireland.[9] As each of the sisters competes for a new perspective, it becomes apparent that escape and transition will not be an option. While the women attain a temporary reprieve through the physical act of dancing, this carnivalesque retreat to the realm of the corporeal serves ultimately to reinforce the dominant social structures with the return to order and suppression.

The window-frame is a device employed evocatively in Paul Vincent Carroll's 1937 Abbey play, *Shadow and Substance*, to explore spirituality and the role of institutional religion against questions of truth and justice. The central character, Brigid, a local Canon's maidservant, experiences vivid visions of St Brigid, and finally causes those around her to confront their own deep-seated prejudices. While the men in the play are regarded, like the Church itself, as hypocritical, selfish and lacking in humanity, Brigid and her Saint are the transformative 'substance' of truth. In the staging, the imagistic drawing-room window, with its '*beautiful long white curtains reaching to the ground*', is where Brigid encounters and embodies her beloved Saint.[10] In Act III: '*The* Canon *stops abruptly to stare at* Brigid *who suddenly comes in by the window. She is dressed all in white...She leans against the curtains – a white picture in a white frame. All turn and stare at her.*'[11] Here, the suggestive site of the window is a portal between the myopia of the clergy and community and the realms of enlightenment and integrity embodied in Brigid.

Máiréad Ní Ghráda's 1964 Irish-language play, *An Triail* (On Trial), shows a young female protagonist, Maura, negotiating the traumatic interface of Church, State and her own sexuality when she crosses the site of the window to meet her lover. Her brother Liam says: 'And oftentimes I hear her slipping out the window in the night time'.[12] Maura pays the ultimate price for her transgression when, after becoming pregnant, she is abandoned by her family and incarcerated in a Magdalen Laundry. In Frank McGuinness's one-act play *Baglady* (1985), the nameless poor old woman of the title, another displaced Kathleen ni Houlihan, wanders the world as she attempts to come to terms with the sexual abuse she endured as a child. As she '*walks along the edge of her space*' she sings a nursery rhyme about a menacing figure at the window:

> Who's at the window, who?
> Who's at the window, who?
> A bad, bad man with a bag on his back
> Coming to take you away.
> Who's at the window, who?
> Who's at the window, who?
> Go away, bad man, with the bag on your back,
> You won't take me with you today.[13]

Here McGuinness indicts the Catholic Church for its silence and collusion with the countless horrifying instances of child sexual abuse in Ireland which came to light in the 1980s and 1990s. Throughout the play

Baglady tries to release the heavy chain around her neck, to fully inhabit a space of her own and to stand before the windows of her past: 'In our house there's a room made of windows. I'm not allowed in, even to see out of it. But I can see it clearly.'[14]

Gregory's and Yeats's *Kathleen ni Houlihan* features at its performative core a woman passing by the cottage window and looking upon the family within, her body separated from the family by the filtering glaze of the window through which she gazes. Gregory and Yeats write: '*An* Old Woman *passes the window slowly. She looks at* Michael *as she passes.*'[15] From this moment, woman is framed on stage within the window of history *as* Ireland, drawing on the tradition of aisling poetry and feminine metonymic references such as the *Shan bhan Bhocht* (Poor Old Woman) and *Róisín Dúbh* (Dark Rosaleen). The aisling was an allegorical form that became especially popular among Irish poets in the seventeenth and eighteenth centuries. The Gaelic word means 'vision' or 'dream image' and evokes a beautiful young woman as metaphor of Ireland. In a letter to Gregory, Yeats claimed that an aisling inspired the idea for the play *Kathleen ni Houlihan*. He says:

One night I had a dream almost as distinct as a vision, of a cottage where there was well-being and firelight and talk of marriage, and into the midst of that cottage there came an old woman in a long cloak. She was Ireland herself, that Kathleen ni Houlihan for whom many songs have been sung and for whose sake so many have gone to their death.[16]

While the majority of nationalists took inspiration from the concept of woman as nation, Eoin Mac Néill was one of the few political activists who recognized the 'danger implicit in a dream image whose force is emotional rather than rational'.[17] In a memorandum to Pádraig Pearse and other members of the Irish Volunteers in February 1916, he wrote:

We have to remember that what we call our country is not a poetical abstraction, as some of us, perhaps all of us, in the exercise of our highly developed capacity for figurative thought, are sometimes apt to imagine – with the help of our patriotic literature. There is no such person as Caitlín Ní Uallacháin or Róisín Dubh or the *Sean-bhean Bhocht*, who is calling upon us to serve her. What we call our country is the Irish nation, which is a concrete and visible reality.[18]

Gregory's and Yeats's Poor Old Woman vividly embodies the unresolved confrontation between symbolic 'Woman' (Mother Ireland) and debilitated physical woman. She is a nameless, homeless wanderer, a simultaneously revered symbol of nation and exilic figure of abjection. Upon first seeing her pass by the window, Michael comments: 'I'd sooner a stranger not to come to the house the night before my wedding.'[19] The Poor Old Woman is initially regarded with suspicion – an unquantifiable 'woman from beyond the world', whose ghostly transformation at the end of the play into 'a young girl [who] had the walk of a queen'[20] has traditionally been regarded as a powerful image of feminine agency related to the nationalist cause. Yet this 'transformation' served to preserve the female wanderer within a frame of sublimated desire. The Poor Old Woman of the play laments her history as homeless symbol of nation since the anti-Catholic Penal Laws of the 1690s, when coded narratives emerged due to the prohibition on explicitly naming Ireland in ballads and poems: '[I]t's long I'm on the roads since first I went wandering. ... There have been many songs made for me.'[21] While Gregory and Yeats are referring to the colonization of Ireland, Peter's comment, 'It's a pity indeed for any person to have no place of their own', can be read in terms of the dislocation of female subjectivity.[22] In a poignant confrontation between 'real' woman and woman-as-nation, Peter's wife, Bridget, says to the Poor Old Woman: 'It is a wonder you are not worn out with so much wandering.'[23]

The lack of accommodation of female subjectivity operates on many levels in this play. Yeats did not publicly acknowledge Gregory's collaborations with him on the script of *Kathleen ni Houlihan*. While Gregory accepted this initially, on the basis 'that his was the name that would sell',[24] she grew to resent Yeats for it as the years went by. In July 1928 she wrote in her journal: 'Rather hard on me, not giving my name with Kathleen ni Houlihan that I wrote all but all of.'[25] Gregory remained unacknowledged as co-author of the play until James Pethica's 1988 essay ' "Our Kathleen": Yeats's Collaboration with Lady Gregory in the Writing of *Cathleen ni Houlihan*' confirmed her co-authorship from manuscript evidence.[26] In *Our Irish Theatre* (1913), Gregory clearly states her collaboration with Yeats: 'Later in the year we wrote together *Kathleen ni Houlihan* ... .'[27] Gregory quotes a letter she received from Yeats in the same passage, where he says: ' "We turned my dream into the little play, *Kathleen ni Houlihan*, and when we gave it to the little theatre in Dublin and found that working people liked it, you helped me to put my other dramatic fables into speech." '[28] Yet, in the Norton Anthology *Modern Irish Drama* (1991), Yeats remains credited as sole author.

Figure 1   Maud Gonne in *Kathleen ni Houlihan* (1902). Courtesy of The Abbey Theatre.

The title role of *Kathleen ni Houlihan* was first performed by the striking nationalist activist Maud Gonne (see Figure 1). The triple convergence of Gonne's commanding physicality, her iconic status as political activist and her mesmerizing portrayal of woman as nation resonated deeply with audiences at the time. In her memoirs actress Máire Nic Shiubhlaigh, who attended the first performance on 2 April 1902 in St Teresa's Hall, Clarendon Street, passionately relates the powerful, almost transcendental, effect Gonne had in the role:

> How many who were there that night will forget the Kathleen ni Houlihan of Maud Gonne, her rich golden hair, willow-like figure, pale sensitive face, and burning eyes, as she spoke the closing lines of the Old Woman turning out through the cottage door .... Watching her, one could readily understand the reputation she enjoyed as the most beautiful woman in Ireland, the inspiration of the whole revolutionary movement. She was the most exquisitely-fashioned creature I have ever seen. Her beauty was *startling*. Yeats wrote *Kathleen ni Houlihan* especially for her, and there were few in the audience who did not see why. She was the very personification of the figure she portrayed on the stage.[29]

The fact that, as Christopher Morash points out, 'Maud Gonne arrived ten minutes before curtain went up, unprofessionally (but impressively) sweeping through the audience in full spectral costume as the Poor Old Woman' shows in a very vivid sense how the boundaries between performance, nation and woman were dissolved for the audience at the time.[30]

Seventeen years later, in March 1919, Lady Gregory played the title role of *Kathleen ni Houlihan* for three nights at the Abbey Theatre when actress Máire Walker (Máire Nic Shiubhlaigh) was unable to get to Dublin (see Figure 2). In an attempt to convince herself to perform, Gregory wrote in her journal: 'after all what is wanted but a hag and a voice?'[31] The *cailleach* (old hag) effect was created by painting, Gregory tells us, 'my face with grease paint – white with black under the eyes and red inside the lids – dreadful! Luckily my own hair is grey enough without a wig.'[32] Despite suffering from an attack of nerves before every performance, Gregory was quietly proud to have completed the challenge and wrote after her first night: 'I had two curtains all to myself.'[33] One wonders how secretly satisfied she must have felt to act in her

Figure 2   Lady Augusta Gregory in *Kathleen ni Houlihan* (1919). Courtesy of The Abbey Theatre.

own play – even if no-one knew it was hers. She excitedly records how Synge felt there was 'thrill' in her performance the following night, and mentions that Maud Gonne, 'a former Kathleen', and her daughter Iseult were there too.[34] Yeats's dismissive reaction to her performance on that March evening reveals, whether consciously or unconsciously, the innate superiority and self-importance he felt in relation to his long-term friend. Gregory's innermost feelings are expressed in her journal when she says of her co-author: 'And Yeats came up to the gallery afterwards and said coldly it was "very nice, but if I had rehearsed you it would have been much better".'[35]

Yeats's attitude to Lady Gregory throughout the course of their acquaintance and collaborations clearly highlights gendered issues of authorship and authority, as well as the overall disempowerment of women in mainstream channels of artistic expression. In what has come to be regarded as a dramatic tradition of almost exclusively male play-wrights (Dion Boucicault, Oscar Wilde, G. B. Shaw, Yeats, J. M. Synge, Sean O'Casey, Samuel Beckett, John B. Keane, Tom Murphy, Brian Friel, Thomas Kilroy, Frank McGuinness), it is crucial to consider the ways in which canon-formation enables an implicit set of cultural norms and standards to materialize, which perpetuate hegemonic structures, and which are based upon historically contingent values. If artistic canons are 'a history of cultural authority', then, as Jill Dolan observes:

> patriarchal/canonical authority has determined the canon's selection and then mystified its terms, so that this reified body of work seems always to have been in place. The invisibility of both its constructors and the origins of its construction render the canon peculiarly (but purposefully) remote from question or attack.[36]

Elizabeth Grosz observes that the overwhelming phallocentricity of historically privileged discourses is not merely 'an oversight', but an action of 'strategic amnesia [which] serves to ensure the patriarchal foundations of knowledges'.[37] It is crucial therefore to identify the means by which cultural value systems operate, and to challenge them. A close analysis of theatre-reviewing over the period of the last century is one way to identify how dominant attitudes materialize and construct norm-ative standards. The process of theatre-reviewing is inextricable from that of canon-formation, where works are either accepted or rejected by the *soi disant* critics in operation at that time. Cathy Leeney makes this point in relation to plays by women in the early twentieth century:

Audiences for the premieres of new plays sport a variety of blinkers. When plays such as Dorothy Macardle's *The Old Man* or Teresa Deevy's *Katie Roche* did make it to the stage, audience expectations, the reputation of the author, or current conventions of staging or of characterization skewed critical responses, so that critics reflected back conservative values associated with the maintenance of existing power structures in society and culture.[38]

Problematically, contemporaneous critical responses become part of a greater, monolithic 'theatre history' which positions the work from that moment as either a success or a failure. In this sense, it is 'profoundly misleading to judge old plays by old reviews [and] it is certainly impossible to judge plays written by women through old reviews; nor can we deem such plays unworthy of production if they were deemed unworthy in the past.'[39] In a 1993 essay, 'Cathleen Ni Houlihan is Not a Playwright', Victoria White observes that, 'The influential critics in the Dublin papers are nearly all men…. The critics have a fairly reliable tendency to make short work of feminist or woman-oriented plays.'[40] This has been the case throughout the twentieth century, where the chief commentators on plays by men and women have almost exclusively been male. Eleanor Methven, co-founder of Charabanc Theatre Company, remembers how the press referred to them as ' "the best all-women theatre company in Ireland". That wasn't much of a compliment. We are the only one. Why can't they just say we're one of the best theatre companies in Ireland?.'[41] It is only recently, in the late twentieth and early twenty-first centuries, that feminist scholars are recovering lost or forgotten texts, critically engaging with the work of women playwrights on their own terms and interrogating the political processes by which 'meaning' and the 'canon' are enabled and sustained.

The project of recovering plays by women is crucial to the renegotiation and pluralizing of Irish theatrical traditions. In terms of this recuperation, it is important that gaps are not merely filled-in by feminist scholarship, as this simply affirms the authority of the preceding structures. There needs to be a thorough interrogation of the very *process* of what constitutes the 'canonical' and of the premises upon which such standards are judged and validated. When approaching previously lost or forgotten plays, diverse evaluative and ideological criteria need to be taken into consideration in conjunction with an awareness of histories other than the printed word (where it exists) – such as production and reception and cultural contexts regarding gender, sexuality and the body. Furthermore, Edna Longley makes the crucial point that, when considering recovered texts and women's writing in general, we must always distinguish between 'critical discrimination and positive discrimination' and be aware that 'inequality should not obscure quality',[42] something which Marina Carr also pays caution to in the Foreword of this book.

While predominantly focusing on plays and productions by Irish women, this volume looks at the ways in which the politics of performance and representation have reflected and infected cultural notions of woman and gender. In the 1990s a number of articles began to explore women's activity in theatre. *Theatre Ireland* devoted an entire issue to the subject in 1993, edited by Victoria White.[43] Up until then, as Anthony Roche points out, the common perception had been that, while central to performance, 'women did not write plays.'[44] An issue of the *Irish University Review*, edited by Christopher Murray, was dedicated to Teresa Deevy and Irish Women Playwrights in 1995. Cathy Leeney edited a volume of six new plays by women, *Seen and Heard*, in 2001 and the *Field Day Anthology of Irish Writing Volume V: Irish Women's Writing and Traditions* (2002) incorporates a valuable section on the work of contemporary women playwrights.

This book explores the rich legacy of Irish women playwrights over the course of the twentieth century, ultimately challenging the notion that Irish drama is primarily a site of male authorship and authority. The volume investigates representations of woman by female playwrights, and also by a smaller number of male playwrights in order to re-evaluate familiar themes and contexts. This book does not aim to provide a survey of the twentieth century but is, rather, a cultural and political intervention. The volume is both a work of retrieval and critique, and while opening up the immense contribution of women to Irish theatre practice, it is only the beginning of the journey, revealing how much more research needs to be done in this field. Each chapter and piece of writing in the volume was specially commissioned and the chapters are placed chronologically in terms of the periods under investigation in order to enable the historical, social and thematic contexts to emerge organically. The three Interchapters do not denote sections in any formal sense but seek rather to provide overviews, further background on women in Irish theatre and culture and to contextualize the critical evaluations. In choosing to employ a temporal structural framework, moments of intersection and thematic interrelationships have materialized in the volume of their own accord. Throughout the collection threads emerge between the chapters as entanglements of location, history, gender and performance interweave explicitly and obliquely in the plays and periods under investigation. Inevitably it was not possible to include chapters on all of the playwrights that I would have liked, such as Mary Manning, Christine Longford, Máiréad Ní Ghráda, Margaretta D'Arcy, Christina Reid, Marie Jones, Emma Donoghue and many others and it is beyond the scope of this volume to consider in any depth the extraordinary legacies of Irish women designers, directors and actors.

The interplay between space (both on-stage and imagined off-stage), gender and authority is especially relevant when considering women on the Irish stage. Perhaps unsurprisingly given that women have been marginalized from Irish theatre history and practice, a concern with location plays an important role in the volume as a whole. Many of the chapters explore the symbolic dialectics of interior and exterior spaces, and ontological 'placelessness'. Moments of intersection emerge particularly in relation to the idea of travelling, or movement, whether physically or conceptually, or both. Lisa Fitzpatrick shows how women 'take their own road' in the imaginative and actual *picaresque* journeys of the female protagonists of the early twentieth century. Maddy Rooney's wanderings in Beckett's *All That Fall* are read as similarly *picaresque* by Anna McMullan, and Brian Singleton points out how Stella Feehily's *Duck* centres on the female protagonists' *Thelma and Louise*-like gritty adventures on contemporary urban streets. Anthony Roche discusses the evocative Irish phrase 'ag gluaiseacht' in *Dún na mBan Trí Thine*, literally translated as 'movement', which he reads as combining 'a sense of freedom, of impulse, of wandering hither and thither, along with a determination, a drive, of psychological impetus'.

Conceptual modes of alterity, such as the realm of the supernatural and the worlds of myth, folklore and storytelling are evoked to incorporate the energies (sexual and creative) of many of the women characters in the plays of the twentieth century. This vitality is reflected in the ways in which the playwrights frequently push the borders of dramatic Realism, renegotiating the very frame of the 'real' and pre-ordained social structures. As Janelle Reinelt observes in the Preface, 'the writers shape their dramaturgy to reveal the structures which constrain them', testing the boundaries of entrapment dramatically and ideologically. Singleton similarly observes that many of the younger playwrights 'challenge the myth-making of the realist form as a dramaturgical strategy to disrupt the time-space continuum and thereby open up new vistas and possibilities for change.' Women's creative energy manifests in many of the plays in a rendering of mythic or fantastic figures – from Brian Boru's encounter with the female spirit 'Aoibhell' (meaning 'blissfulness' but pronounced 'evil') in Gregory's *Kincora* to the horned 'fairy women of the fort' in *Dún na mBan Trí Thine*. Stewart Parker depicts a haunting Phantom Bride in *Northern Star* while McGuinness conjures up 'File' the poetess-magician in *Mutabilitie*. Pre-Christian beliefs and folk-practices, such as the trope of the changeling – a kind of 'double woman or child' – traditionally held as a threat to the foundations of patriarchy, emerge in plays such as *Dún na mBan Trí Thine* and Dorothy Macardle's *Witch's Brew* (1928).

Sites of water occur with remarkable frequency in plays by Irish women in the twentieth century. Rosalind Clarke observes how in Irish culture: 'The evidence shows overwhelmingly that most place-names, particularly for wells and other bodies of water, refer to women.'[45] Water and the fluid can be seen as a potent metaphor for exceeding boundaries and flooding and diluting dominant structures. Luce Irigaray writes of the potential of the fluid to 'disconcert any attempt at static identification [and how] fluid is, by nature, unstable. ... Thus fluid is always in a relation of excess or lack *vis à vis* unity. It eludes the "Thou art that." That is, any definite identification.'[46] Characteristic of water is its compulsion to overflow, to transgress demarcated boundaries. Water and notions of fluidity in these plays by women thus signify the tension between containment and escape, and the possibility of challenging and redefining the socially prescribed borders of patriarchy. In Ní Dhuibhe's drama, the *mise-en-scène* features a prominent well which Roche observes, is 'the locus of interchange between ordinary people and the others, between the living and the dead'. In Eva Gore-Booth's *The Buried Life of Deirdre* (1916), the eponymous woman looks into a pool of water to gain knowledge and to see the future and the past, while in *Witch's Brew* the potion itself denotes intoxicating female energy and agency. Poulgorm ('blue pool'), in Margaret O'Leary's *The Woman* (1929), represents an imaginative and seductive space of refuge and otherness for the protagonist, associated with death and escape. In Carr's *The Mai*, 'Sruthán na mBláth' ('the River of Flowers'), the local folk-myth of Bláth and Coillte and Owl Lake – '*loch Cailleach oíche*, Lake of the Night Hag or Pool of the Dark Witch' are similar repositories of solace, creativity and transformation for female energy.[47] In Carr's *Portia Coughlan* (1996), the Belmont River, named after the River God Bel, is an erotic and thanatotic channel for the protagonist. Similarly, Enrica Cerquoni observes that in Anne Devlin's *Ourselves Alone* (1985): 'The metaphysical realm of the sea, as a boundless room of the spirit, embodies for the three women a releasing space of physical and spiritual nakedness, which binds them together regardless of their disappointing experiences.'

In Chapter 1, Paul Murphy investigates the dynamics of desire and 'Woman as fantasy object' in three early twentieth-century historical tragedies by Lady Augusta Gregory (1852–1932); *Kincora* (1905), *Dervorgilla* (1907) and *Grania* (1912). Murphy addresses the 'sublimation/subordination double-bind which Irish women of all classes and creeds faced on a quotidian basis', as well as Gregory's own 'deep emotional conflict' between desire and responsibility in terms of both sexual and national politics. Murphy points out that: 'In spite of the evidence of her skill as a dramatist, Lady Gregory's plays are hardly ever performed at the Abbey or any other theatre in Dublin or the rest of Ireland.' Lady Gregory was one of the founders of the Irish Literary Theatre in 1899 (with Yeats and Edward Martyn), which led to the opening of the Abbey Theatre in 1904. The author of over 40 plays, translations of Irish sagas, poetry and a collector of folklore, Gregory's legacy has only recently begun to be acknowledged and rigorously examined. Murphy considers Nietzsche's distinction between commemorative history and critical history and makes the valuable point that 'Lady Gregory's plays must also be subjected to a *"critical"* historicization in order for them to be saved from the kind of eulogization which has led to her mummification as a dramatist.'

The plays of Cork dramatists Geraldine Cummins (1890–1969) and Susanne R. Day (1890–1964) are placed in the context of the closing years of British colonialism in Ireland, up to and beyond the formation of the Irish Free State in 1922, in Chapter 2 by Velma O'Donoghue Greene. Pacifist suffragists, Day and Cummins were committed to alleviating the plight of the poor in their communities and co-founded, with Edith Somerville, the Munster Women's Franchise League in 1910. O'Donoghue Greene's cultural materialist reading of their little-known co-authored 1914 drama *Fidelity* opens up a discussion on 'the reality of an oppressively bleak situation of limited choices and rigid social structures' for women at the time. The performative politics of gender and the body can be traced in this play where woman is either contained within the domestic sphere (of patriarchy) or exiled – on the outside of the Symbolic Order, beyond the 'looking-glass' of authorized femininity. There is no record of a contemporaneous production of *Fidelity* (though, as Day and Cummins's plays were not reviewed, this does not mean that one did not take place). O'Donoghue Greene produced the play in 2005 as part of a symposium on Munster Women Playwrights which was attended by relations of Cummins and Day and featured as part of Cork's cultural programme as European Capital of Culture.[48]

Cathy Leeney (Chapter 3) reveals the symbolic possibility of spaces beyond the frame of the patriarchal familial sphere for women in her close reading of two plays, by Eva Gore-Booth (1870–1926) and Dorothy Macardle (1899–1958). Gore-Booth, born to the Protestant Ascendancy class in Lissadell, Co. Sligo, renounced her inheritance and moved to Manchester. She campaigned tirelessly for women's rights throughout her life, adopting a pacifist approach to political change. Drawn to Irish subject-matter, Gore-Booth was a prolific poet as well as a dramatist of the Revival and her work was included in AE's revivalist anthology *New Songs* (1904). Leeney tells us that her play, *The Buried Life of Deirdre* (1916), uses 'performance space to address issues of female subjectivity as inherited from Irish mythic sources, and as related to the role of woman in the emergence of an independent autonomous state'. Educated at University College Dublin, Dundalk-born Macardle was a teacher, writer, historian and political activist. She was dismissed from her teaching post in Alexandra College, Dublin, after her arrest during the Civil War. She spent time in Mountjoy and Kilmainham prisons and participated in the Republican hunger-strike. Her 1928 play, *Witch's Brew*, looks at the allegorical ways in which 'supernatural phenomena express powerful energies that cannot be accommodated in the authorized world of order controlled by church and state.'

Lisa Fitzpatrick in Chapter 4 explores three fascinating Abbey plays, by Teresa Deevy (1894–1963), Margaret O'Leary (no dates) and Augusta Gregory. These dramas, Fitzpatrick tells us, all 'have central female protagonists who seek adventure and who spin new identities and wondrous worlds from their speech' as they attempt to break free from their limiting social environments. Gregory's plays are now receiving the critical recognition that they deserve, as are the plays of Waterford-born Deevy. Very little is known about O'Leary, who was born in West Cork and took an MA at University College Cork. She was a teacher but retired in 1927 and spent time in France and Scotland. O'Leary returned to Ireland and began to write plays, short stories and two novels – *The House I Made*, which won the Harmsworth Prize in 1936, and *Lightning Flash*. Fitzpatrick tells us how Yeats wrote to O'Leary prior to the production of *The Woman* at the Abbey in 1929 requiring a major dramaturgical revision of the play's ending. In a decision which hugely alters the sexual and gender politics of the drama, we see how the woman playwright was artistically restricted in a way that, Fitzpatrick suggests, male playwrights of the time such as J. M. Synge were not.

Anna McMullan (Chapter 5) explores the ways in which Samuel Beckett's 'staging of maternal or matronly figures exposes deep-rooted anxiety around questions of embodiment, reproduction, authorship and origin which can be related to tropes of femininity and the mother in the Irish theatre canon.' She traces Beckett's staging of women in his earliest dramatic works – the unfinished fragment 'Human Wishes' (*c*.1930s) and *Eleutheria* (late 1940s) – which are 'dominated by fleshy matrons', through to his later plays where the corporeality of mother or matron 'dissolves as she becomes the very space and ground of representation, an unseen matrix of semblances'. In so doing, McMullan considers how constructions of the symbolic categories of the feminine and the maternal are 'both other to, and the foundation of, cultural and self-production.'

Mark Phelan (Chapter 6) gives a detailed account of neglected Northern Irish women playwrights, Alice Milligan (1866–1953), Helen Waddell (1889–1965) and Patricia O'Connor (1908–1983). He begins with a call 'for Irish theatre studies to move away from the singularity of "nation" as the dominant conceptual and organizational category of historiography and criticism'. Phelan places Omagh-born Milligan as a 'centrifugal figure of the Northern Revival' in her co-editorship (with Ethna Carberry) of the patriotic newspaper *The Northern Patriot* (1895) and *The Shan Van Vocht* (1896–99). In addition to writing essays, poetry and plays and learning Irish, Milligan's *tableaux vivants* were an inspiration to Maud Gonne and the *Inghinidhe na hÉireann*. She was a founding member of the Ulster Anti-Partition Council and was forced, with her brother William, to leave Ireland under 24-hour threat of execution by loyalists in 1920. Milligan was awarded an honorary degree from the National University of Ireland, presented by Éamon De Valera in 1941, but spent her last years isolated and lonely in Omagh. Phelan evokes the staging, energy and performativity of her *tableaux* which have their roots in the spectacular 'moving picture' world of melodrama. He analyses the little-known dramas of Tokyo-born medieval scholar Waddell, sister of Rutherford Mayne, and Donegal-born O'Connor (pseudonym Norah Ingram) and shows how their personal experiences of sexual discrimination, at university and in their professions, are manifest in their plays.

Rachel O'Riordan (Chapter 8) looks at the evocative triptych of central female characters in Northern Irish Protestant playwright Stewart Parker's *Northern Star* (1984). O'Riordan suggests that Parker (1941–1988) positions the women as central to his interrogation of history, nation and conflict during the life of Henry Joy McCracken, leader of the United Irishmen. The three women are, O'Riordan suggests, 'corporeal sites for the war that is happening in Ireland; between past and present

(Phantom Bride), between myth and logic (Mary Bodle) and between politics and the individual (Mary Anne McCracken)'. Parker interweaves real figures from Northern Ireland's past with 'otherworldly' figures to provide dramaturgical and conceptual links between past and present. One of the figures in the play, McCracken's sister, Mary Anne (1770–1866), established a small muslin business in Belfast and was an active feminist who served on the Ladies' Committee of the Belfast Charitable Society. In this letter, sent in 1797 to her brother during his imprisonment, we see her passionate concern with issues of women's equality:

> If indeed we were to reason from analogy, we would rather be inclined to suppose that women were destined for superior understandings, their bodies being more delicately framed and less fit for labour than that of man. Does it not naturally follow that they were more particularly intended for study and retirement?...there can be no argument produced in favour of the slavery of woman that has not been used in favour of general slavery...[49]

In his chapter on the women characters of contemporary Donegal playwright Frank McGuinness, Eamonn Jordan (Chapter 7) asserts: 'Patriarchy has both prescribed and fictionalized societal, gender, class and race relations, and it has also, to a considerable extent, fashioned and fabricated the dramaturgical practices of Irish theatre in terms of how plays are written, programmed, directed, produced, marketed and consumed.' Jordan considers representations of women and gender in a number of McGuinness's plays, beginning with his first major success, *The Factory Girls* (1982). He argues that McGuinness's theatre adopts a performative epistemology which he denotes as 'a metaphysicality, located in the possibilities, circumstances and the make-up of the mask [and] grounded in the sensibility of the body and its intuition'. Jordan's essay is a compelling study of McGuinness's sympathetic, complex, at times disorientating and challenging women characters whose engagement with 'the collective exuberance of play delineates them as much as their gender'.

Enrica Cerquoni in Chapter 9 focuses upon the work of Northern Irish playwright Anne Devlin (1951–) and considers, in particular, how 'the notion of the "room", the signpost of theatrical realism, is central in Devlin's dramaturgy.' Born in Catholic West Belfast, Devlin moved to England in 1976 and has written extensively for television, radio and cinema. Cerquoni suggests that metaphysical loss, absence, exile and home are central to Devlin's theatrical explorations and that the 'importance of place, of departures and returns, of journeys away, marks all her work'. Cerquoni's meditation on *Ourselves Alone* (1985) challenges previous analyses which have considered the play in terms of a 'certain absolutism and separatism in the thematic and formal development of the subject-matter'. Here, the play is revealed as an 'intersected matrix of outward and inward spaces' which envisages an alternative kind of dramaturgy, disrupting the seams of realism.

Anthony Roche (Chapter 10) explores an Irish language play, *Dún na mBan Trí Thine* (*The Fort of the Fairy Women is On Fire*) (1994) by contemporary Dublin dramatist, novelist, short-story writer and scholar of folklore Éilís Ní Dhuibhne. In his own translation, Roche makes the point that for young women characters in the male-authored Irish plays of the Revival, spaces of possibility are 'frequently imbued with the trappings of folklore'. He intuitively observes that: 'Far from being rejected as outmoded, these concepts have been taken on, refashioned and taken further by contemporary women writers.' Ní Dhuibhne's wonderfully theatrical play draws on the realm of the Otherworld 'to stage the crisis of its 40-something heroine Leiní, a wife and mother who is struggling to be an artist'. Roche utilizes the concept of liminality, and the symbolic potency of the threshold, to show how the drama disrupts chronological succession by moving between the nineteenth-century past and the modern world to the timelessness of the fairy-fort in a feminist 'exploration of the social roles of women in a society caught between tradition and modernity'.

Brian Singleton suggests in Chapter 11 that there is a break-down or 'evanescence' of patriarchy occurring in the work of the younger generation of Irish women playwrights, Ioanna Anderson, Hilary Fannin, Stella Feehily and Elizabeth Kuti. Singleton argues that: 'The essentialized iconic and mythical women of the early nation's male imagination have been replaced by women who reject male authority, seek new lives beyond the strictures of the family unit and refuse to be haunted by the sick, dying and dead patriarchs in their lives.' In the four plays under discussion here, woman is taken out of the country kitchen and placed on the street, the beach and in the garden. As the 'new Irish woman' emerges, this world of reconfigured gender-relations is in a troubled state where, Singleton observes, 'a new surreal set of conceptual values borne out of consumerism has replaced the authority of the Catholic Church.'

My chapter (Chapter 12) explores the thematic and stylistic threads of Marina Carr's plays, beginning with her earliest works up to *On Raftery's*

Hill in 2000. Born in 1964, Carr grew up in Co. Offaly and graduated with a degree in English and Philosophy from UCD in 1987. A member of Aosdána and with 11 plays produced to date, Carr's emergence in the late 1980s and early 1990s coincided with a major moment of visibility and change for women in Irish culture – the inauguration of the first female President of Ireland, Mary Robinson. Carr is exceptionally rare as she is the only Irish woman to have her plays produced on Ireland's main stages in recent years. Her award-winning dramas have been translated into many languages and produced in places as diverse as Siberia, Estonia, Korea, Japan, Slovakia, Bulgaria, Hungary, Iceland, Brazil, Germany, The Netherlands and the Czech Republic, as well as in the United States and London's West End. In this chapter, issues of authorship and authority are explored as well as Carr's illuminating response to Lady Gregory's elision as co-author of *Kathleen ni Houlihan*. The chapter considers the ways in which *On Raftery's Hill* is a radical rewriting of Gregory's and Yeats's 1902 play, 'inverting the actions of the Poor Old Woman in the earlier drama and refusing the myth of an idealized Mother Ireland'. One of the defining characteristics of Carr's dramaturgy is her evocative mingling of the everyday with the otherworlds of myth, folk-tales, ghosts and fairies. This chapter looks at the development of Carr's theatrical voice, the ways in which her linguistic inventiveness imagines new modes of expression and how her plays challenge cultural expectations, bringing us forth into the twenty-first century.

The Appendix of this volume reveals the sheer extent to which women were, and are, writing for the stage in Ireland; north and south, east and west. Yet the fact that most of these plays are unpublished or were never reviewed has contributed hugely to their erasure from theatre history. The Appendix spills over into the twenty-first century and goes back as far as the seventeenth. Many of the earlier plays do not now exist, though most of them were performed at one time, with real actors, props, costumes and painted sets. Others were published, but have never been performed. Sources for the list include the Performing Arts Archive of the Linen Hall Library, the Abbey Theatre Archive, published histories of Irish theatre, anthologies of Irish writing and Irish writers and the Irish Playography. There are unavoidable omissions as dates and venues have not been possible in all cases. At times different sources presented contradictory 'facts', and where this happened I used my judgment and either left out the information or checked it against various sources. This appendix is, above all, a naming of names and another step in the process of a historical recuperation and validation for Irish women playwrights. The research and the critique must now follow if a thorough renegotiation of the landscape of Irish theatre is to occur.

Each play-title in this Appendix is a window into a real woman's life and her particular view of the world. Behind every title there was, at one time, a dramatic narrative; behind every narrative there is a woman and her story. Each play is a tangible trace of a woman who once sat at her table by a window 300 years ago, or last year, and wove a story. Each title is a fragment in time where the agony and the joy behind the writing of the play is contained. How did the play do on its first night? How many people were in the audience? Did they congratulate the playwright or dismiss her? Did they even know that she wrote it? Much of this we may never know, but we can imagine. In imagining these women, they will not be forgotten. It was exciting to watch the number of women's names and their plays grow, each new one being like gold or buried treasure. The list reads like a tantalizing map of the many journeys of women in Ireland throughout the centuries – *The Wonder! A Woman Keeps a Secret* and *A Bold Stroke for a Wife* by Susanna Centlivre (who was perhaps born in Ireland and whose plays were hugely popular in London), Kitty Clive's *The Rehearsal* and Frances Sheridan's *The Discovery* in the eighteenth century; Maria Edgeworth's *The Grinding Organ* in the nineteenth; Jane Barlow's *A Bunch of Lavender*, Alice Maye Finney's *A Local Demon*, Margaret O'Leary's *The Woman*, Una Troy's *The Dark Road* and Olga Fielden's *Witches in Eden* in the twentieth century, all thrill the imagination with their glorious and intriguing titles. Every year this list will be added to as more women write more plays, and more histories are brought to light. Since the Classical Greek theatre, women have been denied the right to self-representation, existing only as patriarchal sign. Philosopher and playwright Hélène Cixous wrote of how she could finally no longer bring herself to go to the theatre, because 'it was like going to my own funeral [where] the horror of the murder scene repeated and intensified with more violence even than fiction . . . a woman must die before the play can begin.'[50] It is now time to consider women's self-image. This book bring us further along the way to discovering women's voices, words and bodies in Irish theatre.

Notes

1. Eavan Boland, *Object Lessons: The Life of the Woman and the Poet in Our Time* (London: Vintage, 1996), p. 66.
2. Maryann Valiulis, 'Neither Feminist Nor Flapper: The Ecclesiastical Construction of the Ideal Irish Woman', in Alan Hayes and Diane Urquhart (eds), *The Irish Women's History Reader* (London and New York: Routledge, 2001), p. 153.

3. Article 3, 1922 Constitution cited by Caitríona Beaumont, 'Gender, Citizenship and the State, 1922–1990', in Scott Brewster, Virginia Crossman, Fiona Becket and David Alderson (eds), *Ireland in Proximity: History, Gender, Space* (London and New York: Routledge, 1999), p. 97.

4. See Catríona Beaumont in *Ireland in Proximity: History, Gender, Space*, p. 97.

5. This discrimination was further solidified in Section 16 of the 1934 Conditions of Employment Bill which sanctioned the right to limit the number of women working in any given industry and to deny further training and promotion to women (on the sexist grounds that they would inevitably marry and therefore be prohibited from further employment).

6. Marina Carr, *Marina Carr: Plays One* (London: Faber & Faber, 1999), p. 158.

7. Gaston Bachelard, *The Poetics of Space* (Boston: Beacon Press, 1994), p. 72.

8. Brian Friel, *Brian Friel: Plays Two* (London: Faber & Faber, 1999), p. 56.

9. *Marina Carr: Plays One*, p. 107.

10. Paul Vincent Carroll, *Two Plays by Paul Vincent Carroll* (London: Macmillan, 1948), p. 178.

11. *Two Plays by Paul Vincent Carroll*, p. 181.

12. Máiréad Ní Ghráda, *On Trial*, trans. Máiréad Ní Ghráda (Dublin: James Duffy, 1966), p. 20.

13. Frank McGuinness, *Frank McGuinness: Plays One* (London: Faber & Faber, 1996), p. 385.

14. *Frank McGuinness: Plays One*, p. 395.

15. Augusta Gregory, *Kathleen ni Houlihan*, in Lucy McDiarmid and Maureen Waters (eds), *Lady Gregory: Selected Writings* (London: Penguin, 1995), p. 305.

16. W. B. Yeats cited in Lady Gregory, *Our Irish Theatre*, The Coole Edition (London and New York: Colin Smythe, 1972), p. 53.

17. Máirín Nic Eoin, 'Sovereignty and Politics, *c.*1300–1900', in *The Field Day Anthology of Irish Writing, Volume IV: Irish Women's Writing and Traditions*, ed. Angela Bourke, Siobhán Kilfeather, Maria Luddy, Margaret Mac Curtain, Gerardine Meaney, Máirin Ní Dhonnchadha, Mary O'Dowd and Claire Wills (Cork: Cork University Press with Field Day, 2002), p. 275.

18. Nic Eoin, in *The Field Day Anthology of Irish Writing, Volume IV*, p. 275.

19. *Lady Gregory: Selected Writings*, p. 305.

20. *Lady Gregory: Selected Writings*, pp. 307, 311.

21. *Lady Gregory: Selected Writings*, pp. 305, 309.

22. *Lady Gregory: Selected Writings*, p. 305.

23. *Lady Gregory: Selected Writings*, p. 305.

24. Roy Foster, *W. B. Yeats: A Life, Volume 1: The Apprentice Mage* (Oxford: Oxford University Press, 1997), p. 247.

25. Roy Foster cites Lady Gregory, from D. J. Murphy (ed.), *Lady Gregory's Journals*, vol. II (Gerrard's Cross: Colin Smythe, 1987), in *W. B. Yeats: A Life, Volume I*, p. 580.

26. James Pethica, ' "Our Kathleen": Yeats's Collaboration with Lady Gregory in the Writing of *Cathleen ni Houlihan*', in Warwick Gould (ed.), *Yeats Annual 6* (London: Macmillan, 1988), pp. 3–31. As established from Pethica's study of the manuscripts, Gregory's preferred spelling was 'Kathleen' and this is the one that will be used hereafter.

27. Lady Augusta Gregory, *Our Irish Theatre*, Coole Edition (London: Colin Smythe, 1972), p. 53.

28. Lady Gregory, *Our Irish Theatre*, p. 54.
29. Máire Nic Shuibhlaigh, *The Splendid Years* (Dublin: James Duffy, 1955), p. 19.
30. Christopher Morash, *A History of Irish Theatre, 1601–2000* (Cambridge: Cambridge University Press, 2002), p. 123.
31. *Lady Gregory: Selected Writings*, p. 436.
32. *Lady Gregory: Selected Writings*, p. 437.
33. *Lady Gregory: Selected Writings*, p. 437.
34. *Lady Gregory: Selected Writings*, p. 438.
35. *Lady Gregory: Selected Writings*, p. 438.
36. Jill Dolan, 'Bending Gender to Fit the Canon: The Politics of Production', in Lynda Hart (ed.), *Making a Spectacle: Feminist Essays on Contemporary Women's Theatre* (Michigan: University of Michigan Press, 1989), pp. 319, 331.
37. Elizabeth Grosz, *Space, Time and Perversion: Essays on the Politics of Bodies* (London and New York: Routledge, 1995), p. 40.
38. Cathy Leeney, 'Violence of the Abbey Theatre Stage: The National Project and the Critic; Two Case Studies', *Modern Drama*, Vol. XLVII, No. 4, Winter 2004, p. 585.
39. Leeney, in *Modern Drama*, p. 591–2.
40. Victoria White, 'Cathleen ni Houlihan is Not a Playwright', *Theatre Ireland*, No. 30, Winter 1993, p. 30.
41. Victoria White, 'Towards Post-Feminism', *Theatre Ireland*, No. 18, April–June 1989, p. 35.
42. Edna Longley, 'Poetry and the Writing of Irish Literary History', Keynote Lecture, *Irish Women's Writing: History Lessons*, Symposium, Queen's University Belfast, 13 May 2006.
43. *Theatre Ireland*, No. 30, Winter 1993.
44. Anthony Roche, 'Essays on Contemporary Irish Drama, Barry, Moore, Yeats and Plath', *Colby Quarterly*, Vol. XXXIV, No. 4, December 1998, p. 274.
45. Rosalind Clarke, *The Great Queens: Irish Goddesses from the Morrígan to Cathleen ni Houlihan* (Gerrards Cross: Colin Smythe, 1991), p. 10.
46. Luce Irigaray, *This Sex Which Is Not One*, trans. Catherine Porter (New York: Cornell University Press, 1985), pp. 111, 117.
47. *Marina Carr: Plays One*, pp. 183, 147.
48. *Fidelity* was performed in Trinity College with the DU Players in April 2004 and again at the Granary Studio (UCC) in December 2005. In both cases it was produced by Velma O'Donoghue Greene and directed by Clare Neylon.
49. *The Field Day Anthology of Irish Writing, Volume V: Irish Women's Writing and Traditions*, pp. 54–5.
50. Hélène Cixous, 'Aller a la Mer', trans. Barbara Kerslake, *Modern Drama*, Vol. 27, No. 4, December 1984, p. 546.

INTERCHAPTER I: 1900–1939

Cathy Leeney

In an overview of Irish theatre history from 1900 to 1939, perhaps no period, as it relates to women, better exemplifies the inverse relationship between the march of the years, and progress. Women who were in the prime of life in the early years of the twentieth century might have had an expectation that their daughters would benefit, as women, from the energetic achievements of their mothers in imagining and organizing an independent Ireland, in conjuring it out of a punishing history of oppression, starvation and defeat, and in creating a cultural and theatrical movement that is still celebrated and written about. This expectation was not met. From the vantage point of the twenty-first century, one looks back to Irish women in theatre in the 1920s and 1930s with sympathy and admiration for their determined survival, and for their ingenious use of theatrical codes and devices to write dramas that could accommodate complex levels of meaning. For the inspiration of role models though, for phenomenal idealism and generosity, for high ambition fuelled by a kind of willed naivety, the first 20 years of the century are the watershed. The early decades encompassed huge political and cultural changes: the height of the cultural renaissance movement, the land reforms of the early century, the revolution of 1916, the Treaty of 1921, the first Irish government, civil war, the consolidation of Fianna Fáil's power as a political force, the rise of fascism in Europe, the Constitution of 1937, and the outbreak of World War Two in 1939.

Feminist scholars have redrawn the developmental map of Irish theatre in these years. The self-conscious appropriations of W. B. Yeats, especially, have been brilliantly illustrated by Roy Foster in his biography, and by Mary Trotter in her pluralist history of the origins of the Irish dramatic movement. Yeats's behaviour, as he worked to control and to represent cultural developments, draws attention to struggles for power in the cultural arena. Yeats placed himself at the centre of the nascent theatre of Ireland, and put the Abbey Theatre at its heart. The attractive simplicity of this version of events elides important contributions, including those of a number of women. Even Augusta Gregory, his supporter and nearest theatrical collaborator, was famously betrayed by him in his Nobel Prize for Literature speech, and, until recently, was robbed of acknowledgement of her work on plays like *Kathleen ni Houlihan*, which he published as sole author. If Yeats has been outed as a ruthless self-publicist, elision of the contribution of groups such as *Inghinidhe na hÉireann* (the Daughters of Ireland) points to the wider, often unconsciously gendered, structures that lead to repeated neglect of women's creativity in cultural and theatrical projects. If women were modest and reticent about their work, they had no need to fear that they would be embarrassed by unwanted recognition from their male comrades. As C. L. Innes further comments, 'too often critics have taken the self-effacement of ... women writers as an excuse for ignoring them.'[1]

Women's role in theatre is a complex set of issues – of writing, producing, performing, of being represented, and of receiving, as audiences, the representations. It is valuable that wider definitions of feminist theatre that include analysis of women working in roles besides writing, and that include issues of representation, in particular performance conditions, are now current. Scholarly analysis of the performance of Kathleen in Yeats's and Gregory's play is a case in point. Such critical approaches have revealed how the central trope of Ireland as a woman impacted on Irish theatre as it developed through the early years of the twentieth century, and how women writing into the 1930s created reactive images in the wake of such powerful icons as the Poor Old Woman, Pegeen Mike and Nora Burke, not to mention the towering mythic females of ancient Ireland. Augusta Gregory interrogated the symbolizing of woman (having co-created the quintessential example with Yeats) in *Grania* (published 1910) and *The Gaol Gate* (1906). She revealed the split between the symbolic woman as she defined nationalist heroism, and the real woman, sacrificing the men she loved, and striving to nurture home and family alone. Irish women playwrights had to deal with a politico-social context where, Trotter points out, 'Irish women became merely passive symbols of the nation – their bodies literally the terrain on which the battle was fought.'[2] In this context, it is no surprise to find women playwrights eager to rewrite, to re-energize these passive tropes.

Realist theatre in Europe had drawn attention to anxieties surrounding women as they sought political representation and full rights as citizens. In Ireland, representations of the 'new woman' were compromised by the concentration of energies on national issues of identity and freedom from English oppression. Where an English woman may have campaigned unproblematically for women's suffrage, a parallel Irish-woman may have joined *Inghinidhe na hÉireann*, founded by Maud Gonne as a conduit for women's political activism, since they were excluded from full participation in overtly political organizations such as the Irish Republican Brotherhood. *Inghinidhe na hÉireann* brought together women's symbolic and real roles as they created perform-ances celebrating Irish icons in *tableaux* and plays, and organized public events. Through their activities they made a nexus of leading players who went on to form the Irish National Theatre Society. As Maud Gonne performed the role of Ireland herself, walking through Dublin streets in a flowing cape with her hound Dagda, the *Inghinidhe* stirred national fervour in crucially influential collaborative events, such as their 1901 programme of *tableaux vivants*, involving playwright Alice Milligan. In June of that year, Milligan's *The Deliverance of Red Hugh*, and *The Harp That Once*, with P. T. MacGinley's *Eilis agus Bhean Deirce* were performed by local actors. To Yeats it was a revelation. His imagination was inflamed by the sound of Dublin accents on-stage, and he reached the realization that, in theatre, language is voice. In 1902, *Inghinidhe* were central organizers of productions of AE's *Deirdre* and Gregory's and Yeats's *Kathleen ni Houlihan*, but by 1903 they had become absorbed into a number of other nationalist organizations, including the company that was to play at the Abbey Theatre.

Limits placed around women's participation in the national move-ment were severely tested by the Gore-Booth sisters, Constance (later Markievicz) and Eva. In contrasting ways, each seriously transgressed the rules of proper feminine behaviour. Constance has bequeathed to us images of the militant woman, pistol in hand, that are deeply unset-tling, and that defy stereotype. Eva was arguably even more radical, since she put issues of women's values and experience before any national interests; in England she was a pacifist suffragist when women's vote had become a prize in exchange for women's support for the 1914–18 war effort. Eva Gore-Booth's imaginative independence marks her out. Her creativity ranged far, and the breadth of her understanding may be seen in the freedom with which she re-figured the mythic tales of her Sligo childhood, of Niamh and Cuchulain, of Deirdre, and of Maeve and Fionavar. If Eva's exile in Manchester exiled her from Irish theatre circles at home, this scarcely put her at a disadvantage compared with other Irish women playwrights determined to take hold of the stage as a public forum.

Geraldine Cummins and Susanne Day had three plays performed at the Abbey Theatre between 1912 and 1917, but did not succeed in consolidating their production record. Cummins wrote many plays that were probably never produced. They are, happily, the subject of ongoing scholarship. The very public vocation of playwright is not an easy one for women in a man's world. Kate O'Brien, better known as a novelist, had considerable success as a playwright with *Distinguished Villa*, produced in London in 1923, but she found the collaborative form of theatre troublesome compared with fiction-writing; novels, she said, you could 'carry on your back.'[3] M. J. Farrell (Molly Keane), likewise, wrote *Spring Meeting* for the London stage in 1938, but waited until 1950 for her next theatre success, *Treasure Hunt*. Both of these authors suffered the censorship of their novels in Ireland. Ironically, the Lord Chamberlain had no control over theatrical presentations on Irish stages, which were policed by forces far harder to identify, but nonetheless powerful for that. The Catholic Church and masculinist post-colonial definitions of Irishness were ingrained to the point where playwrights who challenged hegemonic versions of Ireland, and the constraints placed on its women folk in every aspect of their lives, were either rejected, or learned to write in code. Dorothy Macardle manipulated realist theatrical form to propose women's moral values as fundamentally at odds with men's. She used ideas of the supernatural to create images of women's energy and potential that were not accommodated within a patriarchal realist frame. Teresa Deevy dramatized disempowerment in her young heroines. These characters are sites of remarkable imaginative and creative power, twisted and distorted by their reliance on men and their social vulnerability. Also writing in the 1930s, Mary Manning foregrounded the absurdities of Irishness as a manufactured identity, and the failure of independent Ireland to disrupt conservative notions of women as marriage fodder, or to challenge the social controls of class and gender categories inherited from the English occupier.

1939 is a turning point as Britain and Europe are swept away in the moral catastrophe of World War Two. Ireland's neutrality, arguably, isolated the country not only during the war years but later too, as the legacy of the conflict, its horrors, its losses, its extremity played out in political, social, philosophical and cultural impacts, with which Ireland only belatedly caught up. The effect of the war on women's lives is an issue too. In Ireland, women's situations in a stagnant social order suffered, while partition has continued to divide radical women between republicanism and feminism. In her book on women and nation, Innes aims to reveal: 'Not only the extent of the activities which women undertook, but also to uncover the distinctiveness of what they had to say when all too often their voices had been obscured or subsumed.'[4] Over the 40 years from 1900, the prodigious optimism and inventiveness nurtured by women in the political and social upheavals of cultural renaissance, revolution and civil war, were muffled by consolidation in the nascent state. But women found ways, even under tremendous pressures, to explore through theatre what the *status quo* carefully edited out, ignored or dismissed. For women writers, theatre was a hard path to follow. Their legacy, their plays as blueprints for performance, offers the potential for re-enactment, to test the frailty of the very notion of progress.

Notes

1. C. L. Innes, *Woman and Nation in Irish Literature and Society, 1880–1935* (London: Harvester Wheatsheaf, 1993), p. 179.
2. Mary Trotter, *Ireland's National Theaters: Political Performance and the Origins of the Irish Dramatic Movement* (New York: Syracuse University Press, 2001), p. 76.
3. Kate O'Brien, Interview, *New York Times*, 4 December 1949, p. 22.
4. Innes, *Woman and Nation in Irish Literature and Society*, p. 4.

1
Woman as Fantasy Object in Lady Gregory's Historical Tragedies

Paul Murphy

Barely a year after her death, W. B. Yeats published two poems venerating Lady Augusta Gregory in his collection *The Winding Stair and Other Poems*, 'Coole Park, 1929' and 'Coole Park and Ballylee, 1931', both of which commemorate her legacy to Irish theatre and culture. While Yeats's veneration of Lady Gregory has the effect of canonizing her as a cultural icon, it also has the concomitant effect of ossifying her place in history. Christopher Murray argues that such 'mummifying tributes' tend to 'stiffen her into monumental awesomeness like a building, like Coole House itself or the Abbey Theatre'.[1] What is astounding about Lady Gregory's career is that in addition to the huge effort involved in organizing and sustaining the fledgling Abbey Theatre, she also managed to produce a canon of some 42 plays.[2] The achievement is even more impressive when one considers Lady Gregory's contribution to the writing of plays normally included within the Yeatsian canon, such as *The Pot of Broth* (1904), *Where There is Nothing* and its revision as *The Unicorn from the Stars* (1907), and most notably *Kathleen ni Houlihan* (1902).[3] Colm Tóibín states:

> It is now absolutely clear that ... *Cathleen ni Houlihan*, though credited to Yeats, was written largely by Lady Gregory. The idea belonged to Yeats and Yeats wrote the chant of the old woman at the end. But he could not write peasant dialogue, and the play depends on the naturalistic setting, the talk of money and marriage, the sense of ease in family life in a smallholding. In the manuscript held in the Berg Collection in the New York Public Library, Lady Gregory has written in pencil on the first section of ten pages 'All this mine', and 'This with WBY' at the beginning of the second section.[4]

In spite of the evidence of her skill as a dramatist, Lady Gregory's plays are hardly ever performed at the Abbey or any other theatre in Dublin or the rest of Ireland. While a great deal of scholarship has been produced about the plays of Yeats and J. M. Synge, only a fraction of that amount has been produced about Lady Gregory's plays. As Murray suggests,'[a] pat on the laurelled head from Yeats does not do Gregory justice.'[5]

Scholarship produced on Lady Gregory since the 1960s has generally taken the form of biographical and commemorative work, stressing her significance to the Irish Renaissance in terms of her political and intellectual development, her management skills and her support of other dramatists, particularly Yeats.[6] The scholarship which focuses primarily on Lady Gregory's dramatic work tends to be similarly biographical and commemorative, and avoids rigorous examination of the cultural politics of the plays and their relationship to the social context in which they were written.[7] The commemorative approach conforms to what Nietzsche describes as '*antiquarian*'[8] history, specifically the work of one 'who preserves and reveres' that which has gone before them.[9] In certain ways this approach replicates Yeats's eulogization of Lady Gregory insofar as the antiquarian mode can sometimes 'grow too mighty and overpower the other modes of regarding the past. For it knows only how to *preserve* life, not how to engender it.'[10] While Lady Gregory's *oeuvre* has been (so to speak) well-preserved, it has not been engendered or revitalized in the same manner as the plays of Yeats or Synge. A major reason for the constant revivification of Yeats's and Synge's work is the application of what Nietzsche calls '*critical*'[11] history, which involves 'bringing it before the tribunal, scrupulously examining it and finally condemning it'.[12] The irony here, of course, is that the more the plays of Yeats and Synge have been scrupulously examined and 'condemned' by scholars and audiences, the more their plays have been written about and revived on the stage. The dialectics of critical debate over the years has involved constant reinterpretation and reassessment of their work. In this sense, then, Lady Gregory's plays must also be subjected to a '*critical*' historicization in order for them to be saved from the kind of eulogization which has led to her mummification as a dramatist.

Lady Isabella Augusta Gregory was born into the Protestant Anglo-Irish Ascendancy class; her family, the Persses, were staunch Unionists who owned Roxborough, an estate of significant proportions in southern Galway. The Persses were 'not regarded by the people, the tenantry, as beneficent',[13] to whom they acted as colonial expropriators, gaining from the Great Famine of 1845–49 when other members of their class were almost bankrupted by the catastrophe. As a retaliatory gesture to the Persses's expropriation, the IRA burned down Roxborough House in 1922. In 1880 Augusta Persse married Sir William Gregory, a widower 35 years her senior, who owned Coole Park and had been an MP for Dublin and Galway, and Governor of Ceylon 1871–77. Sir William was responsible for the infamous 'Gregory Clause' of 1847, an amendment to the Poor Relief (Ireland) Act of 1838, 'which denied relief to anyone possessing more than a quarter-acre of land; this boosted the landlord desiderata of land clearance and emigration, and has been credited with "disintegrating the fabric of rural society".'[14] By birth and marriage, then, Lady Gregory was intimately involved with the colonial Ascendancy class and her political evolution from ardent Unionist to strident Nationalist was a slow and difficult one.[15] Sean O'Casey, an unlikely ally considering his political beliefs, crystallized Lady Gregory's predicament in a letter to her in 1928: 'you had to fight against your birth into position and comfort as others had to fight against their birth into hardship and poverty, and it is as difficult to come out of one as it is to come out of the other.'[16]

A pivotal event in Lady Gregory's political development occurred during her travels with Sir William to Egypt in 1881, where she met the poet William Scawen Blunt who was visiting Egypt with his wife. Both Lady Gregory and Blunt developed an interest in the activities of Arabi Bey, an Egyptian revolutionary who was contesting the colonial domination of North Africa by Britain and France, and Lady Gregory's first published work was an account of her meeting with Arabi and his family.[17] From their keen interest in the activities of the anti-colonial Arabi, Lady Gregory and Blunt developed a keen interest in each other and had a passionate love affair which lasted 18 months, starting when Lady Gregory had been married to Sir William for less than two years in total. Lady Gregory's and Blunt's affections were covertly manifested in 'A Woman's Sonnets', comprising 12 sonnets written by Lady Gregory and remodelled by Blunt, which he published near the end of January 1892, barely six weeks before Sir William died.[18] While Lady Gregory's public persona after Sir William's death was an Anglo-Irish version of Queen Victoria after Prince Albert's death, wearing black and maintaining a cool detachment from the world around her, the sonnets reveal the burning desire beneath the cold exterior. A sense of guilt and betrayal pervades Lady Gregory's biography and aesthetics in terms of both sexual and national politics: her love for Sir William and her love for Blunt constituted a deep emotional conflict which troubled her for many years; her loyalty to the Anglo-Irish Ascendancy class and her commitment to Irish anti-colonial Nationalism constituted a similarly difficult impasse.

When one factors in the sublimation/subordination double-bind which Irish women of all classes and creeds faced on a quotidian basis, then one can appreciate the issues which Lady Gregory had to deal with. Indeed, these issues were manifest in her plays, especially in her rendering of the female protagonist as Woman *qua* fantasy object of masculinist and national desire. Three of Lady Gregory's tragedies, namely *Kincora*, *Dervorgilla* and *Grania* conform in many ways to the Classical Greek model, which Aristotle describes as the imitation of 'agents' who are 'admirable' or who are 'better people than we are'.[19] The tragic element lies in an 'error of some kind'[20] which causes a reversal of fortune from an admirable to deplorable state, typified in Sophocles's *Oedipus the King* and Euripides's *Medea*. The admirable agents who undergo such a reversal are invariably members of the aristocracy: Oedipus the King of Thebes; Medea the princess of Colchis and wife of Jason, son of Aeson the King of Iolcus. Lady Gregory's tragedies follow very much in the vein of Classical Greek tragedy in that they involve the same reversal of fortune where the respective protagonists Gormleith, Dervorgilla and Grania are aristocratic women who endure the transition from an admirable to deplorable state.

All three tragedies are effectively history plays dealing with specific junctures in Ireland's long history of conflict with incursionary forces bent on conquering the island. *Kincora* (1905)[21] charts the relationship between Gormleith and Brian Boru in the events which lead up to Brian's legendary victory over the Viking and Danish forces at Clontarf in 1014. The play opens with a prologue where Brian encounters Aoibhell, the 'Spirit' who tempts him to join her in her supernatural realm. Brian has the opportunity to achieve the *jouissance* available in a relationship with Aoibhell, but he rejects her in favour of the possible *jouissance* to be gained in the realization of a united Ireland, which is achievable only after the ordeal of constant war and sacrifice. He could short-circuit the constitutive gap of desire and immediately experience this *jouissance*, but in choosing 'that hard sweetheart Ireland'[22] Brian accepts the pain of successive ordeals. Brian's choice parallels the masochistic etiquette followed by the knight in the classic courtly love scenario where he pretends that his 'sweetheart' is the cruel, inaccessible Lady. As Slavoj Žižek suggests: 'The knight's relationship to the Lady is thus the relationship of the subject-bondsman, vassal, to his feudal Master-Sovereign who subjects him to senseless, outrageous, impossible, arbitrary, capricious ordeals.'[23]

The inaccessible 'hard sweetheart Ireland' takes on material form for Brian in the shape of Queen Gormleith: wife to Malachi, the High King of Ireland; sister of Maelmora, King of Leinster; and mother to Sitric, Leader of the Danes, through a previous marriage. Gormleith's nationality is central to the play insofar as she was born in Ireland, but also has loyalty to the incursionary Danish forces. The combination of Gormleith's potential for 'great trouble' and her 'high beauty' constitutes her as the object cause of desire for both the Irish and the Danish forces who are contesting the ownership of Ireland.[24] In many aspects Gormleith is an incarnation of the Morrígan, the Goddess of Battle, in that she is driven towards (and drives others towards) war and conflict. Gormleith's lust for battle leads her to betray Brian's and Malachi's forces, and to ally herself with the Danes and her brother Maelmora in the battle of Glenmama. Malachi is hell-bent on retribution against Gormleith and her co-conspirators, stating that 'Ireland can have no worse enemies than these', but he leaves their fate to Brian's decision. However, Brian's desire to bring peace through victory and unify Ireland's disparate factions results in an unexpectedly magnanimous gesture after his victory at Glenmama. At the very moment when Brian can finally 'force a peace', he frees Gormleith and her co-conspirators, an act which will ironically lead to further war and ultimately to his death. Just as at the start of the play when Brian can actually achieve *jouissance*, he undermines the realization of that possibility by releasing Gormleith, who Malachi prophetically describes as 'the very seed and root of war', before relinquishing both Gormleith and his High Kingship to Brian.

In the peaceful lull before the final battle at Clontarf, Ireland achieves a measure of unity under Brian's hegemony, revealed to him by Maire, who 'came safely through all' as she travelled from Ulster to Munster, two provinces with a long history of conflict. Gormleith, however, cannot tolerate Brian's peace and shatters it by betraying him again. Once more Brian has a chance to stop the battle before it begins by killing Gormleith, as she herself explains in a moment of repentance: 'You do not understand – there are great hosts coming...they look to me to welcome them – they may turn back if I am not there.'[25] Malachi assures Brian that he should follow Gormleith's advice and when Brian can finally look awry at Gormleith and realize that she is a mortal woman rather than the sublime Woman of his fantasy, he is shattered. On the day of his death Brian accepts the error Gormleith commits as a treacherous, mortal woman, and finally identifies with his symptom as he stops misrecognizing Gormleith as the object of his desire. Like the protagonist of Yeats's Cuchulain cycle of plays, Brian can only achieve the *jouissance* which has tantalized him all his life when he moves from the Symbolic order into the Real in the moment of his death at the end of the battle. Gormleith becomes the object cause of his desire insofar as her status as his *objet petit a*,[26] the traumatic fragment of the Real, is doubly significant in terms of her status as the locus of both national and sexual desire. Brian risks his life and the security of his kingdom for her, just as Brodar of Manannan's Island, Sigurd of Orkney and the Danes risk their lives and fiefdoms for the possibility of union with her. At each juncture Gormleith functions as the fantasy object of masculinist desire which is intimately related to the issue of national sovereignty.

Lady Gregory wrote a revision of *Kincora* which was produced in 1909.[27] The revision is broadly similar to the original but the prologue where Brian encounters Aoibhell the Spirit and refers to 'that hard sweetheart' Ireland is noticeably absent. Brennain's daughter Maire is replaced by the Beggar Girl, and Aoibhell is only referred to a handful of times in the play, once when Brian is talking to the Beggar Girl about the peace he has temporarily brought by uniting Ireland. The Beggar Girl fulfils certain functions that Aoibhell and Maire fulfilled in the earlier version of *Kincora*, insofar as she tells Brian that peace has been achieved and tries to convince him that further conflict is unnecessary. Gormleith's role remains constant however, and while she is certainly an active subject rather than a passive object, her activities oscillate between fealty and treachery to both Ireland and its invaders, so that her only discernable objective seems to be war and bloodshed. Gormleith's *raison d'être* and primary dramatic function therefore is to serve as both goad and goal of the male protagonists, particularly Brian whom she marries and 'in an ambivalent way both betrays him and creates his finest hour at Clontarf'.[28] Gormleith, then, is typical, if not indeed archetypal, of the Woman as fantasy object, who is sublimated insofar as she supports masculinist-nationalist ontology, and yet is simultaneously subordinated as the scapegoat who must accept responsibility for the war and bloodshed concomitant to preserving the structural integrity of both national and masculinist identity. Ultimately Gormleith serves to re-create if not also advocate gender stereotypes of Irish womanhood rather than challenging those stereotypes in any progressive manner.

Dervorgilla (1907)[29] is set outside the Abbey of Mellifont near Drogheda in 1193, during the period of the first wave of Anglo-Norman invasions which involved the 'piecemeal displacement of the native rulers by Anglo-Norman noble families, a process loosely supervised by the

English monarchy'.[30] The play deals with the consequences of Queen Dervorgilla's betrayal of O'Rourke, King of Breffny, in her affair with Diarmuid, King of Leinster, which allegedly had a causal relation to the Anglo-Norman invasion. Dervorgilla is living anonymously at Mellifont, her identity protected by her servants, Flann and Mona, from exposure to the native, colonized Irish who hold her accountable for their predicament. Dervorgilla has devoted her time to charitable exploits in order to ease her guilt-wracked conscience, and has accordingly earned the love of her community: 'MONA: No wonder the people do be saying she will surely get the name of a saint; the darling queen-woman of the Abbey of Mellifont.'[31]

Dervorgilla's status as 'saint' and 'darling queen-woman' is doubly significant when interpreted in Lacanian terms as *le sinthome*, a neologism designed to describe a symptom which endures beyond the fantasy framework which gives it meaning in the first place. In 'Joyce le symptôme' Lacan develops *sinthome* as a synthesis of the traumatic quality of the symptom with the sublime quality of the saint.[32] Žižek suggests that '[w]hat we must bear in mind here is the radical ontological status of symptom: symptom, conceived as *sinthome*, is literally our only substance, the only positive support of our being, the only point that gives consistency to the subject.'[33] In other words, 'symptom is the way we – the subjects – "avoid madness", the way we "choose something (the symptom-formation) instead of nothing (radical psychotic autism, the destruction of the symbolic universe)" through the binding of our enjoyment to a certain signifying, symbolic formation which assures a minimum of consistency to our being-in-the-world.'[34] Dervorgilla functions as the *sinthome* in the play in the double sense as the saint/queen-woman whom her servants and the community at Mellifont revere, but also as the traumatic symptom of the recently colonized population who hold her responsible for their plight.

Dervorgilla is well aware of her status as saint/symptom within the community when, in a moment of bonhomie shared with her servants and neighbours, she is abruptly reminded of her traumatic legacy when Mamie runs in with a dead crane shot by English archers:

Dervorgilla: Was it not I brought the curse upon O'Rourke, King of Breffny, the husband I left and betrayed? The head I made bow with shame was struck off and sent to the English King. The body I forsook was hung on the walls shamefully, by the feet, like a calf after slaughter. It is certain there is a curse on all that have to do with me. What I have done can never be undone. How can I be certain of the forgiveness of God?[35]

Dervorgilla's self-reflection reveals the symbolic nature of her guilt insofar as her sexual betrayal is intimately linked to her national betrayal of her country's sovereignty. Flann explains that it was internecine war and internal division among the factions within Ireland which led to English occupation, but Dervorgilla's guilt at her marital infidelity drives her to internalize the opprobrium of a recently colonized people who are desperate to rationalize the trauma of their oppression. In this sense, then, Dervorgilla functions as the symbolic materialization of her people's immiseration, with her peccadillo with Diarmuid taking on a national dimension in the colonized people's need to create a single scapegoat rather than engage with the political complexities of their situation.

Dervorgilla's traumatic quality comes to the fore as the play reaches its climax when a Songmaker comes to the village and recites the tale of Dervorgilla's transgression to the local English garrison. Dervorgilla asks Flann to send the Songmaker away before he can arouse any further suspicion, but Flann is killed by the English archers for interrupting the Songmaker's performance. When Flann's wife Mona hears of his demise she breaks into grief-stricken lamentations and unintentionally reveals Dervorgilla's true identity to the local villagers. The play ends with the villagers returning all the gifts that Dervorgilla has given them as she resigns herself to her fate as the fallen woman responsible for the nation's woes:

Dervorgilla: There is kindness in your unkindness, not leaving me to go and face Michael and the Scales of Judgement wrapped in comfortable words, and the praises of the poor, and the lulling of psalms, but from the swift, unflinching, terrible judgement of the young! (*She sinks slowly to the ground holding to the chair. The stage begins to darken; the voice of the* SONGMAKER *is heard coming nearer, singing*:)[36]

Dervorgilla, like Gormleith, is a reincarnation of the Woman as object cause of masculinist desire from the ancient Irish sagas and evokes the chauvinistic portrayal of women intrinsic to that period and its liter-ature. The rendering of Dervorgilla and Gormleith as scapegoats for bloodshed and national immiseration are the products of masculinist inadequacy in the face of superior colonialist force. The representation of female characters in these ancient sagas is problematic in that they are made to pay for either the sexual or military impotence of the males, and this is part and parcel of Lady Gregory's dramatization of the sagas insofar as she replicates but does not contest the injustice of their gender typology. It is hard to imagine that Lady Gregory was unaware of this injustice, and her status as a female dramatist would not necessarily require her to overtly engage with gender issues. Indeed, the majority of her dramatic canon does not explicitly engage with the role of women in Irish society. Perhaps Lady Gregory's replication of stereotypical gender ideology in her historical tragedies emerges from an underlying sense of guilt over her infidelity with Blunt.

Dervorgilla's paradoxical status as both sublime queen-woman and traumatic symptom of her country's woes is markedly similar to the eponymous protagonist of Lady Gregory's later play *Grania* (1912).[37] Grania is one of the great *femmes fatales* in Irish mythology and Lady Gregory had engaged with Grania's story long before she wrote the play when she recorded the tale in *Gods and Fighting Men* (1904).[38] In the play, Grania, the King of Ireland's daughter, is initially betrothed to the much older Finn, the leader of the Fíanna. In their opening dialogue Finn asks if Grania ever gave 'a thought to any man in the way of love', to which Grania replies that she was attracted to a man she met briefly 'a long time ago', but 'he was but as if a shadow, that came for a moment and was gone.'[39] When Grania explains that the 'shadow' saved her pet dog from being killed, Finn considers her to be naïve, stating that as far as love is concerned 'I think it is little at all you know of it', and they then engage in a discussion on the politics of desire. The discussion elaborates upon what Lacan refers to as 'the impossibility of the sexual relationship', where the sexual relationship between the two lovers is impossible insofar as they desire what each other represents in the field of desire – namely each other's *jouissance* – rather than what they actually are in the material sense. Love is precisely 'tearing and vexing'[40] because it is unobtainable in the material realm and can only ever be sought after in the fantasy realm as the impossible *objet petit a*. The ironic nature of romantic love is that it depends on misrecognizing the *objet petit a* as the actual person which temporarily materializes or stands in for the fantasy object: 'GRANIA: But the old people say more again about love. They say there is no good thing to be gained without hardship and pain, such as a child to be born, or a long day's battle won. And I think it might be a pleasing thing to have a lover that would go through fire for your sake.'[41] The impossibility of being 'done with [love], and to be safe from its torments'[42] is confirmed when Grania is introduced to Diarmuid, Finn's kinsman and allegedly 'the best lover of women in the whole world, and the most daring in the war.'[43] It transpires that Diarmuid is the 'shadow' which Grania fleetingly encountered long ago, and the desire she had for him quickly returns to divert her affections from Finn. Within a short space of time Grania goes through a rapid desublimation in Finn's eyes, as he accuses her mother of being a prostitute ('some woman of the camp'), calling Grania's explanation a 'false woman's flattering words' and finally castigating her as a 'pitiful hag with the hair matted wild to her knees'.[44]

When Diarmuid gallantly defends Grania's honour by threatening to draw his sword, Finn responds: 'My life is a little thing beside what you have taken!'[45] What Finn accuses Diarmuid of stealing is not Grania the physical woman, but more what she represents as the object cause of Finn's desire. Finn is so consumed with frustration that he faints and collapses, and Diarmuid takes the opportunity to flee with Grania. It takes Finn seven years to catch up with Diarmuid and Grania, who have, as he predicted, fallen in love with one another, but their relationship was neither as easy nor as mutual as Finn had envisaged. Grania explains to Diarmuid that he only fell in love with her out of 'jealousy' when he saw another man, the King of Foreign, desiring her: 'GRANIA: And it was not till you saw another man craving my love, that the like love was born in yourself.'[46] What is striking is not only the transformation of Grania from desexualized 'shadow-shape' or 'hag' to sublime object of Diarmuid's desire, but equally the successive desublimation when he realizes that she desired, albeit fleetingly, the King of Foreign. With that Diarmuid goes off to kill the King of Foreign, and in the afternoon of the same day Finn encounters Grania and explains at length the desire he still has for her: 'Is it not a great wonder the candle you lighted not to have been quenched in all that time? But the light in your grey eyes is my desire for ever, and I am pulled here and there over hills and through hollows.'[47]

In spite of the intensity of Finn's affection for her, Grania is implacable and is devoted to Diarmuid, 'that gave all up for love is the best lover of the whole world'.[48] Diarmuid returns after killing the King of Foreign, but is himself mortally wounded in the battle. Diarmuid's final words are directed solely to Finn as Diarmuid reiterates his loyalty and devotion to his leader: 'That would be a very foolish man would give up his dear master and his friend for any woman at all. (*He laughs.*)'[49] When Grania realizes that Diarmuid has not forgiven her flirtation with the King of Foreign and died professing his devotion to Finn, she performs a volte-face as striking as her turn of affections earlier in the play as she expresses her desire to return with Finn as his wife. When Finn also refutes his earlier declarations of love for her in favour of loyalty to his dead friend, Grania is laughed at by the soldiers, but she ends the play nonetheless defiant: 'GRANIA. How well he kept his own promise to you! I will go to Almhuin in spite of you; you will be ashamed to turn me back in the sight of the people, and they having seen your feet grown hard in following and chasing me through the years.'[50]

Grania's oscillating status in the play as sublime object cause of desire who undergoes a rapid desublimation, constitutes a fascinating engagement with the complexities of Woman as fantasy object. Each of Lady Gregory's tragic heroines shares this commonality of desublimation with the medieval figure of *die Frau-Welt*. Žižek argues that the:

> same experience of desublimation was already well known in the tradition of courtly love, in the guise of the figure of *die Frau-Welt* (the woman who stands for the world, terrestrial life): she looks beautiful from the proper distance, but the moment the poet or the knight serving her approaches her too closely ... she turns her other, reverse side towards him, and what was previously the semblance of fascinating beauty is suddenly revealed as putrefied flesh, crawling with snakes and worms, the disgusting substance of life.[51]

Žižek suggests that the 'gap that separates beauty from ugliness is thus the very gap that separates reality from the Real: what constitutes reality is the minimum of idealization the subject needs in order to be able to sustain the horror of the Real.'[52] In the case of Lady Gregory's heroines, the moment of desublimation occurs when the heroine exercises agency in terms of desiring another lover or choosing a different political allegiance.[53] The heroine's status as either sublime or desublimated object is intimately linked to the performance of her sexual and political desire. Thus, Grania incurs the scorn and hatred of Diarmuid's comrades in the Fíanna when they hear that he has died, and when she hears about their mocking laughter waiting for her outside, she is determined to have the last laugh: 'Give me now the crown, till I go out before them, as you offered it often enough. (*She puts it on her head.*) I am going, I am going out now, to show myself before them all, and my hand linked in your own. It is well I brought my golden dress.'[54]

When Grania goes outside the expected laughing from the warriors in the Fíanna stops abruptly: '(*She opens the door herself.* FINN *puts his arm about her. There is another great peal of laughter, but it stops suddenly as she goes out.*)'[55] Grania's status as object cause of desire is immediately reinstated when she performs the role of Queen and wife to Finn, the leader of the Fíanna. She thus restores the constitutive gap of desire between herself and the Fíanna, turning herself from object of derision to sublime object. Where Gormleith's and Dervorgilla's sexual and political choice ends in a deplorable state, Grania is able to negotiate both her internal conflicts and the external opprobrium from her community and ends the play in a comparatively admirable state. Grania's gesture involves a high degree of self-reflexivity in that she self-consciously utilizes her status as fantasy object to save herself from the deplorable state which befell Gormleith and Dervorgilla. The parallels between the differing trajectories of these heroines and Lady Gregory's own teleology are quite striking in terms of her negotiation of politics in the shift from Unionism to Nationalism, and negotiation of sexuality in the shift from betrayal-born guilt to acceptance and self-reconciliation. The fates of Gormleith and Dervorgilla manifest Lady Gregory's own situation in terms of the difficulty of reconciling her former Unionist politics with her growing Nationalist sympathies, and her infidelity towards her husband Sir William. Grania's tortuous development constitutes a negotiation of the irreconcilable double-bind in which Lady Gregory found herself as the Ascendancy aristocrat turned home-rule Nationalist. The closing image of Grania embracing the fidelity/infidelity dialectic at the heart of her ontology is indicative of the tenuous position Lady Gregory came to occupy as the colonizer who refused[56] her colonial position, while at the same time desiring to maintain a leading role in the shifting sands of Irish cultural politics.

Notes

1. Christopher Murray, *Twentieth Century Irish Drama: Mirror up to Nation* (Manchester: Manchester University Press, 1997), p. 37
2. See Lady Gregory, *Collected Plays, Vol. I: Comedies* (Gerrards Cross: Colin Smythe, 1971); *Vol. II: Tragedies and Tragic Comedies* (Gerrards Cross: Colin Smythe, 1979); *Vol. III: Wonder and Supernatural* (Gerrards Cross: Colin Smythe, 1970); *Vol. IV: Collaborations, Adaptations and Translations* (Gerrards Cross: Colin Smythe, 1979).
3. See Daniel J. Murphy, 'Lady Gregory, Co-Author and Sometimes Author of the Plays of W. B. Yeats', in Raymond J. Porter and James D. Brophy (eds), *Modern Irish Literature: Essays in Honour of William York Tindall* (New York: Iona College Press, 1972).
4. Colm Tóibín, *Lady Gregory's Toothbrush* (Dublin: Lilliput Press, 2002), p. 45.
5. Murray, *Twentieth Century Irish Drama*, p. 37.
6. See especially: Ann Saddlemyer (ed.), *Theatre Business: The Correspondence of the First Abbey Directors: William Butler Yeats, Lady Gregory and J. M. Synge* (Gerrards Cross: Colin Smythe, 1982); Mary Lou Kohfeldt, *Lady Gregory: The*

Woman Behind the Irish Renaissance (London: Andre Deutsch, 1985); Ann Saddlemyer and Colin Smythe (eds), *Lady Gregory, Fifty Years After*, Irish Literary Studies 13 (Gerrards Cross: Colin Smythe; Totowa: Barnes and Noble, 1987).

7. See Ann Saddlemyer, *In Defence of Lady Gregory, Playwright* (Dublin: Dolmen Press, 1966); Elizabeth Coxhead, *Lady Gregory: A Literary Portrait* (London: Secker & Warburg, 1966).

8. Friedrich Nietzsche, 'On the Uses and Disadvantages of History for Life', in *Untimely Meditations* (Cambridge: Cambridge University Press, 1983), p. 67.

9. Nietzsche, *Untimely Meditations*, p. 72.

10. Nietzsche, *Untimely Meditations*, p. 75.

11. Nietzsche, *Untimely Meditations*, p. 75.

12. Nietzsche, *Untimely Meditations*, p. 76.

13. Murray, *Twentieth Century Irish Drama*, p. 40.

14. R. F. Foster, *Modern Ireland* (London: Penguin, 1989), p. 328.

15. See Ann Saddlemyer, 'Augusta Gregory, Irish Nationalist: "After all, What is Wanted but a Hag and a Voice?"', in Joseph Ronsley (ed.), *Myth and Reality in Irish Literature* (Waterloo Ontario: Wilfrid Laurier University Press, 1977), pp. 29–40.

16. Sean O'Casey, *The Letters of Sean O'Casey*, Vol. 1, ed. David Krause (London: Macmillan, 1975), p. 233.

17. The account was published as 'Arabi and His Household', in *The Times*, 23 September 1882.

18. William Scawen Blunt, 'A Woman's Sonnets', in *Love Lyrics and Songs of Proteus with the Love Sonnets of Proteus* (Hammersmith: Kelmscott Press 1892).

19. Aristotle, *Poetics*, trans. Malcolm Heath (London: Penguin, 1996), p. 5.

20. Aristotle, *Poetics*, p. 21.

21. Lady Gregory, *Kincora*, first performed 25 March 1905, by the Irish National Theatre Society, at the Abbey Theatre, Dublin; first published Dublin: The Abbey Theatre, 1905, being Volume II of the Abbey Theatre Series.

22. Lady Augusta Gregory, *Kincora* (1905) [first version], in *Collected Plays, Vol. II: Tragedies & Tragic Comedies* (Colin Smythe, 1979), p. 316.

23. Slavoj Žižek, *The Metastases of Enjoyment: Six Essays on Woman and Causality* (London and New York: Verso, 1994), p. 90.

24. Lady Gregory, *Kincora*, p. 325.

25. Lady Gregory, *Kincora*, pp. 347–8.

26. See Jacques Lacan, 'Of the Gaze as *Objet Petit a*', in *The Four Fundamentals of Psycho-Analysis* (Harmondsworth: Penguin, 1994).

27. Lady Gregory, *Kincora*, revised version, first produced 11 February 1909, by the National Theatre Society Ltd., at the Abbey Theatre, Dublin; first published in *Irish Folk-History Plays, First Series* (New York and London: Putnam, 1912).

28. Murray, *Twentieth Century Irish Drama*, p. 53

29. Lady Gregory, *Dervorgilla*, first performed 31 October 1907, by the National Theatre Society, Ltd., at the Abbey Theatre, Dublin; first published in *Samhain* (1908); first book publication in *Irish Folk History Plays. First Series – The Tragedies* (New York and London: G. P. Putnam's Sons, 1912).

30. David Cairns and Shaun Richards, *Writing Ireland: Colonialism, Nationalism and Culture* (Manchester: Manchester University Press, 1988), p. 1.

31. Lady Gregory, *Dervorgilla* (1907), in *Collected Plays, Vol. II: Tragedies & Tragic Comedies* (Gerrards Cross: Colin Smythe, 1979), p. 95.
32. See Jacques Lacan, 'Joyce le symptôme', in *Joyce avec Lacan* (Paris: Navarin, Diffusion Seuil, 1987).
33. Slavoj Žižek, *The Sublime Object of Ideology* (London and New York: Verso, 1989), p. 75.
34. Žižek, *The Sublime Object of Ideology*, p. 75.
35. Lady Gregory, *Dervorgilla*, p. 98.
36. Lady Gregory, *Dervorgilla*, p. 110.
37. *Grania*, no record of production; first published in *Irish Folk History Plays. First Series – The Tragedies* (New York and London: G. P. Putnam's Sons, 1912).
38. See Lady Augusta Gregory, *Gods and Fighting Men: The Story of the Tuatha de Danaan and of the Fianna of Ireland, Arranged and Put into English by Lady Gregory* (London: Albemarle, 1904; Gerrards Cross: Irish University Press in association with Colin Smythe, 1970).
39. Lady Gregory, *Grania* (1912), in *Collected Plays, Vol. II: Tragedies & Tragic Comedies* (Gerrards Cross: Colin Smythe, 1979), p. 15.
40. Lady Gregory, *Grania*, p. 15.
41. Lady Gregory, *Grania*, pp. 15–16.
42. Lady Gregory, *Grania*, p. 16.
43. Lady Gregory, *Grania*, p. 14.
44. Lady Gregory, *Grania*, ff. 20–1.
45. Lady Gregory, *Grania*, p. 20.
46. Lady Gregory, *Grania*, p. 28.
47. Lady Gregory, *Grania*, p. 38.
48. Lady Gregory, *Grania*, p. 39.
49. Lady Gregory, *Grania*, p. 42.
50. Lady Gregory, *Grania*, p. 45.
51. Slavoj Žižek, *The Plague of Fantasies* (London and New York: Verso, 1997), p. 66.
52. Žižek, *The Plague of Fantasies*, p. 66.
53. Grania's agency is the main reason Lady Gregory decided to write a play about Grania rather than Deirdre because so many plays had 'been written about the sad, lovely Deirdre, who when overtaken by sorrow made no good battle at the last. Grania had more power of will, and for good or evil, twice took the shaping of her life into her own hands.' [Lady Gregory, *Irish Folk-History Plays* (New York, London: Putnam, 1912), p. 283].
54. Lady Gregory, *Grania*, p. 45.
55. Lady Gregory, *Grania*, p. 46.
56. See Albert Memmi, 'The Colonizer Who Refuses', in *The Colonizer and the Colonized* (London: Earthscan, 1990).

2
Writing Women for a Modern Ireland: Geraldine Cummins and Susanne Day

Velma O'Donoghue Greene

Winds of change currently reconfiguring academic perceptions of global history are blowing through the fields of Irish drama and literature. Publications such as *Ireland's National Theaters: Political Performance and the Origins of the Irish Dramatic Movement; The Field Day Anthology of Irish Writing: Irish Women Writers and Traditions, Vols 1V and V*; and the recently published *Dictionary of Munster Women Writers*, constitute examples of a wealth of material evidences that contribute accounts of women's cultural past to a growing body of feminist historiographies.[1] The findings of these and other studies serve to promote a re-evaluation of the historical assumptions regarding women's minimal contribution to Ireland's cultural heritage, particularly in the field of early Irish theatre. They reveal and contextualize previously unrecorded strategies and networking systems, employed by creatively active women in a male-dominated literary world. The texts and autobiographical accounts recovered, document the spaces inhabited by women for the production and dissemination of their ideas, and acknowledge their political acumen and moral arguments regarding issues of gender/class inequality.[2] Historian Margaret Kelleher describes the separate spheres of public and private realms of individuals' activities in Victorian society as ' . . . a cultural and rhetorical construct', arguing that 'it was no less powerful for its fictive basis'.[3] The activities, creative work and autobiographical writings of women of the early twentieth century reveal resistance to sex-prescribed roles, particularly from women of the privileged class, and illuminate ways by which many women challenged the immutable notions of their gender.

Two such women are virtually unknown playwrights Geraldine Cummins and Susanne Day. Cummins hailed from an Anglican middle-class professional background and worked from necessity. In contrast, paid labour was optional for women from privileged Anglo-Irish upper-class families and Day, who chose to work, belonged to this social group. The 'Geraldine Cummins Collection' in the Cork Archives Institute contains material relating to her primary career as a respected and published 'automatic' writer in the field of psychical research. However, a substantial proportion of the collection comprises a body of 24 plays, 12 of which Cummins claims sole authorship for. She wrote three of the early plays in collaboration with Day and four with a friend and colleague in psychical research, Hester Dowden. Susanne Day sole-authored three plays in this collection and the remaining two are in a non-catalogued box of material awaiting examination. These works span a period between the closing years of British colonialism in Ireland up to and beyond the formation of the Irish Free State in 1922. Of the 24 plays in the Cummins Collection, just two, *Broken Faith* (1913)[4] and *Fox and Geese* (1917)[5], were produced professionally in Ireland.[6] Female characters in these early plays resonate with a distinct sense of their co-authors' class and feminist concerns, however, material clues regarding their staging, dramaturgy or reception may never become known in any tangible sense, as the productions were not publicly reviewed.[7]

Susanne Day, along with Geraldine Cummins and the Cork writer Edith Somerville,[8] co-founded the Munster Women's Franchise League (MWFL), a non-militant, non-sectarian suffrage society.[9] Day, like many women of upper-middle-class backgrounds, was also involved in philanthropic activities and was one of the first women elected to serve as a Poor Law Guardian (PLG) in her local parish. The harrowing social conditions she encountered in this capacity, and her struggles to validate her position as a woman operating in the male-dominated public sphere of local government, provide the factual background and humorous material for one of her literary works, *The Amazing Philanthropists*.[10] Written in the form of epistolary letters (from a female 'Guardian' to a close female friend living in England), Day's docu-fiction describes many positive differences she and other Guardians made to the lives of the workhouse residents, whilst clearly illustrating her resourceful and determined nature.[11]

Fidelity is a one-act realist peasant play co-written in 1914 by Cummins and Day.[12] Topical issues of land-ownership, post-Famine emigration and rural marriage patterns of the poorer farming community constitute the social background to this drama. These themes serve to frame other, more subjective authorial concerns in the work and reveal an interesting collision between conformity to, and subversion of, conventional dramatic and social mores. While of the peasant-play genre, this work presents characters and dialogue which disrupt conventional gender representations. *Fidelity* expresses the repressive physical, social and psychological repercussions of the Great Famine (1845–49) on lives and relationships – particularly with respect to women, and the restriction of personal choice. Since the mid-nineteenth century there had been opportunities for some women to receive a measure of equality in education, and this important juncture in women's history had effected an improvement in career prospects for many women from the privileged classes. Both Cummins and Day, beneficiaries of these changes, had strong views regarding the value of financial independence and women's equality in male-dominated professions. Their concern for the education of less-privileged members of society, particularly women, is clear from their documented work in the community and in their personal writings. *Fidelity* operates thematically to suggest the changing conditions in rural Ireland, and reflects the contemporaneous desire of rural women to strive for influence and equal consideration in their society.

The issue of land and prevailing socio-political conditions in *fin de siècle* rural Ireland provide the motivating factors for the characters' actions in *Fidelity*.[13] In the immediate post-Famine decades, Landlords and their agents re-leased forsaken lands to surviving peasant farmers. A two-tiered class of Irish tenant farmers emerged as 'land–hunger' – driven by fear of further disasters – gripped the imagination of the rural populace. The countryside was in constant demographic turmoil, both from the effects of continued emigration and from agrarian unrest.[14] David Fitzpatrick describes how, in the face of overwhelming poverty, land division came to an abrupt halt during the last third of the nineteenth century, replaced by a system of impartible inheritance and 'stem family' succession.[15] Consequently, rural men and women left their homes in droves, seeking opportunities in urban areas in Ireland and abroad.[16] By the turn of the century, in an effort to consolidate family lands and future security, it had become the custom for tenant farmers to arrange marriages for their eldest sons and/or daughters.[17]

It is within the reality of an oppressively bleak world of limited choices and rigid social structures in rural Ireland that events in *Fidelity* take place. The tradition of land consolidation is as central to the situation of Larry Macarthy, the only male character in *Fidelity*, as it had been for his deceased father, Denis, whose absence from the dramatic action does not diminish his continued patriarchal influence on the family. Post-Famine changes in agricultural practices, restoring the land from tillage to pasture, had made farm work less labour intensive. A resultant depreciation of rural women's economic value, the loss of their previous status as shared breadwinner and their relegation to the domestic sphere led to common usage of the term, 'woman of the house' – which resonates with both negative and positive meanings for some commentators. Joanna Bourke argues that notions of an ideal Irish female identity, contributing to the construction of an ideal Ireland, emerged out of ideas propagated by such publications as *The Irish Homestead*.[18] Bourke contends that in the journal the 'affirmations of women's domestic role came to restrict the possibility of their involvement in public life'.[19] In contrast, James MacPherson argues that women 'made the domestic sphere their own and used it as a base from which to gain power through control of the household economy'.[20] McPherson quotes a mission statement from *The Irish Homestead*, which was 'aware of the change in the social and economic status of women and saw the growing power of women as a foundation for a new social order in rural Ireland'.[21] In a further study, Maria Luddy describes how women from across the sectarian/political divide came to work together in rural Ireland to effect progressive change for Irish society in the new century.[22]

In *Fidelity* two female characters, Katie and Ellie, belong to the emergent farming class and, as such, are relentless in their desire to establish a secure position in the new order. While a conventional reading of *Fidelity* suggests a simple melodrama concerning loyalty in affairs of the heart, a closer examination reveals the ambiguities at play in its title and content. The word 'fidelity' has different connotations for the characters in the drama, which concerns the tragic tale of a returning emigrant, Maggie Moynihan, whose dreams evaporate when her fiancé, Larry Macarthy, procrastinates when faced with a choice between Maggie and a younger woman, Katie Drinan, who has been pursuing him in Maggie's absence. Larry's honour is a focal point throughout the narrative, for although he is strongly attracted to Katie, he has waited faithfully for Maggie – who has been working for five years in America. There has been no communication between them, simply an understanding that one day Maggie would return. Larry's dilemma worsens when his sister Ellie reinforces the importance of his familial duty, openly encouraging his relationship with Katie. Maggie returns unexpectedly to the village, in poor health – her former beauty diminished – and Katie proceeds to try to oust her by devious means. When Larry discovers Maggie's presence, he is helpless in the face of stark reality and divided loyalties. In the final scene, Larry has to choose but cannot – and does not. Ultimately, it is Maggie, who determines their future paths, by walking slowly away.

These characters can be seen as representative of the condition of *fin de siècle* rural Ireland – poised between the old and new values of a changing world. Such positions further reveal how these changes particularly affected the personal and political choices for women experiencing the legacy of the Famine. The patriarchal environment of rural Victorian Ireland is evident in the opening scene; Larry Macarthy, enjoying a smoke, is leaning over the half-door, surveying his fields, whilst Katie Drinan sits quietly at the kitchen table. Describing his day at the cattle fair, Larry observes that Katie's father, Matt, did very well. He then speculates on Katie's future inheritance, suggesting that, being female, financial concerns are outside of her sphere:

Larry: ... Old Matt must be making great stores of money these times, 'tis yourself will be the rich woman one of these days.
Katie: Maybe so. I'm not knowing.
Larry: (*laughing*) Matt's close. He wouldn't be telling you anyway I suppose.[23]

The dominant impression of patriarchy in these opening moments, dissolves, however, as the play progresses. Katie and Larry belie the traditional gender roles of masculinity/femininity in Irish society, and in the social realism represented on the Irish stage at that time. Katie Drinan is subservient in neither words nor action. Her social status matches that of Larry, and in her ruthless determination to shape her own future, she not only adopts attitudes traditionally deemed 'male', but is an example of how women in rural Ireland were beginning to demand control of their lives.

Katie, described in the stage directions as '*extremely pretty; about twenty-three years of age*', has just discovered that Larry, the object of her desire, is engaged to Maggie Moynihan – another reputed beauty.[24] Larry pleads against Katie's accusations of duplicity, but admits that his sister Ellie (married to Katie's uncle) had persuaded him to silence. He relates the personal tragedy of his ill-fated romance with Maggie, who was left destitute after the death of her alcoholic father. Larry's father, Denis, in post-Famine, class-conscious prejudice, had vigorously opposed their marriage, threatening to disown Larry if he disobeyed. In tone and language, Larry purports to hold Maggie in high esteem: 'T'was the money *he* was after; but I'd have taken Maggie and welcome, and she without a thraneen to her fortune ... she was ever and always a fine woman was Maggie Moynihan.'[25] Maggie, too proud to marry without a dowry – and in reaction to overpowering cultural imperatives – had made the economic decision to emigrate, with the intention of returning when her financial position improved. While her action of leaving can be viewed as the result of woman's exclusion from land ownership, it can also be seen as an active resistance to female dependency on, and subservience to, a patriarchal system and illuminates the under-explored area of Irish women's emigration histories.[26]

The opening scenes centre on an intertwined preoccupation with physical attractiveness and loyalty or faithfulness. Larry's position is complicated by fidelity to the land he has inherited, and by his responsibility towards perpetuating and strengthening the family hold on that land. Specific stage directions reinforce the attitudes of the characters in the play. Katie's slow response to Larry's revelations regarding his relationship with Maggie suggests a feigned disinterested attitude – revealing both Katie's desire to discover the extent of the threat to her future, and her insecurity, in terms of her physical ability to attract Larry. Having earlier professed his love for Maggie, and admiration for her principles, Larry now confesses that he has been uncertain of his emotions since meeting Katie: 'I never seen a woman in the village to touch her ... but yourself Katie. There was times when I used to think that God Almighty himself couldn't make a comelier woman than Maggie, but then ... I seen you ... (*Speaks slowly – as if realizing Katie's loveliness for the first time.*)'[27]

The arrival of Larry's sister Ellie, and the control that she exerts over her brother, portrays a compliance with patriarchal systems, suggesting the continued presence of their deceased father. However, the provocative image of a strong, pragmatic woman exerting power over an emotional, deluded man also reverses gender perceptions in a style reminiscent of Synge's dominant females – Widow Quinn and Pegeen Mike in *The Playboy of the Western World* (1907). Hosts of unseen characters 'accompany' Ellie's entrance as she describes the activities of various neighbours and regales Katie and Larry with all the local news. The dramatic convention of the messenger/narrator operates here primarily as a structural device to lift the rhythm and tone of the play and also as an opportunity for the playwrights to record local traditions. Ellie gives a rich description of the social codes at the heart of the community:

Ellie: News? Yerra the town's swimming with it ... and Pat Leary has made up that match with that girl of the Delaneys after all. Fifty pounds he's getting with her and God knows it's little enough, and she as ugly as bespoke, and there's only two sheep now and a Government hen between the Cadogans of Keimaneagh and Long Joe Rafferty of the Gap...[28]

Having taken care to ensure that Katie remained in ignorance of Maggie's existence, Ellie had been encouraging Katie's friendship with Larry. She is determined that Larry will produce heirs, and Katie, being young, healthy and attractive, is the obvious candidate to assist him. Ellie tries to be pragmatic about the situation, and to maintain her own integrity:

> There's many the woman has gone to America to earn her marriage portion... but how many have come back, Larry Macarthy? Five years Maggie's gone and small blame to meself or any honest woman to be making a match for you now.[29]

The reference to emigration in Ellie's dialogue suggests a challenge to received notions regarding the boundaries of women's experience and financial responsibilities. There is an ellipsis in the original manuscript, inferring a myriad of possible reasons why Maggie might not return home and positing the notion that many women exceeded prescribed boundaries within the male-dominated industrial world. Ellie's design and intentions for Larry within the world they inhabit are clear. She is a beneficiary of the prevailing system, having married Katie's uncle, and wishes to secure the future of their farmland. In this respect, her deceptions of Katie and Larry are understandable. In a powerful association of woman with the land, Ellie entreats Larry to act:

> There, what did I tell you? T'is you're the fool me boyo, waiting for a woman that maybe you'll never see again in this world or the next, and the prettiest girl in six parishes leaning into your hand. Let you be said by me, Larry Macarthy, cut the oats that's ripe, t'will bring you a better harvest.[30]

Ellie realizes that Katie's assured dowry, and her physical attractiveness indicate that she will not be single for too much longer. A further union between the two families would undoubtedly be preferable to the prospect of Larry unwed and childless, or married to 'dower-less' Maggie. In her unsentimental attitude towards Larry's loyalty to his fiancée, Ellie emerges as a strong advocate of the concept of fidelity to family survival and prosperity. Larry's conflicting loyalties are illustrated when, prior to Maggie's arrival, he is under pressure from Ellie to marry Katie:

Larry: (*very much distressed*) I ... I ... Katie ... I ... God help me ... I ... Katie –
   I can't do it. It's not fair to Maggie ... She's counting on me. Oh, it's sorry I am to hurt you, but I thought you knew all along – Ellie told me you knew – and I promised Maggie. 'Twas over at the style [*sic*] the night before she went away. I told her I'd wait ... and she's counting on me ... she'll be coming back ... and there was never a woman in all the world as beautiful as Maggie Moynihan.
(*He goes out in a sort of blind impulse to escape further argument. Katie turns away to the fireplace.*) [31]

Larry's 'manly' composure in the opening scenes of the play now fragments into confusion by events beyond his control. While contemporary mores considered the display of 'feminine' traits in males as weak and ineffectual, particularly in public, Larry emerges as a caring, if naïve, individual, who elicits sympathy for his predicament by his sensitivity towards both Maggie and Katie.

The value afforded to female beauty and familial concepts of loyalty influence the dilemmas and choices that face the characters. An expectation of Maggie's physical beauty is set in motion from the start of *Fidelity* and she has been the subject of lengthy discussion by the other characters, right up to her entrance midway into the play. She arrives unexpectedly – her former beauty ravaged by work and worry. Her demeanor is one of quiet relief to be home, and complete confidence in her impending marriage to Larry. When this expectation is disrupted, the effect on Katie is one of relief and renewed confidence in a future for her with Larry. Through her character, the conflict in the play between female beauty and honour comes sharply into focus. Katie is aware of Larry's strong sense of loyalty and knows that unless she manages to dispose of Maggie before he returns – her future is uncertain. Despite the fact that Ellie has deceived her, Katie will not deviate from her plan – her resolve to marry supersedes the ethics of her subsequent actions. Stage directions suggest that Maggie's physical decrepitude provides the impelling force behind Katie's impulsive, callous reaction. She assesses Maggie's situation:

Katie: You must have worked very hard in America?
Maggie: (*with a little shiver*) I did ... work hard.
Katie: (*persistent*) But you made money?

Maggie: (*as before*) ... yes ... I made it. With the flesh of me body and the
   sweat of me heart I made it. Early and late, day in, day out. Many's the
   time I'd have given over, only for Larry ... and he waiting. I'd struggle
   on, but God knows I was weary ...[32]

The difficulties that Maggie experienced in America underline the reality
of women who operated outside of conventional familial systems and
gender roles. Having determined that Maggie is not destitute, but otherwise seemingly unmoved by the hardships she describes – or of Maggie's
love for, and fidelity to, Larry – Katie's subsequent actions seem based
on the sure knowledge that she, Katie, will be the more attractive to
him. She hands Maggie a 'looking-glass', stating that Larry could never
love an ugly woman. Once more, the emphasis and clarity of the stage
directions guide character, tone and attitude:

Katie: (*with horrible cruelty*) Look at her, Maggie Moynihan (*she holds the
   glass before Maggie*). Will you believe it now?
   (*Maggie looks in the glass and realizes for the first time the ravages the years
   have made in her face. She gazes horror-stricken, the truth slowly burning
   itself into her brain.*)[33]

On the surface, Katie would appear unnecessarily heartless; however,
the reality of conditions, and in particular the limited opportunities,
for young, single women in rural Ireland, forms the driving impulse
behind her actions. In terms of the marriage stakes, female physical
attractiveness extended beyond a pleasant countenance, to embrace the
requirement of youth, health and the promise of child-bearing ability.
Katie's advantage in this respect is in no doubt. However, in order to
overcome the problem of Larry's sentimental and honourable character,
she resorts to the drastic measures described.

Observation of the harsh realities and survival tactics of the rural Irish
community is illustrated through the unsentimental attitude behind
Katie's crushing words and actions. Maggie realizes she has missed her
chance of marriage to Larry and she is in the process of leaving when he
returns to the cottage. His horrified reaction to her appearance confirms
both Maggie's new fears of his reluctance to honour his promise to
her, and Katie's satisfaction that her future with Larry is certain. Larry
attempts and fails to remain in control of the situation – his conflicting
loyalties render him speechless and unable to respond. In the final scene,
a parodic repeat of their shared history plays out, as Maggie, once again

driven by necessity and external pressures, is the one who takes control and decides to leave.

As Maggie slowly departs, Larry stands by in impotent silence. Katie, who has been anxiously observing the outcome, calls Larry to the table as if nothing had occurred. By thus attending to her domestic duties, Katie would appear to re-establish the patriarchal order disrupted by Maggie's presence. However, the patriarchal images that frame the beginning and conclusion of this play, only serve to reinforce the conditions and systems under which rural Ireland operated at the time. Women's survival, in subaltern terms of preserving a sense of 'self' in male-dominated societies, has taken many forms. By adopting an unsentimental and practical attitude in establishing her new position of authority in the home, Katie represents a different image of Irish rural women, one that defies received gender-models of Ireland's rural communities at the turn of the twentieth century.

In conclusion, it is important to note that while Maggie appears to be a victim of the self-interest of others; her dignity, not to mention her savings, emerges intact. Despite humiliation and rejection, Maggie's experiences and stoicism enable her to rise above adversity, embrace reality and move on – refusing her prerogative to insist that Larry honour his commitment to her. Viewed in this way, she reads as a positive female role model and an advocate for women's economic and emotional independence. Of the two women, Maggie is the worldlier, more experienced, and is now financially independent – albeit through necessity rather than choice. Katie, on the other hand, has no such visible autonomy. In English Common Law, which was in operation at that time, a husband gained control over any estate a wife brought to a marriage; and custody of their children, should the marriage fail. However, as previously described, rural Irish women were shaping their roles and identities within the confines of a patriarchal system, and in the play both Katie and Maggie offer images of women encountering and attempting to overcome the prejudices and expectations of their society.

The female characters in *Fidelity* portray attitudes and/or experiences generally considered the province of males in their society. Katie's determination to succeed, her assertive language and manipulation of events, Ellie's 'land hunger' and Maggie's economic independence are all signifiers of the changes for women that were taking place in modern Ireland. In tandem, the solitary male figure of Larry inverts representations of masculinity in the realist 'peasant play' genre and prompts speculation on Day's and Cummins's perceptions of changing male attitudes.

Their counter-normative representation of gender affords an opportunity to consider and evaluate the specific perspectives, and reflections, of women involved on the fringes of the suffrage and avant-garde movements in early twentieth-century Ireland.

Notes

1. Mary Trotter, *Ireland's National Theaters: Political Performance and the Origins of the Dramatic Movement* (New York: Syracuse University Press), 2001; A. Bourke, S. Kilfeather, M. Luddy, G. Meaney, M. Ní Dhonncadha, M. O'Dowd and C. Wills (eds), *The Field Day Anthology of Irish Writing, Vols IV & V* (Cork: Cork University Press in association with Field Day, 2002); Tina O'Toole (ed.), *Dictionary of Munster Women Writers 1800–2000* (Cork: Cork University Press, 2005).
2. In addition to historians mentioned in the above texts, seminal works by Margaret Ward, Rosemary Cullen-Owens, Carol Coulter and Cliona Murphy have uncovered and documented comprehensive accounts of women's political activities in the feminist and nationalist movements at the beginning of the twentieth century. Equally revealing studies of gender operations in Irish society are by Richard Breen, Damian Hannon, Chris Curtain, Pauline Jackson and Barbara O'Connor amongst others.
3. Margaret Kelleher and J. H. Murphy (eds), *Gender Perspectives in Nineteenth Century Ireland: Public and Private Spheres* (Dublin: Irish Academic Press, 1997), p. 17.
4. Geraldine Cummins and Susanne Day, *Broken Faith* (1913), Unpublished MSS, in the 'Geraldine Cummins Collection', Item 2.35., Cork Archive Institute.
5. Day and Cummins, *Fox and Geese* (Dublin: Maunsel, 1917).
6. *Broken Faith* (1913) and *Fox and Geese* (1917), co-authored by Cummins and Day, were produced by the Abbey Theatre, Dublin. The 'Cummins Collection' contains documentation (unauthenticated to date) claiming that a further two (unnamed) plays, authored separately by Cummins and Day were staged in England, the former by Chanticleer Theatre, London, and the latter by Annie Horniman's avant-garde theatre, The Gaiety, Manchester.
7. The Abbey diarist Joseph Holloway favourably mentions a second run of *Fox and Geese* in his diary of Abbey productions, 'I was at the Abbey last night where an amusing comedy, Fox & Geese was revived with success, with Shadow of the Glen as first piece'; from *Joseph Holloway's Abbey Theatre: A Selection from his Unpublished Journal 'Impressions of a Dublin Playgoer'* (USA: Southern Illinois University, 1967), p. 194.
8. Edith Somerville, 'Geilles Herring' and her cousin Violet Martin 'Martin Ross' achieved considerable literary success as novelists in the years between 1889 and 1949. After Ross died (1915) Somerville continued to cite her as co-author of her creative output. Together with Day, Cummins and other literary women from the Munster region, they provided (through the MWFL) a fertile environment for women's political, social, psychical and literary discourse.

9. Cliona Murphy, in her seminal study of the Irish suffrage movement and Irish society, describes the members of this society as generally middle-class, educated literary women whose primary aim was, as described in 1912 by Susanne Day in her book, *Women in a New Ireland*, 'to obtain the vote for women as granted to men'. Cliona Murphy, *The Women's Suffrage Movement and Irish Society in the Early Twentieth Century* (Dublin: Temple University Press, 1989), p. 21 (re. citation: Susanne Day, *Women in a New Ireland* (Cork: Munster Women's Franchise League, 1912), p. 3).

10. Susanne Day, *The Amazing Philanthropists* (London: Sidgwick & Jackson, 1916),

11. An example of Day's passion is evidenced in this extract from her book, *The Amazing Philanthropists*: 'Jill, as I write, only adjectives like cancerous, infamous, appalling, rise to my mind. I feel that no words in the world are too strong, too ugly, too blasting to be used in description of what experts call the General Mixed Workhouse.... when you see hundreds of little children growing up behind those walls, and know that they will have to go out into the world, branded – well, you just have to...fight like a demon against the conviction that no work you can do will be of any use; that the whole system is wrong from the bottom up, and any attempt at reform is like putting sticking plaster upon a sloughing abscess...' Letter No. 12, p. 47.

12. *Fidelity* was produced by the Dublin University Players at Trinity College in April 2004. This is believed to be the first public performance of the play as there are no contemporary records or reviews. The play was directed by Clare Neylon and produced by Velma O'Donoghue Greene. The play was produced again from 1–3 December 2005 in the Granary Studio UCC and was incorporated into a one-day conference on Munster Women Playwrights (2 December).

13. In pre-Famine years Landlordism encouraged subdivision of tenant farmers' holdings. This practice supported early marriages, larger families and further subdivision of the land. Following the devastation wreaked by poor management; the years of potato blight (1845–49); and the failure of government to address the tragic situation of its subjects, abandoned smallholdings littered the Irish landscape. The subsequent reduction in population (from 8.5 to 6.5 million) through fatal disease and emigration profoundly altered the social and cultural structures of life in rural areas.

14. Land League rent boycotts and destruction of property became a common response to evictions and harsh Landlord practices. The Land League's efforts, alongside Parnell's constitutional, parliamentary strategies, eventually succeeded in securing tenancy rights for Irish farmers in 1881.

15. David Fitzpatrick notes that, 'the favoured son would be encouraged to bring a wife into the family upon the enfeeblement or death of his father. A quite rapid transition followed during which, non-inheritors were compensated, dowered or emigrated...this arrangement meant that a farmer's son was unlikely to marry...until his father had reached his sixties'; from Fitzpatrick, 'Marriage in Post-Famine Ireland', in Art Cosgrave (ed.), *Marriage in Ireland* (Dublin: College Press, 1985), pp. 116–31.

16. Poverty in Ireland was widespread – the workhouses over-populated with dispirited men, women and children. Many women joined religious communities to escape starvation, whilst the Catholic Church at this time was encouraging young men from the farming classes to train for the priesthood.

17. Commonly referred to as a 'match', the marriage contract was usually in the form of an exchange of land from the male with cash (dowry) brought by the female.

18. *The Irish Homestead* was a weekly publication of the Irish Agricultural Organization Society (IAOS).

19. Joanna Bourke, *Husbandry to Housewifery: Women, Economic Change and Housework in Ireland, 1890–1914* (Oxford: Clarendon Press, 1993), p. 268.

20. J. MacPherson, 'Ireland Begins in the Home: Women, Irish National Identity and the Domestic Sphere', in *Éire Ireland: An Interdisciplinary Journal of Irish Studies* (St Paul, MN: Irish American Journal), Vol. XXXVI, Nos. III–IV, Fall/Winter 2001, p. 131.

21. MacPherson, in *Éire Ireland*, Fall/Winter 2001, p. 131.

22. Maria Luddy in 'Irish Women and the Co-operative Movement' writes: 'Nationalist, unionist, suffrage and cultural organizations co-existed in the first decades of the twentieth century and claimed the attention of Irish men and women. Sir Horace Plunkett, the pioneer of the co-operative movement in Ireland, founded the United Irishwoman in 1910, with Mrs Ellice Pilkington...The organization encouraged the development of rural society, and expected women to serve their local communities', in *Women in Ireland, 1800–1918: A Documentary History* (Cork: Cork University Press, 1995), p. 327.

23. Cummins and Day, *Fidelity* (1914), Unpublished MSS, 'Geraldine Cummins Collection', Item: 11/5, Cork Archive Institute, p. 1.

24. Cummins and Day, *Fidelity*, p. 1.

25. Cummins and Day, *Fidelity*, p. 5.

26. For a comprehensive study and documented accounts of Irish women's emigration, see Maria Luddy and Dympna McLoughlin, eds., 'Women and Emigration from Ireland from the Seventeenth Century', in *The Field Day Anthology of Irish Writing, Vol. V*, p. 567.

27. Cummins and Day, *Fidelity*, p. 5.

28. Cummins and Day, *Fidelity*, p. 10.

29. Cummins and Day, *Fidelity*, p. 12.

30. Cummins and Day, *Fidelity*, p. 13.

31. Cummins and Day, *Fidelity*, p. 14.

32. Cummins and Day, *Fidelity*, p. 19.

33. Cummins and Day, *Fidelity*, p. 23.

3
The Space Outside: Images of Women in Plays by Eva Gore-Booth and Dorothy Macardle

Cathy Leeney

European theatre of the nineteenth century presents an image of woman confined by, or negotiating the confinements of, domestic interiors. This image recurs in much of the theatre of the Irish cultural renaissance at the beginning of the twentieth century, primary and influential examples being Synge's *In the Shadow of the Glen* (1905) and *The Playboy of the Western World* (1907), and O'Casey's *Juno and the Paycock* (1924) and *The Plough and the Stars* (1926). This chapter begins by examining *The Buried Life of Deirdre* (1916) by Eva Gore-Booth, concentrating on the playwright's use of spatial images to propose subversive representations of female identity. I will then look at Dorothy Macardle's *Witch's Brew* (1928; publ. 1931), in which ideals of domesticity and the ideological control of femininity are destabilized through images of forces that invade the stage. Macardle characterizes these forces as supernatural, and as representative of ancient, but powerful energies denied by patriarchal hegemonies.

The role of the imagined space off-stage, the space outside the walls of social control, may be defined in terms of the challenges and potentials facing female characters who are unable to sustain active subjectivity and fulfil their desires within the framework of the patriarchal familial sphere. This sphere is often represented architecturally on-stage. Both Eva Gore-Booth and, later, Dorothy Macardle explored ways of dramatizing notions of inside and outside in selected plays written in the 1900s, 1910s and 1920s, using performance space to address issues of female subjectivity as inherited from Irish mythic sources, and as related to the role of women in the emergence of an independent autonomous state.

Eva Gore-Booth radically re-created mythic figures like Maeve, Cuchulain, Deirdre and Naisi. Her daring use of theatrical form and style, paralleling that of W. B. Yeats, creates a stage world that works non-mimetically, as an imaginative alternative beyond the shadowy real world of appearances. Her dramaturgy liberates representations of the female into realms of new possibility, challenging the limitations of conventional tropes such as Mother Ireland. Writing in the late 1920s, Dorothy Macardle employs more conservative theatrical means to express the limits placed on women by the nascent state. In her play *Witch's Brew*, supernatural phenomena express powerful energies that cannot be accommodated in the authorized world of order controlled by Church and State. Drawing these plays within the boundaries of critical discourse reveals the gendered limits of theatrical conventions of representation onstage, and how those limits may be ruptured and opened to the space outside. As Richard Kearney observes: 'Myth becomes exemplary and consequently *repeatable*, and thus serves as a model and justification for all human actions...'[1]

In common with a number of other writers of the Irish dramatic renaissance, Gore-Booth chose to write about the heroes, and more especially, in her case, the heroines of Irish mythology. The notion of Ireland as a woman as expressed through sovereignty myths and the *banfheisrígí* or marriage of sovereignty, gave women a central position in myths which were allegorical of the life of the nation.[2] Thus, as Proinsias MacCana remarks, 'while the goddess depended upon the advent of a worthy prince for the preservation or recovery of her beauty and youthful vigour, hers was the discretion to decide whom she would legitimize by mating with him in the *hieros gamos* or sacred marriage.'[3] The proactive desire of the sovereignty figure proved disturbing to nineteenth century sensibilities and was side-stepped in a number of ways. Gregory rewrote the sovereignty function in *Grania*, and drawing from her work on translating the Cuchulain cycle of tales, reformulated the figure of the Morrigán in *Kincora* (1905). Gore-Booth, in appropriating the Deirdre myth, redrew the contours of the sovereignty function most radically, without losing a sense of the person of Deirdre as symbolic of a source of ethical and spiritual power. In doing this, Gore-Booth writes the drama of Deirdre in a non-tragic mode. This is significant since it draws attention to the tragic function of sovereignty figures in other versions where the source of inevitable doom is attributed to the central female character. Such women are prey to ambivalence since they are seen 'both as images of an ideal order which they [the writers] sought to restore and as images of an Ireland that had been betrayed, or had collaborated in its own betrayal.'[4] Gore-Booth refocuses the heroine as the active subject at the centre of the drama. In *The Buried Life of Deirdre*, the heroine refuses altogether the role of tragic catalyst, appropriating instead the roles of protagonist and *deus ex machina* in her own story.

The spatial implications of Gore-Booth's dramaturgy are central to her rewriting of the female subject in Irish myth. By drawing together Michael Issacharoff's distinction between mimetic and diegetic emphasis on the close relationship between theatrical space and the representation of women, I will explore Gore-Booth's choices regarding space in *The Buried Life of Deirdre*.[5] In the play, the organization of space, both on-stage (mimetic), and imaginative or off-stage (diegetic), fore-grounds the heroine's role as arbitrator of ritualized spaces 'without' that represent an underlying, parallel world beneath the illusory world of men. In her confrontation with destiny one can say that for Deirdre, 'the pliability of stage space and time map the possibilities available to her.'[6]

The Buried Life of Deirdre was developed over a period of years, from 1908 to 1912. According to Anne Marreco, it was performed at the Gaiety Theatre in 1911 but this version of events cannot be confirmed.[7] In her introduction to the play Gore-Booth puts forward her particular spin on the story:

> The idea of reincarnation is not so exclusively an Eastern doctrine as many people think. Mr Douglas Hyde, in his *Literary History of Ireland* points out its place in Irish literature, and explains that it seems to have been part of the Druidic teaching. It may be that the thought itself has the recurrent, re-incarnating power of truth.[8]

For human existence to have a larger frame, beyond the fevered trajectory between birth and death, was a cherished belief of the playwright. In *The Buried Life of Deirdre* this is the predominant theme. Repetition, mirroring and layering, shape the form, the action and the philosophical impulse of the piece. Gore-Booth plunders the Deirdre tale and rebuilds it into a very different kind of theatre from, say, Yeats's version of 1906, or Synge's of 1909. There is no indication that either version influenced Gore-Booth's work. Yeats wished to telescope the emotional impact of the love triangle and confine the action of his *Deirdre* to the couple's doomed return to Emain. Contrasting strongly with this, Gore-Booth opens out the structure; in place of a tragedy of passion and jealousy building towards its catastrophic crisis, here in *The Buried Life of Deirdre* is a surprising enactment of redemption through experience, a placing of the 'sad children of life and death' in a space beyond the teleology of a purely linear narrative.[9] In this sense,

Gore-Booth, in rewriting Deirdre as the genius of the play, creates, in Kristeva's words, [a] 'female subjectivity [that] would seem to provide a specific measure that essentially retains *repetition* and *eternity* from among the multiple modalities of time known through the history of civilizations.'[10] *The Buried Life of Deirdre* is, in fact, a re-enactment. It is part of a cyclical structure, outlined by Deirdre herself: 'Yet have I found the hidden sorrow in my soul, the sorrow of the past. Is not this dream the shadow of my deed, this terrible deed that has been crying out against me for a thousand years?'[11] The play characterizes, on the one hand, the 'cycles, gestation, the eternal recurrence of a biological rhythm which conforms to that of nature... whose regularity and unison with what is experienced as extra-subjective time, cosmic time, occasion vertiginous visions and unnameable *jouissance*' and, on the other hand, 'a monumental temporality, without cleavage or escape, which has so little to do with linear time...: all-encompassing and infinite like imaginary space....' [12] It is these two types of temporality that Kristeva links with female subjectivity. It is no coincidence that Gore-Booth maps *The Buried Life of Deirdre* as a cyclical action, which fulfils itself outside the teleology of tragic narrative, and enters, thereby, monumental temporality, calling to mind 'the vestige of an anterior or concomitant maternal cult.'[13]

The consciousness of Gore-Booth's Deirdre so overarches the entire action of the play that one might almost imagine the mythical figure as her own dramaturge. If James Flannery complains that Yeats's Deirdre appears to know too much too soon, 'thus depriving her of the conflict within her own soul', by comparison Gore-Booth's Deirdre seems virtually omniscient.[14] In this sense the action of the drama is ritualized, and conventional psychological conflicts and resolutions are deeply undermined. Deirdre cannot be said to confront her destiny in any emotionally tragic way since her identity as a reincarnated king from long ago, a mirror-image of Conor, undercuts the tragedy of her loss of Naisi. How does Gore-Booth rewrite the Deirdre myth so that it becomes an expression of a pacifist philosophy, with a ritual, religious base? Gore-Booth makes major interpretative changes in two ways. First, the aspect of the story involving Naisi's conflict of loyalties, his love for the woman, and his allegiance to his prince or leader, is underemphasized to such an extent that it seems scarcely to figure; Naisi's role is very much as a function of the narrative, and as foil to Deirdre's vision. The effect of this change is to remove the element of Conor's betrayal of Naisi as retributive, and to keep the central focus firmly on the heroine as the active subject of the drama. This latter aspect of the representation of

Deirdre finds further corroboration in the concept of dreaming back, and in Deirdre's control of the symbolic world created through the dialogue. Thus, Gore-Booth's version breaks with the family of tales in which erotic love for a woman conflicts with chivalric fealty, the same dilemma which, as MacCana points out 'was...to capture the imagination of Europe in the romance of Tristan and Iseult and profoundly influence western attitudes to erotic love in art and society down to our own day'.[15]

The theme of erotic love brings us to Gore-Booth's second major departure from precedent. The centrality of love is maintained by Gore-Booth, but it is love of a very particular kind. Deirdre insists on a form of love that overrides jealousy or possessiveness. It is a neo-platonic, Christian ideal, in Eliot's phrase, an 'expanding of love beyond desire'.[16] Thus, the core impulse of the action is, in Gore-Booth's version, ethical rather than erotic, and this poses interesting challenges in defining the genre of the play. The status of the tale as a mythic tragedy, upheld in varying degrees by Synge and Yeats, relies upon the sense of Conor, Deirdre and Naisi as prey to passions that lead them helplessly towards a doomed destiny, both for themselves and for Emain. The conflict between vengeance and forgiveness, between possessive love and platonic love is woven into *The Buried Life of Deirdre* through the imagery of the Gods, Mannanan and Angus. Mannanan is worshipped by Deirdre and identified with images of atonement and peace. Angus is the God of Conor and Naisi, the God of vengeance, war, blood and possession. Gore-Booth's attempt is to create a dramatic schema through which the inevitability of violent resolution is challenged, even as it is enacted.

In *The Buried Life of Deirdre*, as the title indicates, the action presents a realm of existence which is, in a sense, already dead, is over and is now being repeated. Through the reincarnated Deirdre, Gore-Booth proposes the possibility of a present which is at once the past and the future, and the freeing, in that present moment, of human power from a cycle of violence, possessiveness and retribution. Like Matthew Arnold, Gore-Booth thought of the buried self as a source of truth and oneness, a resistance to 'bondage of the flesh and mind...or some fantastic maze/ Forged by the imperious lonely thinking power.'[17] How such a magnificent idea might be made to work theatrically requires the figuring of a parallel, but alternative dimension which is represented imaginatively in the play. In Gore-Booth's version Deirdre's identity is, to use Kristeva's terms, the 'recognition of an irreducible identity,...exploded, plural, fluid '.[18] The space in which the tragedy is played out is revealed in all its restriction by reference to a wider space beyond, which is also temporally fluid and free. Arnold writes:

> And in our individual human state
> Go through the sad probation all again,
> To see if we will poise our life at last,
> To see if we will now at last be true
> To our own only true, deep-buried selves,
> Being one with which we are one with the whole world[19]

Throughout *The Buried Life of Deirdre*, there is repeated reference to a passage underground. It leads to 'the palace of another King'; it is 'very low and dark and long, but in the end it reaches the open country'.[20] The passageway is identified with Mannanan, the God of peace, and it is by this route that Deirdre and Naisi escape from Conor at the end of Act I. In Act III, when the lovers are threatened by Conor, again it is the underground passage that offers refuge from the jealous king. In a confusion of darkness though, Deirdre is killed, and then Naisi. Gore-Booth redefines the passageway at various points and in Act III it is refigured as the way to death, reminding the audience of Deirdre's *alter ego*, the old king, a mirror image of Conor himself. Thus, the underground passage begins to represent the notion of reincarnation, and of lives and fates understood through monumental time, beyond the limits of a single life. The female association with the passageway as an image of birth is emphasized by Deirdre's and Lavarcam's knowledge of it. In this way, Gore-Booth suggests a gendered aspect to the opposition between Angus, God of war and retribution, and Mannanan, God of gentleness and peace.

The suggestion of a parallel, alternative dimension in *The Buried Life of Deirdre* is central to the working of the play. This dimension is spatial and temporal. Gore-Booth uses natural elements as conduits to it. Act I is set in a wood. There is a stone altar, grass and a pool of water. Deirdre enters carrying a torch to burn an offering to Mannanan, but Conor has destroyed the altar, and the ritual cannot be completed. Deirdre uses the pool of water to see into the future, which is also the past. She prays to Mannanan and describes her vision, in which she is identified with an old king, 'The King's voice is the voice of Deirdre, the King's eyes are the eyes of Deirdre... there is a sword red with blood, in the hands that are the hands of Deirdre.'[21] Deirdre sees the 'terrible deed that has been crying out against me for a thousand years' and nature is identified as the source of her knowledge.[22] Gore-Booth appropriates the identification of the feminine with the natural world, and creates a new definition of the natural as the repository of history and culture. It seems crucial that the mirroring of Deirdre in the figure of the old king be dramatized, rather than merely described, at this point.

If the theme of prescience through reincarnation is to be exploited fully, and a sense of the great temporal arch of the play be captured, the actual stage space needs to reflect the larger vision available to Deirdre through the element of water. This vision is verbally embodied in the trope of the underground passage, but again, requires visual reference as a metonymic principle underlying the entire action. Gore-Booth creates opportunities for the expression of this larger vision through the permeability of space in all three acts. In Act II, the combination of *'sunset'* and *'a fog … rising from the sea'* creates a context of the natural world that elicits Deirdre's explanation of her previous life to Naisi.[23] The fog invades the stage, and with it comes Fergus, whose belief in Conor's integrity obscures the inevitability of the resolution, and Deirdre's fears.

In Act III the combination of indoor and outdoor is repeated in the stage directions, and the space is oddly described as *'a room in the forest'* and is lit not by natural light but by torches.[24] There is a new sense of confinement and with it come images of the inevitability of violence, 'a little blood shed by the wayside can stain the feet of the passers by after a thousand years.'[25] *The Buried Life of Deirdre* dramatizes the destructiveness of cycles of violence based on retribution. As Deirdre herself says, 'I, who am very old,/ Know that the slain must slay.'[26] Her overarching prescience and her fluid identity are reflected in the extension of stage space and time through the tropes of visions and underground passages and spatial permeability. By these means the conceptual frame of the play is privileged over its familiar source narrative. Gore-Booth's manipulation of the original tale disrupts Deirdre's role as the doom-bearing heroine, and proposes a model of shared responsibility for violence across gender divisions, but a refusal of the normalization of violence, and finally a utopian image of alternative possibilities identified with respect for Mannanan.

Throughout the late 1910s and up to the late 1930s Dorothy Macardle wrote non-fiction, fiction and journalism, as well as plays. She was alert to the medium of theatre as collaborative, as reflective of, and reflective on, society and, in Ireland particularly, as undeniably linked with the nation's history:

The theatre, communal in its origins and in its appeal, remains sensitive to communal moods and the mind of the dramatist is a kind of weather-vane.... Irish drama, even more than that of most countries, has been conditioned by the nation's history.[27]

So Macardle wrote, from the vantage point of the 1930s; she was identifying a new wave of theatrical energy at the Gate Theatre. However, she had begun her work as a playwright earlier, in 1918, at the Abbey Theatre. Macardle's participation in culture and politics betrays complex explorations of an individual's ethical values as they are swept up in history, and in her fiction and playwriting she dramatized the situation of women in relation to the national project. Her interest in supernatural forces may, I believe, be read allegorically, as an oblique expression of the hidden power of women in a patriarchal structure which allows them no place or recognition. The apparent certainties of her political life, and of her role as an Irish historian, are significantly complemented and deepened by the moral and gender conflicts in her plays. Her subversive dramaturgy shows in the stresses visible between her female characters and the dramatic narratives in which they are placed. In the post-revolutionary 1930s Ireland, how woman might be represented as powerful was a question which, as Gerardine Meaney expresses, disclosed certain anxieties: 'Anxiety about one's fitness for a (masculine) role of authority, deriving from a history of defeat or helplessness, is assuaged by the assumption of sexual dominance.'[28]

Macardle's engagement with the nationalist cause (at its height from 1921 to the founding of Fianna Fáil in 1926) coincides with plays such as *Atonement* (1918) and *Ann Kavanagh* (1922) and speaks of this playwright's abiding sense of the need to create a locus of female agency which is defined as outside the ordinary limits of social and psychological materialism. Her attempt in these plays to explore women's relation to ideology and violence may be described as an important period in her work; yet, it is only one part of a continuum of her preoccupation with placing female subjectivity in relation to supernatural powers that are impossible to control. These powers combine with potential catastrophe; they cannot be accommodated within the boundaries of rational, conscious reality, yet they are undeniably present.

The relationship between femininity and this sense of hidden or occluded power in Macardle's work tells of the changing position of women during the consolidating stage of Irish independence. Theatrically, Macardle's plays illustrate a straining at the limits of realist style, and with *Witch's Brew*, a return to folkloric sources to find a mode of expression for female energy that is powerfully transgressive. Mary Condron states: 'Irish indigenous culture retreated into a steadfast form of nationalism where the links with the Roman Catholic Church provided the only symbolic force the Irish had against the might of the British Empire.[29] The topoi of Church and motherland were crucial sites in the consolidation of national identity in the Ireland of the 1920s and 1930s. In *Witch's Brew* Macardle allegorizes the crisis of women in this symbolic framework. The play is in the neo-Celtic revivalist mould, and the old pagan values are set against those of the 'new' Christianity. The most radical expedition into this territory had been perhaps, Synge's *The Well of the Saints* (1905). Gregory dealt with the clash in *Kincora*. Like the latter, *Witch's Brew* is safely distanced by its archaic setting, but the bric-a-brac of wattle, skins and earthen vessels does little to disguise the oppressively polarized and conservative representation of women. Here, the embryonic female subjectivity, present in Macardle's earlier work, is obliterated in a Manichean struggle between good (as represented by Christianity in the person of Kiaran, a hermit monk) and evil (embodied in the figure of Blanid, a girl of the forest). The obliteration is embedded in the narrative; it is also enacted in Una, the central female character, the victim of a mysterious and unspecified illness. Una is an incarnation of the hysterical woman. Macardle frames the etiology of her symptoms within the power struggle between pagan 'old' culture and Christian 'new' culture, resolving her enigma in a closing alliance of Church and family.

Witch's Brew was rejected by the Abbey Theatre in January 1929, and was published two years later. At the opening of the action, Una lies almost lifeless, while her mother-in-law, Áine and her sister-in-law, Nessa, look on helplessly. Áine says: 'At dawn, when the pulse of the world is faint and sluggish, she will die.'[30] Outside a great storm is raging; its din interrupts the dialogue and adds to the embattled atmosphere. Both watchers are awaiting the return of Una's husband Phelim, who has ventured out in search of Kiaran and the 'blest water'.[31] Áine decides to look for help to the 'old Gods'.[32] Against Nessa's will she brings Blanid into the house to make her 'witch's brew', one drop of which can bring Una back to life. Una revived is very different from the loving, saintly, death-bed Una. She is selfish, complaining and contemptuous. Before Phelim and Kiaran return a dispute develops between the women and there are accusations of 'murderess'.[33] Una accuses Nessa of stealing her silver ring, and attacks her, exclaiming, 'Blood! Red and shining! I will have blood!'[34] Kiaran intervenes and deliberately allows Una to wound him. Her reaction is the desired one: '*She drops the knife, screams and shudders as though a possessing demon was leaving her body, and falls.*'[35] The play ends with the family kneeling in prayer around Kiaran.

The theme of possession by spiritual forces occurs in Macardle's short story 'The Return of Niav' and in several of her novels.[36] The trope of the changeling, which is its folkloric expression, may be read as an example of 'the popular epistemology of the double woman: frail saint and animalistic whore.'[37] In the case of *Witch's Brew*, the place of sexuality in this equation is occluded and may be read only through the semiotics of Una's hypnoid state and the striking significance of Blanid as she conjures her brew from fire, blood and milk. This representation of the double woman dramatizes the contest for power between the symbolic woman and the literal woman in the context of this play, the question is – which is which? Una, who is described as being '*very beautiful*' opens and closes the action as a saintly, gentle and loving figure, everything that the 'good woman' should be.[38] As such, she is a powerful symbol of woman as angel of the house (read nation), nurturer and upholder of Christianity. Is this a new version of a sovereignty figure where folkloric, and therefore pagan, associations have been replaced by reliance on the power of the 'blest water', the Church which, in the play, metaphorically wounded itself in order to save Ireland? If so, then Una is trapped within this image; her 'real' self, which appears under the influence of the witch's brew, is seen as degenerate, self-pitying, defeatist and, in the play, defeated.

This is the way the equation of the double woman is worked out in *Witch's Brew*. However, there are several points where the stage picture presents vital and energizing images of the 'old' culture. There is a clear association between the pagan and the female, as represented by Áine and Blanid. When Áine sets out to fetch Blanid, she is described as: '*Standing erect, the lantern in her hand, she speaks strongly, like one freed from fear.*'[39] She cries out to Mananaan, Dagda and Baal, the ancient deities of women's power. Visually, and from the point of view of staging, Blanid's entrance and her preparation of the potion are the most exciting actions in the play: '*Out of the darkness, her black hair and streaming rags wet and dishevelled, Blanid, the witch-girl, runs in, noiselessly, as though blown by the wind.*'[40] Blanid's cauldron is full of 'the colour of blood', it is 'writhing like serpents'.[41] Before adding milk to the mixture, Blanid remarks, 'They say Patrick has put the snakes out of Ireland, but there are snakes in Ireland still.'[42] Theatrically, this scene offers potential for strong visual images, and could, in performance, pose a challenge to the resolutions enacted in closure.

Una's illness is never explained. Her unconsciousness declares, paradoxically, the difficulty of expressing an authentic subjectivity in relation to the controlling functions of religion, the family and, by extension, the state. Una can only express her resistance in her unconsciousness, in her longing for death, 'I cannot stay. My soul is a wild bird; it is craving for the air and the light!'[43] Una's secret is not her virtue, but her sexuality, her femininity, which can only be expressed obliquely in the play, and which is codified in her physical beauty and in Blanid, and in the witch's brew itself, giving the play its title. She herself cannot speak it. Her subjectivity is incompatible with the 'new' politico-religious order. *Witch's Brew*, like Yeats's *The Only Jealousy of Emer* (1919), opens with a vigil around a seeming-dead figure. In the latter, Emer says: 'Although they have dressed him out in his grave clothes/ And stretched his limbs, Cuchulain is not dead.'[44] In Cuchulain's case we are told the reason for his swoon, but in the case of Una no explanation is offered. *Witch's Brew* is set with significant detail. Furniture is described; there are '*hunting knives and axes,*' '*a low brazier*' and, significantly, '*no windows*'.[45] This places emphasis on the door as the only threshold space on-stage. The bed on which Una lies, holding a crucifix, is positioned with '*the foot below the centre of the room*', that is, dominating the stage.[46] Unlike the fluidly representational space of Yeats's play, and of Gore-Booth's discussed earlier, where the action is framed by theatrical ritual, *Witch's Brew* takes place within a claustrophobic space which is closed off from outside, and is threatened by the intrusive noise of the storm. When Áine unbars the door and ventures out she is passing into the world of nature, of the old Gods, of danger; it is also Blanid's world. There her power resides, in the herbs which go to make her magic and in the association established by Macardle between the fire power of the storm and Blanid's use of fire. Here, Macardle's use of the identification between woman and nature is ambivalent. Elizabeth Cullingford identifies how: 'Images of women that originated as the projections of male anxieties and aggression are used as evidence of the need to control and subordinate the whole female sex.'[47]

Blanid invades the stage space and dominates it, turning it red with fumes and flames. The theatrical impact of Blanid, and her impact on Una, creates an unstable dramatic structure. It is not until the entrance of Phelim and Kiaran, and the symbolic sacrifice of Kiaran, when his hand is cut, that order is restored. René Girard says: 'Blood serves to illustrate the point that the same substance can stain or cleanse, contaminate or purify, drive men to fury and murder or appease their anger and restore them to life.'[48] Blood which was, at first, identified with Blanid, and with Una's madness, is now transformed into a Christian symbol of redemption. At the sight of Kiaran's cut hand, Una returns to 'herself'. She '*lies in Phelim's arms, apparently lifeless*' once more, and

ends the play speaking '*wistfully*' once more of death.[49] Before Kiaran
asserts the new order by his recital of the 'Agnes Dei', he defines Áine's
sin as 'too much love for the life of the body, and too little care for
the soul.'[50] Macardle creates a stage space that works allegorically as a
representation of the nation, sealed off from, yet not immune to, the
huge cultural and political energies without. Written in the wake of
the introduction, in 1928, of the *Censorship of Publications Act*, the play
enacts 'the continuing disassociation of body and spirit as campaigners
sought to impose upon all Free State citizens an ethic which viewed the
desires of the body as a menace to the prospect of eternal life.'[51] The
irony of Macardle's representation lies in the element of performance. By
representing Blanid through such a theatrically compelling action the
playwright creates a drama which, at once, celebrates in performance,
and obliterates through narrative, the mechanisms of closure.

Read allegorically, as an exploration of the intersection of religious
traditions old and new, *Witch's Brew* does not comfortably accommodate
the revivalist notion of ancient Irish religious and cultural icons as
touchstones in the projection of a national future. Rather, Macardle
dramatizes the rejection of these forces, and does so in a way that associ-
ates certain representations of femininity with the defeated powers. This
is, perhaps, the most compelling aspect of the play for a present-day
audience. Macardle used theatre to interrogate the impact of ideology
allied with violence, and women's place in relation to both. Her belief in
the special relationship between theatre and the nation's history, even
into the 1930s, invites allegorical readings of her plays, straining within
the frames of realist and melodramatic convention. The power of the
supernatural, which had informed Macardle's fiction from the beginning, becomes an issue in her later plays. *Witch's Brew* was written in the
period of national consolidation when conservative forces placed Irish
women as 'other of the ex-other', effectively erasing their presence in
public life, and confining their role within the terms of Catholic ecclesiastical misogyny.[52] Macardle then turns to supernatural forces, characterized as pagan in *Witch's Brew*, as a metaphorical expression of the
occluded passions and energies of women. In this play she realized the
dramatic potential of transgressive female figures in performance, even
when they are framed by a narrative that asserts their defeat. A theatrical
dialectic is thus established, between radical representation and conservative form. It is a measure of the cautions that hedged around the
process of representing the female on stage. Concomitantly, cultural reliance on the control of female iconography becomes visible. *Witch's Brew*
was not produced. The violence which had fed revolutionary upheaval

and civil war, but which had failed to emancipate women (beyond their winning of the right to vote), has turned inwards and the earlier, spacious experiments of Gore-Booth are narrowed to images of confinement and alienation.

Notes

1. Richard Kearney, 'Myth and Terror', *Crane Bag*, Vol. 1, Nos. 1–2, 1978, p. 276.
2. Prionsias MacCana, 'Women in Irish Mythology', *Crane Bag*, Vol. 4, No. 1, 1980, p. 521.
3. MacCana, *Crane Bag*, Vol. 4, No. 1, 1980, p. 521.
4. C. L. Innes, *Woman and Nation in Irish Literature and Society, 1880–1935* (London: Harvester Wheatsheaf, 1993), p. 178.
5. Michael Issacharoff, 'Space and Performance in Drama', *Poetics Today*, Vol. 2, Spring, 1981, pp. 211–24.
6. Geraldine Cousin, *Women in Dramatic Space and Time: Contemporary Female Characters on Stage* (London: Routledge, 1996), p. 201.
7. Anne Marrecco, *The Rebel Countess: The Life and Times of Constance Markievicz* (London: Weidenfeld & Nicholson, 1967), p. 134.
8. Eva Gore-Booth, *The Buried Life of Deirdre*, in *The Plays of Eva Gore-Booth* (San Francisco: EMText, 1991), p. ix.
9. *The Plays of Eva Gore-Booth*, p. 215.
10. Julia Kristeva, 'Women's Time', in Toril Moi (ed.), *The Kristeva Reader* (London and New York: Routledge, 1986), p. 191.
11. *The Plays of Eva Gore-Booth*, p. 165.
12. *The Kristeva Reader*, p. 191.
13. *The Kristeva Reader*, p. 191.
14. James Flannery, *W. B. Yeats and the Idea of Theatre* (London: Yale University Press, 1976), p. 46.
15. MacCana, *Crane Bag*, Vol. 4, No. 1, 1980, p. 523.
16. T. S. Eliot, *Four Quartets* (London: Faber & Faber, 1959), p. 55.
17. Matthew Arnold, 'Empedocles on Etna: A Dramatic Poem', in *Poems: Dramatic and Later Poems* (London: Macmillan, 1988), p. 173.
18. *The Kristeva Reader*, p. 198.
19. Arnold, *Poems: Dramatic and Later Poems*, p. 173.
20. Gore-Booth, *The Plays of Eva Gore-Booth*, pp. 171–2.
21. Gore-Booth, *The Plays of Eva Gore-Booth*, p. 165.
22. Gore-Booth, *The Plays of Eva Gore-Booth*, p. 165.
23. Gore-Booth, *The Plays of Eva Gore-Booth*, p. 173.
24. Gore-Booth, *The Plays of Eva Gore-Booth*, p. 192.
25. Gore-Booth, *The Plays of Eva Gore-Booth*, p. 200.
26. Gore-Booth, *The Plays of Eva Gore-Booth*, p. 178.
27. Dorothy Macardle, 'Experiment in Ireland', *Theatre Arts*, 1934, p. 124.
28. Gerardine Meaney, *Sex and Nation: Women in Irish Culture and Politics*, LIP Pamphlets (Dublin: Attic Press, 1991), p. 7.
29. Mary Condron, *The Serpent and the Goddess: Women, Religion and Power in Celtic Ireland* (San Francisco: Harper, 1989), p. 184.

30. Dorothy Macardle, *Witch's Brew* (London: H. F. W. Deane, 1931), p. 4.
31. Macardle, *Witch's Brew*, p. 4.
32. Macardle, *Witch's Brew*, p. 6.
33. Macardle, *Witch's Brew*, p. 15.
34. Macardle, *Witch's Brew*, p. 17.
35. Macardle, *Witch's Brew*, p. 18.
36. Macardle, *Theatre Arts*, pp. 56–71.
37. Elin Diamond, *Unmaking Mimesis: Essays on Feminism and Theatre* (London: Routledge, 1997), p. 21.
38. Macardle, *Witch's Brew*, p. 3.
39. Macardle, *Witch's Brew*, p. 6.
40. Macardle, *Witch's Brew*, p. 9.
41. Macardle, *Witch's Brew*, p. 10.
42. Macardle, *Witch's Brew*, p. 10.
43. Macardle, *Witch's Brew*, p. 7.
44. W. B. Yeats, *The Only Jealously of Emer*, *Collected Plays*, 2nd edn (London: Macmillan, 1952), p. 283.
45. Macardle, *Witch's Brew*, p. 3.
46. Macardle, *Witch's Brew*, p. 3.
47. Elizabeth Cullingford, 'Thinking of Her…as…Ireland', *Textual Practice*, Vol. 4, 1990, p. 2.
48. René Girard, *Violence and the Sacred*, trans. Patrick Gregory (Baltimore: John Hopkins University Press, 1979), p. 37.
49. Macardle, *Witch's Brew*, pp. 18, 19.
50. Macardle, *Witch's Brew*, p. 19.
51. David Cairns and Shaun Richards, *Writing Ireland: Colonialism, Nationalism and Culture* (Manchester: Manchester University Press, 1988), p. 116.
52. Ailbhe Smyth, 'The Floozie in the Jacuzzi', *Irish Review*, No. 6, 1989, p. 10.

4

Taking their Own Road: The Female Protagonists in Three Irish Plays by Women

Lisa Fitzpatrick

This chapter explores three plays by Abbey Theatre playwrights; *Grania* by Augusta Gregory (variously dated 1910 or 1912[1]), *The Woman* by Margaret O'Leary (first staged in September 1929) and *The King of Spain's Daughter* by Teresa Deevy (premiered in April 1935). These plays were written during those decades of the twentieth century when Ireland's political status as an independent nation, and the gender relationships legislated by the new state, were still in flux. All three plays have central female protagonists who seek adventure and who spin new identities and wondrous worlds from their speech; ultimately, however, none of the three is fated to go 'romancing through a romping lifetime' like Christy Mahon, the playboy of the Western world.[2] Inspired by Christopher Murray's and Lionel Pilkington's readings of the Irish theatre as a 'mirror up to nation', and as a public forum for the representation and exploration of key issues for the new administration, this chapter will explore whether these three plays similarly reflect the status of women in the decades following 1916.[3]

If Gregory's and Yeats's 1902 drama *Kathleen ni Houlihan* can be read, as Robert Welch suggests, as the foundation stone of modern Irish theatre, this dramatic representation of the Woman-Nation might seem to reinforce the symbolic consonance between woman and land in a public and definitive act of representation. Welch describes the text as 'a scene of transformation; what the play accomplished was also an act of translation, whereby emblems and figures out of the Irish cultural memory were carried over into the twentieth century and given immediate and shocking relevance. Modern Irish theatre begins here.'[4] However, it is significant that the part of Kathleen was first performed by Maud Gonne, a woman well known to her audience as both a Nationalist and as a feminist. Gonne's presence in the title role is a

69

complicating element in reading the performance, as is the recognition of Gregory's role in the writing of the piece. Antoinette Quinn suggests that in this play, Gregory 'represented nationalism's devastating impact on the well-being and continuity of family life in small-farm Ireland and showed how women lose out to the woman-nation.'[5] Quinn's reading may be counter-intuitive, but the figure of Kathleen does not in itself promote an ideal of self-sacrificing, self-abnegating femininity; Kathleen, passionate and imperious, commanding the destinies of many, might instead offer an ideal of femininity more akin to Granuaile than to the Victorian 'Angel in the House'.[6]

The early decades of the twentieth century saw vigorous debates about the civil rights and proper role of women, both in Ireland and internationally, although throughout Western Europe and North America the advances that women made during this time were largely reversed in the post-World War One years. As the new Irish state established itself and began the process of forming and reforming its social and legislative structures, gender identities were correspondingly revised, reformulated and often prescribed. The debates that accompanied these processes, and women's resistance to some of the legislation, had largely been ignored until the 1970s, when scholars of women's history, such as Margaret MacCurtain, Margaret Ward and Maria Luddy, amongst others, began publishing their historical research. In the past few years, Rosemary Cullen Owens's *A Social History of Women in Ireland*, Diane Urquhart's and Alan Hayes's *Irish Women's History Reader* and the *Field Day Anthology* Volumes IV and V among others, have all extended knowledge of this field, while Diarmaid Ferriter's *The Transformation of Ireland 1900–2000* is one of relatively few 'mainstream' histories that considers the experience of women as integral to the history of the state. This scholarship offers new interpretations of the period, uncovers previously ignored documentation, and focuses attention on the organized resistance to retrogressive pieces of legislation. The Proclamation of 1916 and the Constitution of the Free State of 1922 had guaranteed certain equalities of treatment and status to both sexes before the law, identifying equal rights and duties of citizenship. But the following years saw the introduction of legislation that increasingly limited women's participation in public life.[7] In 1937, the only newspaper edited by a woman was *Prison Bars*, a small publication for the Women's Prisoners Defence League, which published objections to the proposed Constitution from Hanna Sheehy-Skeffington, Kathleen Clarke, Kate O'Callaghan and Maud Gonne MacBride. All of these women saw the article regarding the status of women (Article 41.2) as 'a betrayal of the 1916 promise of

"Equal Rights and Equal Opportunities guaranteed to all citizens" ', and 'a grave danger to the future position of women'.[8]

Viewed retrospectively, the years that Gregory conceived and wrote *Grania* were a time of pre-revolutionary Nationalist and feminist tension, when the promise of Irish independence seemed to offer a new model of a utopian society. The gradual erosion throughout the 1920s and 1930s of the choices available to women, however, is reflected in the plays discussed here. To describe these works as feminist would be inaccurate; rather, the plays address a discomfort or uncertainty regarding the unjust social position of women. Recent scholarship on Teresa Deevy's play *Katie Roche*, which was first staged at the Abbey Theatre in March 1936, argues that the heroine's abrupt and unconvincing volte-face at the end expresses the impossibility for the devoutly Catholic Deevy of writing the only convincing outcome for her heroine: that of leaving her marriage.[9] Instead, Katie submits to the isolation and loneliness of life with her older husband. This is the only expression of heroism, of 'something great to do' that is available to her.[10] Similarly, in *The King of Spain's Daughter*, the heroine is left to choose between servitude in the factory, and marriage to a man she does not love; like Katie Roche, she attempts to find the passion she craves in a loveless marriage.

The King of Spain's Daughter is a one-act play set entirely 'on a grassy road in Ireland during the dinner-hour of a day in April'.[11] The characters are Annie Kinsella, her father Peter, who is angry because she is late with his dinner and Jim, the young man who hopes to marry her and whom she is eventually forced to accept. The other figures are Mrs Marks, an older woman from the community who acts as mouthpiece for the traditional role of women, and Roddy, another of Annie's boyfriends, whom she kisses in view of Jim, Mrs Marks and the audience. Since Annie does not appear on stage until approximately half-way through the play, the opening dialogue focuses mainly on her behaviour, of which the other characters disapprove, and on a local wedding that was performed that morning, before the play begins. These topics allow the range of meanings in operation in this community to emerge, as well as forming the basis for the audience's impression of the central protagonist.

One of Annie's key characteristics is her romantic imagination, which finds expression, for instance, in her description of the bride's gown: she variously describes it as 'flamin' red', 'shimmerin' green' and 'pale, pale gold'. Jim tells her angrily that the bride wore grey.[12] As this dialogue about the bridal gown continues between Annie and Jim, her longing for romance is further expressed through her identification with the heroine in the poem she quotes – 'The King of Spain's Daughter'. She apparently often quotes its verses, for Jim tells her, 'I'm sick of that thing! Who's the King of Spain's daughter?', and he laughs when she replies, 'Myself'. She explains, 'It is myself I seen in her – sailin' out into the sun, and to adventure.'[13] In reality, her brutal father beats her and offers her a choice: she must either sign a five-year contract with the local factory, or marry Jim, whom she had rejected as a husband two years earlier. The play ends with Annie realizing that Jim has saved two shillings a week for four years in the hope that she will marry him. This discovery provides her with a strange comfort, as the final lines of the play should make clear, when she exclaims, 'He put by two shillin's every week for two hundred weeks. I think he is a man that – supposin' he was jealous – might cut your throat. (*Quiet, exultant, she goes.*)' Mrs Marks, left alone on the stage, responds to the possibility of jealous violence that attracts Annie, saying, 'The Lord preserve us! that she'd find joy in such a thought!'[14] But for Annie, it is the only possible hint of adventure or passion in her future.

Sean Ó Meadhra, a theatre critic with *Ireland Today* in the 1930s, writes of *The King of Spain's Daughter* that 'this character study by Teresa Deevy in the Schnitzler or Molnar mode is worthy of more praise than it has received. "Katie Roche", first produced some months ago, is merely a successful expansion of it. Its subtlety is too much for the Abbey, and the staging was the last word in bathos.'[15] Both Ó Meadhra and Joseph Holloway praised Ria Mooney, who performed the title role. Holloway writes, 'Ria Mooney as the wayward one, "Annie Kinsella", lay bare the fluttering thoughts that filled her head with great artistry and tact. John Stephenson was a trifle hard and wooden as "Annie's" father, "Peter Kinsella", and Cyril Cusack as "Annie's" lover, "Jim Harris", in thinking of his accent lost much of the naturalness of the part.'[16] The ending, however, was often misinterpreted in performance by the critics of the time. Holloway concludes that 'the romantic ideas of a labourer's daughter are nearly brought to a commonplace end by her somewhat brutal father, but she runs away from it all.'[17] *The Irish Times* review similarly misunderstands the action. Its reviewer explains Annie's reports of the wedding as her dreamy longing for her own wedding. He or she sees Annie's decision to marry Jim as a sensible choice to settle down with a hardworking man, and the review ends: 'She could run away, of course; and finally she did. A man who could save two shillings every week for four years could be a jealous man – one who could cut a throat. That was the thought on which she fled.'[18] In fact, Annie does not flee, and Deevy makes use of the set to establish from the opening scene that escape is impossible for any of her characters. The stage directions read, *'An open space on a grassy road. At each side road-barriers with notices, "No Traffic", and "Road Closed".'*[19] Thus the signs immediately contradict the meaning of the open, natural space. A wall with a small door standing open is at the back; the fields can be seen through the door. This does not represent an escape either, however, since it is through this door that Annie Kinsella enters from the village. The road reaches the wider world, and it is closed at both sides. It appears therefore that Holloway and the unnamed reviewer from *The Irish Times* are reinterpreting the action to conform to the dominant social attitudes of the time.

In her study of the emergence of the subject and of signifying practice, Catherine Belsey writes: 'Meanings are not the record of experience, though they may define the conditions of its possibility... the meanings in circulation at a given moment specify the limits of what can be said and understood.'[20] Her argument continues, defining the subject as one who controls the discourse, but who is in turn produced discursively and therefore both controls and, paradoxically, is bound by signifying practice: 'The subject is held in place in a specific discourse, a specific knowledge, by the meanings available there.... Subjectivity is discursively produced and is constrained by the range of subject-positions defined by the discourses in which the concrete individual participates.'[21] Belsey describes the movement beyond the prescribed range in a given society as 'psychotic'. She explains: 'Utterance – and action – outside the range of meanings in circulation in a society is psychotic. In this sense existing discourses determine not only what can be said and understood, but the nature of subjectivity itself, what it is possible to be.'[22] Similarly, Valerie Traub, Lindsay Kaplan and Dympna Callaghan list interiority, agency and status as defining marks of the individual subject, with the qualifying statement that the individual 'makes claims for cultural recognition only through available means'.[23] Belsey observes that: 'Signifying practice is never static [it] is also the location of resistances. Since meaning is plural, to be able to speak is to be able to take part in the contest for meaning which issues in the production of new subject-positions, new determinations of what it is possible to be.'[24] Reading *The King of Spain's Daughter* in the light of her argument, it seems that Annie Kinsella's speech and behaviour transgress the range of meanings commonly shared in 1930s Ireland, both within the world of the play as seen in the other characters' responses to her, and in the (usually male) critics' reading of the performance in the actual world.

Annie Kinsella resembles the heroine of Margaret O'Leary's 1929 play *The Woman*, in her dreams of far away and her thirst for passionate love.[25] Ellen Dunn, 'the woman' of the title, is a girl from a poor family comprising her widowed mother and layabout brother William. The Dunns occupy a marginal position on the edge of their village, and on the edge of respectability; there is a rumour that the father was a 'Tinker' (Act I). The main characters are the relatively prosperous and respectable O'Haras; John and his wife Mary, their widowed son Maurice, and Mary's brother James Deasy. Set in a hamlet in Cork, the action takes place entirely in the contrasting domestic spaces of these two families. Maurice, recently bereaved and now the sole parent of two infants, is already courting Ellen, to the fury of his family. His father is so distressed by the liaison that he threatens to disown him if he persists with the relationship (Act I). Mary O'Hara even attempts to bribe Ellen's family with money for the girl's passage to America, but the family only takes the money and keeps it for themselves. Ellen, for her part, wants Maurice to elope with her to 'the lovely country where all the sun is' (Act II), and demands that he abandon his parents, the land and even his children to prove his love for her. She asks him, 'Do you love me more than everything you have?...More than your father, and mother, and house, and lands, and cattle, and money, and everything? (Act II).

Maurice's family favour Kitty Doyle as a match for him. Even though Maurice's mother, Mary, is consistently kind to Ellen, her interaction with Kitty is notably warm and welcoming. The pencil notes in one of the rehearsal copies of the manuscript record that when Kitty first appears on stage in Act I, Mrs O'Hara 'pushes' her the armchair, then takes a chair from the table and sits next to her. As the scene unfolds, they move to the table, and drink tea together; they then go to sit by the fire (Act I). When the dialogue turns to Kitty's love for Maurice, Mrs O'Hara *'hitches her chair closer'*. The scene charts the development of their regard for each other from the friendly and informal welcome, to the significance of sharing food, to the final scene by the fireside. Kitty is symbolically welcomed into the family through her invitation to both table and hearth, and the moving of Mrs. O'Hara's chair closer expresses their willingness to share confidences. There are no such intimate moments shared between Mrs. O'Hara and Ellen.

The plot follows Maurice's struggle to reconcile his love for his parents, his children and the land, with his sexual passion for Ellen. Although he claims that 'she was made for me from the beginning of the world', in the same scene he also admits that he 'loves the land as good as anyone ever loved it' (Act I). Ellen is fascinated by Poulgorm, a pond in which her grandmother drowned, and this morbid longing foreshadows her fate. In fact, 'the lovely country where all the sun is' (Act II), gradually becomes intertwined in her imagination with Poulgorm and with her concept of the afterlife, while Poulgorm is linked in her speech to her longing for love. She remarks to Maurice that 'your arms around me will be as soft as the dark waters of Poulgorm' (Act II). However, at the climax of the play, Maurice remains on the farm to deal with a crisis, rather than meeting Ellen. His failure to give himself to her, body and soul, prompts her to leave, proclaiming 'away my own road I must be going now – by myself, not thinking of any of ye...And 'tis grand and shiny the water in Poulgorm will be now, and so soft – (*moving into the night*) – so soft!' (Act III).

Although *The Woman* was never published, there is evidence that an earlier draft was submitted to the Abbey sometime before April 1929 (the play was staged the following September, see Figure 3). According to a letter written by W. B. Yeats to Lennox Robinson in April 1929, the original ending of the play had Ellen leaving to wander the roads. In his letter to Robinson, Yeats insists that 'the heroine must die and we must know she dies; all that has been built up is scattered, and degraded, if she does not come to the understanding that she seeks something life, or her life, can never give.'[26] In the same letter, he writes, 'Miss O'Leary should be the best realistic peasant dramatist who has yet appeared', and judges that, if the ending is reworked as he suggests, she will have written 'a most powerful play'. In a letter O'Leary implies that these changes were made.[27] Revisions to the original draft include that the heroine is now clearly understood to kill herself by drowning. However, this is never confirmed either mimetically or in the diegesis, and no body of the dead woman appears on stage. Ellen leaves, having spoken the lines quoted above, and the play ends with Maurice dashing off, having just realized what she intends to do.

The popular Abbey actress Eileen Crowe performed the part of Ellen at the premiere. Holloway comments that her performance 'developed into a sort of female "Playboy of the Western World", in the grand flow of flowery talk she gives tongue to'.[28] This invocation of Christy Mahon, coupled with the original open ending of the play, and O'Leary's resistance to staging any confirmation of Ellen's death in the iconic form of the tragic drowned body, provokes questions about the gender roles inscribed in the text. In comparison to the eponymous heroine of Gregory's *Grania*, who commands her own destiny, or to Annie Kinsella, who is completely dispossessed of choice or opportunity, Ellen Dunn

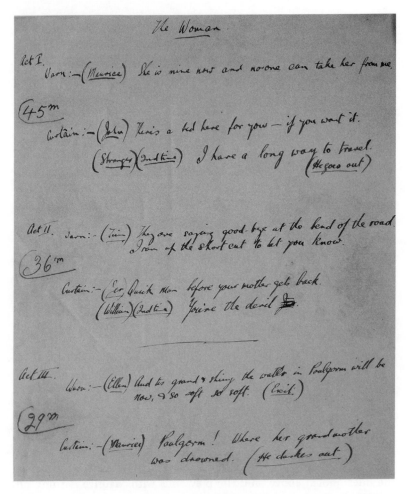

Figure 3 Stage Management Records of *The Woman* by Margaret O'Leary, 10 September 1929. Courtesy of the Abbey Theatre.

occupies a kind of middle ground. Ellen is an agent in the dramatic action, but her ultimate (presumed) act of agency is radically destructive. It seems that the time for women to wander out of the home and shape their own destiny – as Nora Helmer does in *A Doll House*, or Nora Burke does, albeit reluctantly, in *The Shadow of the Glen* – had passed. The choice to leave is daring: the open ending, which Yeats believed would weaken the play, asserts that there is a choice beyond submission or death. Furthermore, it refuses to identify female rebellion – particularly sexual rebellion – with madness; and it refuses to punish the character for transgressing patriarchal mores. By changing the resolution, O'Leary allows her character to be safely contained within the mythos of the woman who was beautiful and mad, and tragically killed herself. Ellen's despair thus becomes an individual tragedy, rather than the tragedy of women as a class. It is significant, however, that O'Leary does not confirm the death of the protagonist: the audience is denied the final satisfaction of the elimination of the threatening element and a safe conclusion.

Like Annie Kinsella, Ellen Dunn seeks overwhelming passion; she explains to Maurice that she needs 'an awful lot of love' (Act II). But, as in *The King of Spain's Daughter*, the dramatic world characterizes this kind of love as aberrant, as a sickness, while in *Grania* it is seen as the harbinger of grief and pain. In these fictional worlds, sexual love is to be abjured in the interest of social stability. In *The Woman*, the men bond with each other in their dread of women, and female sexuality is abjected. Similar to Annie Kinsella in Deevy's play, Ellen does not appear on stage until Act II, the first act dealing with her effect on men. The play opens in the O'Hara's kitchen, in the middle of an argument about Maurice's relationship with an unnamed 'black-eyed slut' and 'jade'[29] (a disreputable woman) (Act I). This early dialogue centres on Ellen's perceived sexual immorality. James denounces her as a 'light woman' who is known to have had a number of lovers. Later, two other male characters, who have been in thrall to her, speak of her in demonic terms. One warns Maurice, 'She will bring a curse on any man who looks into the black fire of her eyes.... She is a woman of flame. She will suck the youth out of you. And she will finish with you soon –' (Act I). Even Maurice, when he believes her to be unfaithful, calls her 'slut... serpent... spawn of Hell' (Act III). Ellen believes in her power over men, using it in the final scenes to pronounce a curse on Maurice:

> Often in the night time you'll wake up out of your sleep, and you'll turn your back on the good wife sleeping beside you, and every drop of your blood will cry out for me. There will be no hunger like that hunger, and no thirst like that thirst. You will be parched and burning, and your eyes will drop scalding tears.
>
> (O'Leary, *The Woman*, Act III)

While regarding romantic love and desire primarily as weakness or disease, the male characters turn their love towards the land. This emerges very clearly in an impassioned scene in Act I, in which Maurice's uncle and father appeal to him to think of his farm and his home and give up Ellen:

(John goes over to the chair on the right of the table, sits down, and with his elbows resting on the table, addresses Maurice plaintively. His voice sometimes breaks.)

JOHN: Listen here, son. The land – our land – don't play a dirty trick on it. For a dirty trick it would be to turn your back on the land for the sake of a woman. The land that the men who went before us watered with their sweat! The land that is more to you than a mother – that stands by you from cradle to grave – that feeds you – and that puts a roof over your head – and a coat on your back. The darling land – always with a welcome for you – and you digging the potatoes out of her! And her fields of ripe yellow corn! And she always so fresh – and clean – and – and – why, man, just like God Almighty Himself!

(John covers his face with his hands. They are all touched. Silence for a few moments. Brokenly): and you are thinking of leaving all that.

(O'Leary, The Woman, Act I)

Maurice resists his father's appeal, saying, 'A greater love has come to me.' But later in the same scene, Maurice is discovered to have a fever, and is sent away to bed. His reckless talk of love is attributed by the other characters to his delirium, a dramaturgical choice that confuses, since in this context neither the audience nor the other characters can confidently distinguish love from sickness. Yet, by setting the land in opposition to Ellen – the land whose love is wholesome, true and godly, against the tainted love of physical woman – and having Maurice choose Ellen – O'Leary asserts the ascendancy of the actual over the mythological woman, and breaks the symbolic consonance that links Ireland-Woman-Land into interchangeable units of meaning.

For the male characters, Ellen represents the abjected qualities of the feminine. Defining the concept, Julia Kristeva writes:

There looms, within abjection, one of those violent, dark revolts of being, directed against a threat that seems to emanate from an exorbitant outside or inside, ejected beyond the scope of the possible, the tolerable, the thinkable. It lies there, quite close, but it cannot be assimilated. It beseeches, worries, and fascinates desire, which, nevertheless, does not let itself be seduced. Apprehensive, desire turns aside; sickened, it rejects.'[30]

The excessive rage and disgust that James Deasy and John O'Hara express in the opening scenes represent Ellen as, quite literally, a spawn of the devil; they accuse her of putting spells on Maurice, and their language recalls that of the witch-hunts. John says, 'She put her spells on him... It's her and her like that do the divil's work.' James concurs, 'That's the devil's work and no mistake' (Act I). Ellen's power to unman her rejected suitors recalls the popular belief that a witch could steal a man's penis through the power of magic. Ellen's rejected suitor at the end of Act 1 warns Maurice that she will 'suck the youth out of you', a terrifying threat. The text makes clear that Ellen's sexuality is perceived as the source of her terrifying power, and O'Leary draws a sharp distinction between the kindness that the female characters show to her, and the fearful anger of the men. The power that is attributed to her is both a testimony to her unusual beauty and an unsettling articulation of misogynistic disgust. All the characters comment on her loveliness, and the stage directions describe her as moving '*with quick, rhythmic, feline grace. When at bay, she elongates her neck and throws up her head in a manner which suggests a beautiful untamable* (sic) *bird. Her voice is flexible, vibrating and extremely sensitive to all her varying moods.*' Nonetheless, the male characters' mingled fascination and revulsion hints at their realization that Ellen's love is death-dealing, something that the female characters only dimly perceive. Her final demands on Maurice are that he must travel with her to 'the lovely country where all the sun is' (Act II), which is gradually identified with death over the second and third acts, and her description of his embrace as 'as soft as the dark waters of Poulgorm' (Act II) reinforces this morbidity. In the final scene, after Ellen has left the stage, Mary O'Hara remarks, 'Tis her and her likes that the grand stories of the world are about, like Helen the Beautiful and Deirdre of the Sorrows.' To this, her husband responds, 'The woman that brings destruction!' (Act III).

While their protagonists share a hunger for adventure and experience, the dramatic worlds of *The Woman* and *The King of Spain's Daughter* differ sharply from each other in their evocation of a social and emotional landscape. *The Woman* is a far less pessimistic work; there is at least space in its dramatic world for affection of a warm, domestic nature. Mary O'Hara is a kindly older woman, who never condemns Ellen for her flightiness, as the men do. Mary's own home life has been happy, as she explains to Ellen in the final act of the play, defining love in everyday terms: 'love is just feeding your man well, and keeping a warm shirt on his back.' Ellen, horrified, replies that her husband has 'broken her in', and proclaims, 'no man will ever break me in'. But Mrs O'Hara disagrees; God broke her in, she says: 'You let go of yourself – and you get knitted in with everyone around you – and God too – all together – in one swim – and you lose yourself – for others. (*Knitting again: brightly.*) And there's such a lot of them to be taking care of.' As a girl, she confides, she was 'a bit fidgety – like all young girls – wanting love, and romance, and all sorts of foolish things' (Act III). Kitty Doyle, Ellen Dunn's *alter ego* – Kitty is even plump and fair while Ellen is small and dark – is similarly kind, gentle with Maurice's children, and warm and generous in her love for Maurice.

In contrast, *The King of Spain's Daughter* is unrelentingly grim in its representation of male-female relationships, although it also portrays women as complicit in their own dispossession, and compliant in the misogyny of their society. Mrs Marks, an older woman and a widow, is the first to denounce Annie as 'a shame and a sin!' and 'a bold wild thing'.[31] Of her own marriage she says, 'It is a thought would sadden anyone', yet she situates the wedding day as the pivotal moment in a woman's life: 'For twenty years you're thinking of that day, and for thirty years you're lookin' back at it.'[32] Later, she does speak more kindly to Annie, urging her to make the best of her marriage, but rebuking her for her reluctance, 'Did you think you needn't suffer like the rest of the world?' she asks, adding, 'You have a right to be grateful.'[33] Annie's disturbing hope that her husband will be brutal suggests that in the absence of any other path to an intensity of experience, she will welcome violence as a substitute. She thus resigns herself to a fate she despises, but which Mrs Marks reminds her is the most she may expect. It seems that the play's exploration of the possibilities available to women is frustrated as surely as Annie is: every attempt at escape is labelled a sin, and submission to social norms is enforced by all the members of society.

As characters, Ellen and Annie are out of joint within their fictional worlds; their speech is consistently misinterpreted, does not make sense to the other characters and their attempts to act upon their desires are dismissed as lying, wickedness or madness. They function as disruptive elements, as does Gregory's eponymous Grania. Significantly, what all three women clearly disrupt are the patriarchal norms governing their communities, which are expressed primarily through the homosocial and familial bonds between the male characters. They do this through the fact of their femaleness: it is the male characters' awareness of the protagonist's beauty and sexual desirability that produces the discord for which they are blamed. Notably, both Annie and Ellen resort to sexual relationships to express passions which are not, of themselves, primarily sexual, and in so doing they invite further condemnation. It is notable that these two protagonists rebel against domesticity and child-bearing, since the plays are written at a moment when women in Ireland were, in the legislation, increasingly being classified as wives and mothers, and limited in their opportunities outside of the home.

The community in *The King of Spain's Daughter* finally 'solves' the problem of what to do with Annie by forcibly marrying her to Jim, a resolution that brutally reinstates the patriarchal order and erases Annie's difference from the other villagers. Her tragedy is that she sees what her fate will be; she says bitterly '(*to herself*) I couldn't bear that I'd be no more than any other wife.'[34] *The Woman* similarly solves the problem of Ellen by eliminating her, the conclusion favoured by Yeats, and one that places the play in the genre of melodramatic tragedy. But *Grania*, in comparison to these two later plays and in sharp contrast to most of the Irish Revival plays based on myth, has at its centre a strong and indomitable female protagonist who refuses, in the end, to be defeated. Unlike the two protagonists in these later plays, Augusta Gregory's Grania is fully the author of her own destiny. Writing in the late 1920s, Andrew Malone laments that *Grania* has never been produced, and praises its 'characterization, dialogue, and construction'.[35] In fact, it was Gregory who denied the play a production during her lifetime, apparently because of its autobiographical significance.[36] Malone believes that this is her 'highest achievement in historical tragedy', and continues, 'here she is superior to the Ibsen of The Vikings at Helgeland, the Strindberg of Gustavus Vasa, or the Hauptmann of Florian Geyer.'[37]

Grania tells the story of the young woman who is betrothed to Finn, King of Ireland, but who elopes on her wedding night with the young warrior Diarmuid, Finn's kinsman. The play begins with Grania's initial arrival at Almhuin, to marry Finn. In the opening scene, she states that she has chosen her husband herself: 'My father was for the King of Foreign, but I said I would take my own road.'[38] Her phrase, 'my own road', implies far more than a choice of husband: it is an imperious statement of Grania's determination to chart her own path through life. When Finn asks her if she was ever in love, she gives a frank response, telling of a young man she saw once and her 'thoughts went with him for a good while'.[39] When she sees Diarmuid, she recognizes him as that young man. Having previously chosen her husband, she now actively woos Diarmuid, telling him, 'I am not ashamed. Was it my fault at all? I will light now this candle, I will dare to show you my face.'[40] Finn, enraged by his bride's infidelity, blames Diarmuid, with the result that Diarmuid and Grania leave together, and wander for seven years. But following the death of Diarmuid, Grania decides to return to Finn, without pausing to mourn or bury her lover. She insists that she will marry Finn, telling him, 'It is with you I will go to Almhuin. Diarmuid is no more to me than a sod that has been quenched with the rain.'[41] Although he refuses at first, Finn eventually agrees to marry her, but he warns her that she will be mocked for seeking to marry 'in the shadow of your comrade's wake'.[42] When she first emerges into the public space on Finn's arm the warriors do laugh at her, and she *'falls back and crouches down'*, but she conquers her fear and goes out again: 'I am no way daunted or afraid. Let them laugh their fill and welcome ... (*She opens the door herself. Finn puts his arm around her. There is another great peal of laughter but it stops suddenly as she goes out.*)'[43]

Gregory said of her heroine that 'Grania had more power of will [than Deirdre of the Sorrows], and for good or evil twice took the shaping of her life into her own hands.'[44] As in the other plays, the primacy of the homosocial bonds between men act to limit their sexual engagement with women. Diarmuid swears to Finn that he will not marry Grania until Finn freely lets her go, and he remains true to his word for seven years, before Grania finally overcomes his resistance by letting him find her with 'the King of Foreign'. Finn tells her at first that he will not marry her, because his loyalty to Diarmuid extends beyond the grave, for even though she and Diarmuid were not married, they were 'man and wife to one another'.[45] Like the men in *The Woman*, who turn to the land rather than to human women to express their love and sexuality, or the men in *The King of Spain's Daughter*, who seek fellow-feeling in their shared contempt for women, Finn and Diarmuid reserve their greatest passion and commitment for each other.[46]

But Grania is not subject to what others say about her. Unlike the protagonists of the two later plays, who are characterized and condemned before they appear, Grania is present on stage throughout almost all of the three acts and is on stage at the beginning of the play. If others speak of her, their speech is only reported when it is recounted to her, and she is impervious to criticism. She thus controls the discourse within the play. Although all three protagonists progress the dramatic action, only Grania can resolve the conflict to her own advantage. Cathy Leeney argues that Grania does so at the expense of passion. Grania also does so by entering into the language of the men, and never veering from it. Annie Kinsella and Ellen Dunn are inassimilable in part because they speak outside the range of accepted codes and meanings of their communities, but Grania speaks plainly and fearlessly throughout the drama. From the opening scene, where she responds fearlessly to Finn's question about love, to her wooing of Diarmuid, and her eventual return to Finn, she expresses her desires openly and directly. Unlike the heroines of the two later plays, she neither hides her sexual desire, nor does she confuse it with a desire for power or adventure. A comparison of the love scene in *The Woman* with Grania's early scene with Diarmuid, illustrates the difference. In *The Woman*, Ellen draws Maurice into a declaration of love without putting her own feelings or thoughts into words. '*Putting her cheek against his*' and '*nestling up to him*', she asks if he loves her, and leads him from his first, taciturn response 'You know I do', to romantic visions of a world of just the two of them. Finally, Maurice declares, 'I love you more than all I have in the world, more than all the world holds. If I were to get all the riches of the world without you, I would be poor. If I was to have nothing at all only you, I would be rich' (Act II). But Ellen does not reciprocate; on the contrary, her imagination is turned towards a 'lovely country were all the sun is' (Act II), the place that Maurice will bring her. Grania, in contrast, wooing Diarmuid, calls him first by name, in a direct address. When he does not respond, she 'speaks a little louder', saying simply 'Give me your help now. I cannot wed with Finn … It would be a terrible thing, a wedded woman not to be loyal – to call out another man's name in her sleep.'[47] There is no ambiguity in her speech and, although her desires are regarded as immoral and her behaviour eventually draws the mockery of Finn's soldiers, she never ceases to voice her desires and demands.[48] Interestingly, after she and Diarmuid first make love, his question, 'And did you love me ever and always, Grania?', is a stereotypically feminine request for reassurance.[49] The same question is asked by Ellen of Maurice, in Act II of *The Woman*. Grania replies, with perhaps a note of impatience, 'Did I not tell you long ago, my heart went down to you the day I looked from the high window, and I in my young youth at Tara.'[50] This implies that it was Diarmuid's beauty that first captivated her, which casts her in the role of the pursuer, and makes him the passive object of her desiring gaze.

The reading of these three plays explores the ways in which each reflects the issues or problems of the contemporaneous society. The fact that Deevy's work repeatedly returned to the situation of the unhappily married woman and to the lack of choices available to women, that O'Leary reworked the material of this play again in a novel published ten years later, and that Gregory denied her play a production during her lifetime supports such a reading.[51] Many of the realistic dramas by women of the 1920s and 1930s quite clearly engage with and represent the dearth of choices facing women, or grapple with the relationship between the real woman and her needs and desires, and the twin feminized abstractions of the nation and the land, which are represented as dominating the emotional lives of the men. The fictional worlds of all three of the plays, although very different from each other, share a number of features, including the primacy of the relationships between men over any other social or personal relationships. These factors come to be represented in more and more oppressive terms as the century unravels and the Irish State establishes its increasingly male-dominated power structures.

In the short 25-year historical arc of these dramas, the independent and adventurous heroine is increasingly an inassimilable element. Grania may shape her own destiny in 1910, in the midst of highly contested and various models of femininity and nationality that leave some space to imagine the Irishwoman of the post-Independence nation. But both the character of Ellen Dunn, and the apparent dramaturgical revision of the text prior to production at the instigation of Yeats, suggest that in the theatre of the time, the tragic heroine was in ascendance over the free, adventurous character who might seek her own destiny. Increasingly in the decades after independence, female characters in Irish plays are confined to the domestic space. Moving from *The Woman* to *The King of Spain's Daughter* brings a representation that is yet more pessimistic in terms both of the choices available to the protagonist, and to the tone and shading of the dramatic world. It can be no coincidence that, at the time when legislation was increasingly confining women to the domestic sphere, there should appear on stage so many female-authored heroines who long for, and are denied, a life of freedom and adventure.

Notes

1. Cathy Leeney, 'Augusta Gregory's *Grania* and the Codification of Sexuality in Irish Theatre', *Irish Theatre Forum*, Vol. 1, No. 1, Summer 1997, gives the date as 1910. Mary Fitzgerald, Introduction to *Selected Plays of Lady Gregory*, Irish Drama Selections Vol. 3 (Gerrard's Cross: Colin Smythe, 1983), p. 17, dates the play as 1912.
2. John Millington Synge, *The Playboy of the Western World*, *The Complete Plays* (New York: Vintage Books, 1935), p. 80.
3. Christopher Murray, *Twentieth Century Irish Drama: Mirror up to Nation* (Manchester: Manchester University Press; New York: St Martin's Press –

now Palgrave Macmillan, 1997); Lionel Pilkington, *Theatre and the State in Twentieth Century Ireland* (London and New York: Routledge, 2001).

4. Robert Welch, *The Abbey Theatre: 1899–1999* (Oxford: Oxford University Press, 1999), p. 16.

5. Antoinette Quinn, 'Ireland/Herland: Women and Literary Nationalism, 1845–1916', in Angela Bourke, Siobhán Kilfeather, Maria Luddy, Margaret MacCurtain, Gerardine Meaney, Máirín Ní Dhonnchadha, Mary O'Dowd and Clair Wills (eds), *The Field Day Anthology of Irish Women's Writing and Traditions Vol. V* (Cork: Cork University Press in association with Field Day, 2002), p. 899.

6. Granuaile, or Grace O'Malley (1530–1603) was a 'Pirate Queen' from Connaught. This extraordinary figure – independent, intelligent and obviously extremely strong-willed – is in clear contrast with the Victorian ideal of femininity eulogized in the popular poem by Coventry Patmore, 'The Angel in the House' (1854). Virginia Woolf comments that 'Killing the Angel in the House was part of the occupation of the woman writer' in her 1931 lecture to the National Society for Women's Service.

7. Rosemary Cullen Owens, *A Social History of Women in Ireland* (Dublin: Gill & Macmillan, 2005), pp. 251–79.

8. Kathleen O'Callaghan, *Prison Bars*, July 1937, quoted in Margaret Ward, *In Their Own Voice: Irish Women and Nationalism* (Dublin: Attic Press, 1995), pp. 164–8.

9. Judy Friel, 'Rehearsing *Katie Roche*', *Irish University Review*, Vol. 25, No. 1, Spring/Summer 1995, pp. 117–25.

10. Teresa Deevy, *Katie Roche, Three Plays* (London: Macmillan, 1939), p. 111.

11. Deevy, *Three Plays*, p. 120.

12. Deevy, *Three Plays*, pp. 127, 130, 132.

13. Deevy, *Three Plays*, p. 133.

14. Deevy, *Three Plays*, p. 142.

15. *Ireland Today*, Vol. 1, No. 4, September 1936, p. 63.

16. Joseph Holloway, *Joseph Holloway's Irish Theatre*, Vol. 2, 1932–1936, ed. Robert Hogan and Michael J. O'Neill (Dixon, CA: Proscenium Press, 1968), p. 59.

17. Holloway, *Joseph Holloway's Irish Theatre*, p. 59.

18. *The Irish Times* 2000, Waterford City History. Available online at http://members.tripod.com/waterfordhistory.

19. Deevy, *Three Plays*, p. 121.

20. Catherine Belsey, *The Subject of Tragedy* (London and New York: Routledge, 1985), pp. 5–6.

21. Belsey, *The Subject of Tragedy*, pp. 5–6.

22. Belsey, *The Subject of Tragedy*, pp. 5–6.

23. Valerie Traub, M. Lindsay Kaplan and Dympna Callaghan, *Feminist Readings of Early Modern Culture* (Cambridge: Cambridge University Press, 1996), pp. 1–2.

24. Belsey, *The Subject of Tragedy*, p. 6.

25. *The Woman* was never published. All quotations contained in the text are taken from the manuscript, held by the National Library of Ireland: MS 29446.

26. William Butler Yeats's letter to Lennox Robinson dated 16 April 1929. Reprinted in 'Publisher's Note' to Margaret O'Leary, *Lightning Flash* (London: Jonathan Cape, 1939), pp. 7–9. *Lightning Flash* is O'Leary's second novel. It reworks the material of the play, adding considerably to the fore-story but keeping the same plot and characters.

27. Margaret O'Leary's comments are interspersed in the above letter, in parentheses: '[N.B. That was the ending of the first version of the play. M.O'L.]'

28. Joseph Holloway, *Joseph Holloway's Irish Theatre*, Vol. 1, ed. Robert Hogan and Michael J. O'Neill (Dixon, CA: Proscenium Press, 1968), p. 52.

29. 'Jade' is an Irish-English colloquialism for a disreputable or promiscuous woman. According to the Oxford English Dictionary, it is Middle-English and is archaic in standard British English.

30. Julia Kristeva, 'Powers of Horror', in *The Portable Kristeva*, ed., K. Oliver (New York: Columbia University Press, 2002), p. 229.

31. Deevy, *Three Plays*, p. 125.

32. Deevy, *Three Plays*, pp. 125–6.

33. Deevy, *Three Plays*, pp. 140–1.

34. Deevy, *Three Plays*, p. 141.

35. A. E. Malone, *The Irish Drama*, (London: Constable, 1929), p. 160.

36. Mary Fitzgerald, 'Introduction', *Selected Plays Lady Gregory*, Irish Drama Selections Vol. 3 (Gerrard's Cross: Colin Smythe, 1983), p. 17. 'In 1912, Lady Gregory experimented with a three-act drama involving only three characters. *Grania*, based on a classic and tragic romantic triangle in Irish legend, had such strong autobiographical significance for its author that she did not allow its production during her lifetime'. The reference here is presumably to Gregory's marriage to a much older man, and her reputed love affair with Wilfred Scawen Blunt during her marriage.

37. Malone, *The Irish Drama*, pp. 160–1.

38. Augusta Gregory, *Grania*, *Selected Plays of Lady Gregory*, Irish Drama Selections Vol. 3 (Gerrard's Cross: Colin Smythe, 1983), p. 181.

39. Lady Gregory, *Selected Plays*, p. 183.

40. Lady Gregory, *Selected Plays*, p. 189.

41. Lady Gregory, *Selected Plays*, p. 211.

42. Lady Gregory, *Selected Plays*, p. 213.

43. Lady Gregory, *Selected Plays*, p. 214.

44. Malone, *The Irish Drama*, p. 161.

45. Lady Gregory, *Selected Plays*, p. 205.

46. Leeney, *Irish Theatre Forum*, Vol. 1, No. 1, Summer 1997, discusses the homosocial and possible homoerotic tensions underlying *Grania*.

47. Lady Gregory, *Selected Plays*, p. 188.

48. Lady Gregory, *Selected Plays*, p. 214.

49. Lady Gregory, *Selected Plays*, p. 192.

50. Lady Gregory, *Selected Plays*, p. 192.

51. Margaret O'Leary, *Lightning Flash* (London: Jonathan Cape, 1939).

INTERCHAPTER II: 1940–1969

Melissa Sihra

Lady Augusta Gregory died in 1932 and from that period the Abbey Theatre consisted of an all-male directorate – Yeats, Kevin O'Higgins, Ernest Blythe, Brinsley MacNamara, Lennox Robinson and Walter Starkie. Blythe, an Irish-language revivalist and politician, would now remain on the inside of the Abbey for many years to come. Issues of artistic policy remained primarily within Yeats's domain, but with his death in 1939 the position of power was open and Blythe took over as Managing Director in 1941, remaining in that post until 1967. Earnán de Blaghd, as he preferred to be known, espoused a conservative ethos and the board as a whole was highly restrictive artistically. While the work of a significant number of women dramatists was produced during these decades (see Appendix pp. 223–4), this period in the Abbey's history is associated predominantly 'with kitchen farce, unspeakably bad Gaelic pantomimes, compulsory Irish and insensitive bureaucracy'.[1] The move from the 1930s into the 1940s saw the consolidation of Éamon De Valera's Fianna Fáil administration. *Bunreacht na hÉireann* (The Irish Constitution) was established in 1937, the same year that Samuel Beckett moved to Paris. During this time women activists sought political representation and equal rights as citizens of the Irish Free State, particularly with regard to the 1932 marriage bar. In 1938 Hannah Sheehy-Skeffington, a prolific feminist campaigner and member of the Women's Graduates' Association, argued that the constitution was based on 'a fascist model, in which women would be relegated to permanent inferiority, their avocations and choice of callings limited because of an implied invalidism as the weaker sex'.[2] A fully independent Republic of Ireland came into being in 1949, in a decade that was framed by De Valera's patriotic speech: 'The Ireland that we dreamed of'. From the shadows of World War Two, he addressed the nation on St Patrick's Day, 1943, as 'a land whose countryside would be bright with cosy homesteads, whose fields and villages would be joyous with the sounds of industry, with the romping of sturdy children, the contests of athletic youths and the laughter of comely maidens'.[3] In this period of high unemployment and mass poverty, De Valera's ideological *tableau vivant* had very little to do with the everyday realities of vulnerable and marginalized people such as orphaned children, single women, emigrants, the elderly and scrimping small farmers.

Change was gradual but constant at this time. The electrification of Ireland from the 1930s onwards impacted psychologically as well as practically upon the lives of women and men, and denoted the symbolic and actual advent of modernity. This was a time when *piseogs* (malevolent spirits) and fairies – 'the beyond crowd' – still roamed the mindscape of the predominantly rural population whilst appliances such as refrigerators, washing machines and electric cookers were being introduced into the home. Social and political groups such as the National Council of Women, the Joint Committee of Women's Societies and Social Workers, the Irish Countrywomen's Association and the Irish Housewives' Association enabled some sense of a collective identity and outlet for women during these years. Diarmaid Ferriter observes:

> Contemporary publications aimed at women were well aware that Irish women desired modernity in a new consumer era, not just in obvious areas like electricity and running water, but in respect of recreation, appearance and relationships. The best-selling *Woman's Life* magazine in the 1930s and 1940s offered as role models not only independent unmarried working women, but women in arts, culture and sport.... [4]

While the Catholic Church promoted large families, sexuality was something that was repressed and very much under the surveillance of the Church and State. As the plays by the women whose work was produced at this time show, life was extremely restrictive for the majority of the population, and women in particular. While Teresa Deevy (1894–1963) emerged in the 1930s, her career was stifled due to rejection by the Abbey in subsequent decades, causing her to withdraw from the stage and write radio plays (even though she became completely deaf in her twenties). Deevy's rejected play, *Wife to James Whelan* (written in 1937), was eventually staged in October 1956 at Madame Desirée Bannard Cogley's Studio Theatre Club, Upper Mount Street, Dublin, and was directed by Madame Cogley. The script was missing for a number of years but finally turned up at Deevy's family home, 'Landscape',

Co. Waterford, and is published in a special issue of the *Irish University Review*.[5] Fiona Becket writes: 'In *Wife to James Whelan,* rejected by the Abbey in 1937, the figure of the young mother Nan Bowers represents Irish women's economic vulnerability outside the family, but also shows the modern family unit itself subject to the vicissitudes of physical health and economic fortune.'[6] Deevy died in 1963 and so did not live to see the revival of her best known work, *Katie Roche,* on the Abbey main-stage in 1975, directed by Joe Dowling with Jeananne Crowley as the eponymous heroine (see Figure 4).[7]

The Constitution that De Valera produced was heavily influenced by the social teachings of the Catholic Church, particularly the 1891

Figure 4 Jeananne Crowley as Katie Roche and Bill Foley as Stanislaus Gregg in the 1975 Abbey Theatre production of *Katie Roche* by Teresa Deevy. Photo: Courtesy of Fergus Bourke.

Rerum Novarum Papal Encyclical and Pope Pius XI's *Quadragesimo Anno* of 1931, which were fundamentally opposed to contraception. The Catholic Church continued to induce a palpable anxiety about sexuality and the body throughout these decades and reacted strongly to the perceived immorality of pastimes such as dancing. Myrtle Hill points out how, as recently as 1960, the Archbishop of Cashel and Emly advised dance promoters operating in his jurisdiction that:

No dances should be held on Saturday nights, eves of holy days, Christmas night, or during Lent (except for St Patrick's night for traditional Irish dancing or where dancing has already been customary on that night)... Concern for the moral welfare of those who dance will surely be accepted as no more of an interference with legitimate amusement than concern for their health and physical safety.[8]

State oppression in the 1950s was rife with censorship laws cultivating a climate of anti-intellectualism which only began to be alleviated in the 1960s. Church and State agendas ensured that 'books and magazines were banned on two basic grounds – that they were "indecent or obscene" or that they advocated contraception and abortion.'[9] One venue that was outward-looking rather than insular was Dublin's Gate Theatre, founded in 1928 by Micheál Mac Liammóir and Hilton Edwards. This theatre exuded an *esprit* of European style, modernity and visual flair which was in broad contradistinction to the Abbey, which 'had became both narrowly national and dully ruralist'.[10] Mac Liammóir and Edwards formed the Gate Theatre Company, enlisting the talents of actress Coralie Carmichael, and audiences were attracted to the sophisticated, stylish feel of the newly designed theatre in the eighteenth-century Assembly Rooms next to the Rotunda Hospital. With its thinly disguised, repainted standard kitchen box-set, the Abbey seemed regressive by comparison. Mary Manning's (1906–1999) *Youth's the Season–?* was produced at the Gate on 8 December 1931, when she was in her twenties. Robert Hogan cites Mac Liammóir, who remarked that Manning's,

'brain, nimble and observant as it was, could not yet keep pace with a tongue so caustic that even her native city... was a little in awe of her.' That incisive perception and satiric wit were beautifully evident in *Youth's the Season–?* which still comes near to being the most sophisticated and yet poignant study of young people to come out of modern Dublin.[11]

Her subsequent plays, the one-act *Storm Over Wicklow* (1933) and *Happy Family* (1934), were also produced at the Gate.[12] Manning was born in Dublin of an Anglo-Irish Kerry background. She studied acting at the Abbey school and performed with the Irish Players in England, and at the Abbey in Dublin, before joining the Gate. In the 1930s Manning left Ireland for America and turned to novel-writing. *The Voices of Shem,* her adaptation of *Finnegan's Wake,* was first produced by the Poets' Theatre in Cambridge, Massachusetts, in 1955. Hogan praises Manning's first play effusively, while not being able to remove himself from the fact of her gender: 'Dublin had never seen a play quite like *Youth's the Season- ?,* and perhaps it has not seen one since. Such a strong and smoothly written play would have been remarkable no matter who had written it, but it was even more remarkable for a girl barely out of her teens.'[13]

Chairman and main financial backer of the Gate Theatre at the time was Edward Arthur Henry Packenham, the sixth Earl of Longford, who founded Longford Productions, presenting plays by both himself and his wife Christine. In 1936 Lord and Lady Longford broke away from the Gate while Mac Liammóir, Edwards and other members of the company were on a tour of Egypt. Longford Productions then played in the Dublin building for six months of the year, with Edwards and Mac Liammóir using it for the rest of the year. Christine Packenham's (1900–1980) plays were of a superior quality to those of her husband and her works fall into three categories – adaptations of novels, such as *Pride and Prejudice*; sparkling comedies satirizing Irish life such as *Mr. Jiggins of Jigginstown* (1933) and *The Hill of Quirke* (1953); and historical dramas such as *Lord Edward* (1941), *The United Brothers* (1942), *Patrick Sarsfield* (1943) and *The Earl of Straw* (1944), which is set in 1600 and 1601 during the time of the Earl of Tyrone's rebellion against Queen Elizabeth.[14] The Longfords' investment in the Gate was not only financial but also involved a commitment to gruelling rounds of provincial touring. When Lord Longford died in 1961, Lady Longford handed the theatre back to Edwards and Mac Liammóir, who then made her Chairperson of the board.

A number of women had their plays produced in the 1940s and 1950s, such as, Winnifred Letts, Patricia O'Connor, Margaret O'Leary, Una Troy (Elizabeth Connor), Olga Fielden, Maura Laverty, B. G. MacCarthy and Anne Daly. However, from the 1960s to the 1990s the Abbey Theatre became an almost exclusively male preserve. In Northern Ireland, theatrical production was equally male-dominated. The organization that carried on the tradition of the Ulster Literary Theatre was the Group Theatre, which was founded in the early 1940s by Joseph Tomelty, Gerald Morrow and others. Anna McClure Warnock and Janet McNeil had their plays produced there at this time. One woman who made a lasting contribution to the face of theatre production in the North of Ireland is Mary O'Malley who co-founded, with Pearse O'Malley, the Lyric Players in 1951 and opened a new theatre for poetic drama in Belfast in 1968. This theatre remains Northern Ireland's only producing house.

In the mid-century a number of powerful, striking and very popular women emerged as actresses and also as directors and producers. Ria Mooney (1904–1973), a member of the Abbey Company who famously played prostitute Rosie Redmond in the premiere of *The Plough and the Stars*, directed *Red Roses for Me* in London and Dublin in 1946. Mooney toured America with Molly Allgood and remained in New York for some years as assistant director of the Civic Repertory Theatre. On her return she joined the Gate Theatre Company and then became director of the Gaiety Theatre School of Acting. Mooney then returned to the Abbey Theatre as its first woman producer and remained the theatre's resident director from 1948–63 (the title of Artistic Director was not used until the 1970s), directing up to 12 shows every year, such as O'Neill's *Long Day's Journey into Night* in 1962.

Phyllis Ryan (1921–), award-winning actress, producer, artistic director and director began her long and illustrious career on the Abbey stage as a child actor. In 1937, at the age of 16, Ryan got her big break playing the role of Brigid in Paul Vincent Carroll's powerful and evocative play *Shadow and Substance* at the Abbey, in which she 'caused a sensation'.[15] Ryan went on to form her own company, Orion Productions, and in 1958 co-founded Gemini Productions with Norman Rodway. In the 1950s Ryan produced plays in the old Pocket Theatre, Ely Place, Dublin. She then moved to the Globe Theatre, Dun Laoghaire, and subsequently, with Gemini Productions, to the Eblana Theatre. As well as performing on all of the main stages in Ireland, and in the West End and America, Ryan spent much of her career nurturing emergent writers and producing new plays by John B. Keane and Hugh Leonard among others. At the 2002 ESB Irish Theatre Awards, Ryan was presented with a Special Tribute award for her remarkable and on-going contribution to theatre.

Lelia Doolin, a television producer and Director of the Irish Film Board, served as Artistic Director of the Abbey Theatre for over a year in the early 1970s. Actor and producer Shelah Richards founded her own company at the Olympia Theatre and directed the world premiere of *Red Roses For Me* in March 1943 at the Olympia Theatre. Richards joined Radio Téilifís Éireann (national television network) as a drama producer in 1962. Siobhán McKenna (1922–1986) began performing in Galway's Irish-language theatre, An Taibhdhearc, playing leading roles and translating G. B. Shaw into Irish. She is considered, along with her friend May Craig, to be one of the most outstanding actresses of the Abbey Theatre. McKenna was directed by Shelah Richards in the role of Pegeen Mike in *The Playboy of the Western World* in 1951 to major critical acclaim. She took London by storm in *St Joan* at the Arts Festival in 1954 and then starred on Broadway. In the 1960s McKenna performed her one-woman show *Here are Ladies*, but she will be remembered in recent years for her magnificent last performance as Mommo in *Bailegangaire* in 1985, an intense and demanding role written for her by Tom Murphy and directed by Garry Hynes.

The 1950s and 1960s heralded rapid change. The old Abbey building burnt down in 1951, the Dublin Theatre Festival was launched in 1957, Radio Téilfís Éireann (RTÉ) began transmission on New Year's Eve 1961, and the new Abbey building was ceremonially opened by De Valera in 1966 (after the company's 15-year sojourn at the dilapidated venue of melodrama, the Queen's Theatre on Pearse Street). In 1963 Deirdre O'Connell founded the Focus Theatre, Dublin, which became a home for classics and new writing, including the plays of Ena May and Mary Elizabeth Burke-Kennedy. Yet even with all of these changes, a moral conservatism prevailed. Hill observes:

> The so-called sexual revolution of the 1960s, which undermined the traditional 'taboos' involving restraints and limitations on sexual conduct, was slow to impact on the South, where family life was highly valued and where, despite the liberalising tendencies of the Second Vatican Council launched in 1962, the Catholic Church retained a tight control over moral and sexual behaviour.[16]

In 1953 Carolyn Swift co-founded, with Alan Simpson, the tiny avant-garde Pike Theatre in Dublin, famously staging the Irish premiere of Beckett's *Waiting for Godot* in 1955 and the plays of Brendan Behan. The theatre is known for the controversy that occurred surrounding an ironically 'invisible' condom (mentioned in the script) of their 1957 production of Tennessee William's *The Rose Tattoo*. This incident, and the subsequent arrest of Simpson, is one of the major events in the nascent liberal consciousness of modern Ireland and a symbol of the fight between freedom of choice and the repressive power of the conservative orthodoxy of the time.

The decade of the 1950s was also a period in which the systematic and illegal incarceration of unmarried mothers in institutions such as the notorious Magdalen Laundries occurred. Certainly, 'the majority of young women throughout Ireland who became pregnant while unmarried in the 1950s suffered profound shame and guilt.'[17] Many young women were forced, or at the very least, coerced to enter the institutions, which were run by religious orders, and did not have the option of keeping their babies. It is estimated that, in exchange for money, '2100 children were sent to America under this scheme between 1949 and the end of 1973'.[18] Women only began to speak about their experiences in these institutions in the last decade or so of the twentieth century. Patricia Burke-Brogan's 1992 play *Eclipsed* looks at the lives of young women in the homes as does the film *The Magdalen Sisters* and June Goulding's 1998 memoir, *The Light at the Window*, is dedicated, 'To all those thousands of unmarried mothers and their babies who were incarcerated in that horrendous Home [Bessboro, Cork].'[19] The laundries and state-run orphanages, 'industrial schools', form the backbone of the hidden Ireland that was enabled by a culture of silence and denial. What emerges from the stories of these single mothers is the sense of penance and stigmatization which they had to endure on a daily basis, whether in the constant arduous, unpaid task of cleaning dirty laundry, or by not being administered pain relief during childbirth, as part of their moral 'atonement'.

One playwright who wrote about such oppression at the time is Máiréad Ní Ghráda. Born in 1899 in Co. Clare, Ní Ghráda was an active member of Cumann na mBan (the women's version of the Irish Volunteers) and personal secretary for a time to Ernest Blythe during the first Dáil. She also had a thriving career in radio production and was the first female announcer in Ireland and Britain. Ní Ghráda married in 1923 but refused to give up her career. Finally her husband's employer required that she resign, forcing her to leave programming and production at 2RN (the predecessor to Radio Éireann) in 1935. Ní Ghráda wrote her first play in the Irish language, *An Uacht (The Will)*, in 1931, which was produced by Mac Liammóir at the Gate. Her play *An Grá agus and Gárda (Love and the Policeman)* was performed at the Peacock Theatre and published in 1937. Her best-known play, *An Triail*, was produced in Irish in the Damer Hall, Dublin, in 1964. Ní Ghráda translated the play and it was performed the following year in English under the title of *On Trial* in the Eblana Theatre, produced by Phyllis Ryan, with Fionnuala Flanagan in the lead role as Maura Cassidy. In this powerful and intensely moving drama, the unmarried pregnant protagonist is set against society, which puts her, literally and figuratively, 'on trial'. She is abandoned by her family, her lover and the community at large, and her only option is to enter an institution. The play charts her painful and brave negotiation with intolerance and culminates in her and her child's escape through death. Ní Ghráda died a few years later, in 1971. Her play is especially deserving of a major production, capturing as it does the sense of abandonment of many women and children at this time, and the autocratic and confining ethos of the conservative Church and State influence during these mid-century decades.

Notes

1. Brian Fallon, *An Age of Innocence, 1930–1960* (Dublin: Gill & Macmillan, 1998), p. 134.
2. Hannah Sheehy-Skeffington, *Irish Independent*, 11 May 1938, cited in Caitríona Beaumont, 'Gender, Citizenship and the State, 1922–1990', Scott Brewster, Virginia Crossman, Fiona Becket and David Alderson (eds), *Ireland in Proximity: History, Gender, Space* (London and New York: Routledge, 1999), p. 100.
3. Eamon De Valera, 'The Ireland That We Dreamed Of', Radio Broadcast, 17 March 1943, in Maurice Moynihan (ed.), *Speeches and Statements by Eamon De Valera, 1917–1973* (Dublin: Gill & Macmillan, 1980), p. 466.
4. Diarmaid Ferriter, *The Transformation of Ireland, 1900–2000* (London: Profile Books, 2004), p. 424.
5. *Irish University Review*, Silver Jubilee Issue 'Teresa Deevy and Irish Women Playwrights', Vol. 25, No. 1, Spring/Summer 1995.
6. Fiona Becket, 'A Theatrical Matrilineage? Problems of the Familial in the Drama of Teresa Deevy and Marina Carr', in *Ireland in Proximity: History, Gender, Space*, p. 86.
7. Teresa Deevy, *Teresa Deevy: Three Plays* [*Katie Roche, The King of Spain's Daughter, The Wild Goose*] (London: Macmillan, 1939). *The King of Spain's Daughter and Other One-Act Plays* (Dublin: New Frontier Press, 1948).
8. Myrtle Hill, *Women in Ireland: A Century of Change* (Belfast: Blackstaff Press, 2003), p. 140. By 1967 all prohibitions on dancing were rescinded. It was only in 1973 that the Fifth Amendment of the Constitution Act removed the special position of the Catholic Church within the Constitution.
9. Fallon, *An Age of Innocence, 1930–1960*, p. 10.
10. Fallon, *An Age of Innocence, 1930–1960*, p. 138.
11. Robert Hogan (ed.), *Seven Irish Plays: 1946–1964* (Minnesota: University of Minnesota Press, 1967), p. 9.
12. Mary Manning, *Youth's the Season-?*, in *Plays of Changing Ireland*, ed. Curtis Canfield (New York: Macmillan, 1936). *The Voices of Shem* (London: Faber & Faber, 1957).
13. Robert Hogan, *After the Irish Renaissance* (London: Macmillan, 1986), p. 120.

14. Christine Packenham, (Lady Longford), *Mr. Jiggins of Jigginstown*, in *Plays of Changing Ireland*, ed. Curtis Canfield (New York: Macmillan, 1936). *Lord Edward* (Dublin: Hodges Figgis, 1941), *The United Brothers* (Dublin: Hodges Figgis, 1942), *Patrick Sarsfield* (Dublin: Hodges Figgis, 1943), *The Hill of Quirke* (Dublin: P. J. Bourke, 1958).
15. Christopher Fitz-Simon, *The Abbey Theatre: Ireland's National Theatre* (London: Thames & Hudson, 2003), p. 85.
16. Hill, *Women in Ireland: A Century of Change*, p. 145.
17. Hill, *Women in Ireland: A Century of Change*, p. 131.
18. Ferriter, *The Transformation of Ireland, 1900–2000*, p. 515.
19. A first reading of Patricia Burke-Brogan's play *Eclipsed* took place at 'Inisfail', 42 College Road, Galway City, 1988. It was first produced by Punchbag Theatre, Galway, 1992. *The Magdalen Sisters*, Dir. Peter Mullan, 2003. June Goulding, *The Light in the Window* (Dublin: Poolbeg Press, 2004).

5

From Matron to Matrix: Gender, Authority and (Dis)embodiment in Beckett's Theatre

Anna McMullan

While there are no Kathleen ni Houlihans or Mother Irelands in Beckett's theatre, which was written and produced after he moved to Paris in 1937, Beckett's staging of maternal or matronly figures exposes a deep-rooted anxiety around questions of embodiment, reproduction, authorship and origin which can be related to tropes of femininity and the mother in the Irish theatre canon.[1] I will argue that Beckett's theatre foregrounds the construction of the symbolic categories of the feminine and the maternal as both other to, and the foundation of, cultural and self-production. Yet his drama also displays the cultural encoding of gender, and the later plays present ghostly or fragmented bodies that disarticulate the relationship between gender, embodiment and the subject.

Beckett's first performed and best-known play, *En Attendant Godot* (*Waiting for Godot*), which premiered in Paris in 1953, has an all-male cast, but his earliest theatre writing features several female figures who are important for an understanding of Beckett's presentation of gender on stage. Beckett's first attempt at dramatic writing, the unfinished fragment, 'Human Wishes', written in the 1930s, presents three women from the household of the eighteenth-century English writer Dr Samuel Johnson: Miss Carmichael, a former prostitute, the straight-laced Mrs Desmoulins and the domineering Mrs Williams. This combination of matrons and a younger female recurs in Beckett's first full-length play, *Eleutheria*, written just before *Godot* in the late 1940s (though Beckett withdrew the performing rights and they remain unavailable). In these early texts, gendered embodiment is foregrounded and linked to Beckett's struggle with theatrical form and convention.

As Mary Bryden[2] and Linda Ben-Zvi[3] have argued, there is a marked evolution in Beckett's staging of women from the earlier drama dominated by fleshly matrons to the ghostly shades of later plays such as *Come and Go* (1966) or *Footfalls* (1976) and the disembodied Mouth of *Not I* (1972). I will investigate Beckett's changing incarnations of gender in particular plays, including the fragment 'Human Wishes', *Eleutheria*, the radio play *All That Fall* (1957) and the stage plays *Happy Days* (1961) and *Footfalls*, focusing on the figure of the mother or matron, whose flesh dissolves as she becomes the very space and ground of representation, an unseen matrix of semblances. I will therefore be investigating not only particular female characters in Beckett's drama, but also the engine or dynamic of gender as it operates through the media of theatre and radio and engages the politics of embodied and disembodied representation.

'Human Wishes': a comedy of manners and mortality

From Beckett's first attempt at dramatic writing, gender and embodiment are linked to the realm of the visible: what does or does not appear on stage. 'Human Wishes' was initially conceived as a dramatic exploration of Dr Johnson's complex and ultimately doomed relationship with his friend and companion, Mrs Thrale. Beckett compiled copious research about Dr Johnson and his private circle, and as Linda Ben Zvi,[4] Ruby Cohn[5] and Fred Smith[6] have noted, Beckett abandoned the project as his interest shifted from the story of Johnson and Mrs Thrale to Johnson himself, and in particular, his physical ailments and mental anguish. All that remains of the projected play is a fragment of a few pages with no Dr Johnson.[7]

The fragment is set in Johnson's private residence, Bolt Court, and opens with three women engaged in various silent activities: Mrs Williams is contemplating, Mrs Desmoulins knitting and Miss Carmichael reading. The first line of the fragment refers to its central male absence: 'He is late' (presumably Dr Johnson). The dialogue has period vocabulary: 'You are knotting, Madam, I presume' (p. 155), and the decorum of an eighteenth century interior is initially suggested: 'God grant all is well' (p. 155), though the relationship between the women quickly becomes highly fractious. Mrs Williams is a powerful matriarch who describes herself as 'old...blind, halt and maim'(p. 156), but who wields authority over the household with the help of her stick – a female precursor of Hamm in *Endgame*: Mrs W: '(*striking the floor with her stick*). Be seated; and let your scurrility be the recumbent scurrility of polite society' (p. 156).

While Mrs Desmoulins is a much more retiring matron, she also monitors middle-class etiquette in the play, complaining of Miss Carmichael's language and dubious background. Miss Carmichael is a feisty, irreverent presence. Her response to the taunting of Mrs Desmoulins is to laugh heartily and to call her 'an insupportable hag' (p. 156), setting up generational and class tensions between the women. However, while the women often disturb the very domestic and social civility which Mrs Williams and Mrs Desmoulins insist they observe, the drunken appearance of another of Dr Johnson's exceedingly hybrid circle, Dr Frank Levett, is even more of a disruption. Levett briefly enters the room, but leaves after emitting '*a single hiccup of such force that he is almost thrown off his feet*' (p. 160). Indeed, it is the male flouting of corporeal rectitude (even though Levett is '*slightly, respectably, even reluctantly drunk*') that shocks the women, who respond with: '*Gestures of disgust. Mouths opened and shut*' (p. 160). The male characters are marginalized or absent from this interior, domestic space whose manifestly artificial social and theatrical conventions are associated with, and upheld by, matrons.

'Human Wishes' also reproduces a highly gendered set of associations of the feminine with the 'womb-tomb' of death. The women's dialogue continually revolves around death and the threshold and processes of dying as they disagree about which eighteenth-century playwrights are or are not dead (including references to Oliver Goldsmith and Hugh Kelly). Mrs Williams asserts that 'I am dead enough myself, I hope, not to feel any great respect for those who are so entirely' (p. 162), and Miss Carmichael cites at length from Jeremy Taylor's *The Rule and Exercises of Holy Dying*, which enumerates the ways in which 'death enters in at many doors' (p. 165). While the mortal condition of embodiment is not gender specific, women here (like the three fates or witches or Marys which they recall) constitute guardians not only of the corporeal and social patterns of living, but those of dying.

Looking at Beckett's early dramatic work both confirms and complicates the picture of the linear development of women as grotesquely embodied suffocating creatures in the early work to more subjectively complex subjects in the late work. Mrs Williams is certainly a matriarch of the hearth, who is implicitly contrasted with Johnson the eminent writer and author of 'The Vanity of Human Wishes', in her creation of doggerel verse. Yet we are given glimpses of a more reflective side to Mrs Williams, when she muses (after Proust's '*intermittences du coeur*') that her father's death only registered with her affectively several months after it had occurred: Mrs W: 'For years, for how many years every day, dead, whose name I had known, whose face I had seen, whose voice I had heard, whose hand I had held, whose – but it is idle to continue' (p. 164). Miss Carmichael, even in the few pages of the fragment, is a spirited and articulate character. However, the overall tone references the genre of comedy of manners – there is little room for identification with any of the figures on stage. This may be one reason why the tormented writer Johnson is not presented as a realized, embodied character. It was the interaction between the material condition of embodiment and the subjective experience of it which had begun to fascinate Beckett and which would in the future dominate his theatre. However, at this early stage, he had not yet found the dramatic means to present this dilemma, which he would achieve through an exorcism of a dramaturgy of the domestic interior.

Eleutheria and the masquerade of home

The trope of matrons as domestic enforcers of the social norms of their milieu is intensified in *Eleutheria*, where the family home is presented as a place of entrapment and alienation for the male members of the Krap family, especially the son, Victor. Written in French in 1947, and set in contemporary post-war Paris, the play parodies the social and theatrical conventions of bourgeois domestic drama. The title *Eleutheria* is the Greek word for freedom, and the play was written after Beckett's return to Paris after his experiences in the French Resistance, his flight from Paris to Roussillon where he and his future wife, Suzanne Deschevaux-Dumensil, waited for the Liberation, and his post-war aid and reconstruction work in St Lô, Normandy. The title, however, is ironic, as the characters in the play are entirely trapped and blinkered by their conventional middle-class environment.

The central character, Victor, the only son of Monsieur and Madame Krap, has left the family home and is living in a miserable rented room. The action of the play revolves around the vain attempts of the family and their allies to get Victor back into a socially conventional mould. *Eleutheria* can be linked to what Gerardine Meaney describes as the trope of the 'literary subversive-in-exile', where women, and especially mothers, represent the 'nets' of home/nation/language which must be escaped in order for the male self and artistic voice to be generated.[8] Peter Boxall has noted that Beckett transposed certain autobiographical details rooted in his youth in Dublin into the French language, and into a Parisian setting.[9] However, the play presents a general critique of the perceptual, ethical and ideological limitations of a middle-class world, whether located in Ireland (which had remained neutral during World War Two) or post-war Paris. Indeed, this supposedly respectable environment accepts the 'hideous' Dr Piouk as husband to Victor's aunt, though his aim is to exterminate humanity through such 'solutions' as euthanasia programmes, recalling the recent horrors of the Nazi regime and the Holocaust. Victor's rejection of his familial environment is a refusal of the parameters of a social and theatrical world which remains impervious to human suffering both in recent times and throughout history. While the Krap salon is dominated by three matrons: Mme Krap, her sister Mme Piouk and her friend, Mme Meck, the focus shifts in Act III to a meta-theatrical discussion of dramatic structure and convention which is led by the Pirandello-like characters of the Glazier and the Spectator who enter Victor's room. Counterpointing the female guardians of the bourgeois home, these male guardians of dramatic *bienséance* are prepared to subject Victor to violence, even torture, in order to force him to conform to their habitual norms. While the Kraps' salon and Victor's room share the stage in Acts I and II, by Act III, the bourgeois salon has been dispensed with. At the end of the play, Victor has ejected everyone from the bare space of his room, and his last gesture is to turn his 'emaciated' back on the audience, on theatre and, indeed, on 'humanity' as currently constituted.

With the exception of Victor, the play foregrounds gendered modes of embodiment in heightened, grotesque ways. The characters have scatological names: Krap, Piouk or Skunk. Male and female procreative and sexual organs are particularly satirized; M. Krap has problems with his prostate, and the three older women are at different stages of the menopause; Mme Piouk is on the threshold but still fertile (Dr Piouk wants a child in spite of the sterility he wishes to impose on everyone else), Mme Meck and Mme Krap have prolapsing and prolapsed wombs, respectively. M. Krap has been a writer of the 'shit genre' (p. 37)[10], recalling Jarry's *Ubu roi*, and anticipating a future Beckettian character also named Krapp. Like his son, M. Krap experiences the female dominated domestic environment as suffocating: 'My freedom diminishes daily. Soon I shan't be allowed to open my mouth' (p. 20). Yet, in his attitude towards his wife, which is at times murderous, and in his sexism towards Mlle Skunk, his misogyny is so overt that it becomes highly theatricalized. Mlle Skunk is treated by M. Krap uniquely in terms of her body and her sexual charms: he commands her to lift her skirt and open her jacket. When she bursts into tears, revealing a suffering subjectivity rather than surface sexuality, M. Krap is extremely annoyed. This seems to frame M. Krap's very construction of Mlle Skunk as a sexual stereotype, suggesting Beckett's consciousness of gender, especially femininity, as performed masquerade, rather than a naturalized or essentialized quality.

However, in *Eleutheria*, all existence is masquerade. The specific historical moment of post-World War Two and post-Holocaust France and

Europe produced an aesthetic crisis which questioned the ability of any form of representation to articulate the horror of recent history. Victor approaches the footlights on several occasions and tries to communicate with the audience: 'I must tell . . . I'm not . . . *He falls silent* . . .' (p. 66). The only space for Victor to tell 'how it is' occurs in what is left unsaid, stuttered or articulated off-stage. The feminized space of the home is presented as collusive with a dramatic aesthetic and a social world which naturalizes and incorporates violence in order to secure conformity, and excludes the realities of existence beyond the visible boundaries of the stage. In terms of his portrayal of gender and embodiment, it was *All That Fall* that enabled Beckett to get inside the consciousness of a female persona, via the medium of radio and the fable of a post-menopausal matron in a post-lapsarian world.

All That Fall: post-menopausal metamorphoses

All That Fall is Beckett's most culturally grounded dramatic work, set in Boghill, a recognizably translated Foxrock, the place of Beckett's birth, on the outskirts of County Dublin. Yet, as a radio play, the whole world evoked is an illusion created by sound and language. Beckett resisted frequent requests to stage this piece, saying that 'Even the reduced visual dimension it will receive from the simplest and most static of readings . . . will be destructive of whatever quality it may have and which depends on the whole thing coming out of the dark.'[11] Beckett related this specific quality to the fact that *All That Fall* was written: 'for voices, not bodies'.[12] Beckett exploited the intimacy of radio, which, as Everett Frost has argued, can take the listener into Maddy's mind: 'nothing that occurs in *All That Fall* is independent of Maddy Rooney's awareness of it.'[13] The experience of radio also freed him from the material representation of the body on stage, and made him aware of the possibilities of exploring diverse subjective and perceptual apprehensions of corporeality.

The play is dominated by the sonic evocation of the excruciating corporeal effort involved in any physical exertion on the part of Maddy Rooney, who is in her seventies. Although she is unwell, she has arisen from her sickbed to walk to Boghill station to meet her husband, Dan, from the 'slow and easy' train, because it is his birthday. In many ways, she confirms the association of the female with the fleshly body and emotional excess: 'Oh I am just a hysterical old hag I know, destroyed with sorrow and pining and gentility and churchgoing and fat and rheumatism and childlessness' (p. 175).[14]

The sense of Maddy's bulky body is emphasized at various points, especially getting into and out of Mr Slocum's car: 'As if I were a bale, Mr. Slocum...Oh!...Lower!...Don't be afraid!...We're past the age when...There!' (p. 178). Yet, though Maddy Rooney is verbally evoked as 'two hundred pounds of unhealthy fat' (p. 191), her body is not seen. The focus is rather on her subjective experience of corporeality. Indeed, her body is in constant vocal metamorphosis:[15] not just an abject encumbrance, but a protean material, both corporeal and subjective, which shifts its shape to match her affective and psychic state: 'Oh let me just flop down flat on the road like a big fat jelly out of a bowl and never move again! A great big slop thick with grit and dust and flies, they would have to scoop me up with a shovel' (p. 174) Or again: 'What's wrong with me, what's wrong with me, never tranquil, seething out of my dirty old pelt, out of my skull, oh to be in atoms, in atoms! (*Frenziedly.*) ATOMS!' (p. 181).

Dan has also been in progressive corporeal decline since he first met Maddy: 'The day you met me I should have been in bed. The day you proposed to me the doctors gave me up...The night you married me they came for me with an ambulance....But I am no worse. Indeed I am better than I was. The loss of my sight was a great fillip. If I could go deaf and dumb I think I might pant on to be a hundred' (p. 192). However, if the experience of corporeality torments both Maddy and Dan, female reproduction is the target of particular violence in the play. When Maddy asks Mr Tyler about his daughter, he explains: 'They removed everything, you know, the whole...er...bag of tricks. Now I am grandchildless' (p. 175). Maddy herself is childless, and muses that even her daughter, 'little Minnie' would have been: 'In her forties now...I don't know, fifty, girding up her lovely little loins, getting ready for the change' (p. 176). Maddy identifies herself with a number of post-reproductive female animals she encounters on her journey to the railway station and back, including Christy's hinny,[16] and a hen squashed by Mr Slocum's car: 'then – bang! – all her troubles over. [*Pause.*] All the laying and the hatching' (p. 179). Any source of fertility, human or animal, is subject to recurring violence from a series of male-driven increasingly technologized machines, from bicycle to train.

Sarah Bryant-Bertail brilliantly analyses Maddy as *picara*:

> Like the *picaro* who is her male counterpart, the *picara* walks over a physical yet symbolic landscape, and the people she meets along the way constitute a social milieu and a metaphysical universe.... Like Chaucer's Wife of Bath, Maddy is used as a mouthpiece and

embodiment of misogyny, yet undermines it by her vivid material struggle to go on in spite of it. She tries to make the best of what she cannot change, and in voicing the misogynist discourse that would make of her a monster, exposes the discourse itself as monstrous.[17]

While Maddy indeed embodies a negation of female reproduction, she does, as Bryant-Bertail notes, become: 'the mouth that produces the landscape, the matrix through which creation *takes place*'.[18] However, unlike the language of the pretty woolly lambs which 'has not changed since Arcady' (p. 194), Maddy's naming of the animals of Boghill (usually associated with Adam in the biblical story of creation) brings them into aural existence at the moment of their subsidence into silence and exhaustion:

Mrs Rooney: The wind – (*Brief wind.*) – scarcely stirs the leaves and the birds – (*Brief chirp.*) – are tired singing. The cows – (*Brief moo.*) – and sheep (*Brief baa.*) – ruminate in silence. The dogs – (*Brief bark.*) – are hushed and the hens (*Brief cackle.*) sprawl torpid in the dust. We are alone.

(p. 192)

Seán Kennedy has linked the play's emphasis on extinction to Beckett's depiction of the moribund cultural community of the post-independence suburban Protestant upper-middle class in Ireland.[19] He notes Maddy Rooney's confusion: 'Now we are the laughing stock of the twenty-six counties. Or is it thirty-six?', Dan's bemused comment on the toilets which are now marked 'Fir', and Maddy's reference to the death of the Gaelic language, which may indicate a scepticism towards the Free State's official policy of Gaelicization, evident in the renamed toilets. Miss Fitt eventually agrees to help Maddy up the stairs to the railway platform as: 'I suppose it is the Protestant thing to do' (p. 183). *All That Fall* is a rare instance in Beckett's post-*Eleutheria* drama where the body of the community is evoked, though it vocally appears only in order to subsequently disperse, leaving Maddy isolated until Dan joins her for the walk home (to the other terminus). The play's atrophy of reproduction certainly contrasts with the value of corporeal and cultural reproduction in both Nationalist and, Kennedy notes, some post-independence Protestant pronatalist rhetoric. The soundscape and verbal texture of the play is haunted by loss, from the hen run over by Mr Slocum's car to the death of Maddy's daughter, and the child fallen on to the tracks and killed by the train (pushed, perhaps by the blind Dan?). The vocal landscape evoked by the childless Maddy is used by Beckett to explore a terminal creation, in which death and loss are interwoven into the sonic texture of the play.

Unlike the matrons in *Eleutheria*, Maddy's vision can see beyond the conventional confines of respectable Protestant Boghill:

> The entire scene, the hills, the plain, the racecourse with its miles and miles of white rails and three red stands, the pretty little wayside station, and even you yourselves, yes I mean it, and overall the clouding blue, I see it all, I stand here and see it all with eyes... (*The voice breaks.*)...through eyes...oh if only you had my eyes...you would understand...the things they have seen...and not looked away...this is nothing...nothing...
>
> (p. 185)

In *All That Fall*, Beckett transformed the maternal trope from suffocating corporeality and conventionality to an indomitable voicing of self, world and body doomed already to extinction. The medium of radio enabled him to exploit a disjuncture between the vocal and the visible, the image of the body and the complex experience of embodiment that surely informed the later stage play, *Happy Days*.

Happy Days to *Footfalls*: from matron to matrix

The play script of *Happy Days* presents another childless, post-menopausal woman, in this play stuck up to her waist, and later, to her neck, in a mound of scorched earth with only the contents of her bag and the occasional interjections of her companion, Willie, to help her pass the time. Linda Ben-Zvi has emphasized that: 'Gender is scripted into the roles Beckett's characters play.'[20] Winnie's gendered rituals include applying lipstick, combing her hair and raising her parasol. However, she is self-consciously aware of how she is perceived, of the feminine 'masquerade' of appearance in a gendered scopic economy, and indeed both she and the woman in her story return the male gaze:

> Well anyway – this man Shower – or Cooker – no matter – and the woman – hand in hand...standing there gaping at me – at last this man Shower – or Cooker...What's she doing? he says – What's the idea? he says – stuck up to her diddies in the bleeding ground – coarse fellow – What does it mean?...And you, she says, what's the idea of you, she says, what are you meant to mean?'
>
> (p. 156)

On the one hand, therefore, Winnie performs the spectacle of embodied femininity, but, on the other, as in *Eleutheria*, Winnie is presented in relation to an economy of representation which is patently a simulacrum. Beckett's remarks about *Happy Days* to Alan Schneider reveal a great deal about his decidedly non-naturalist approach to setting: 'What should characterize the whole scene, sky and earth, is a pathetic unsuccessful realism, the kind of tawdriness you get in third-rate musical or pantomime, *that* quality of *pompier*, laughably earnest bad imitation.'[21] Though Winnie presents herself as (sexual) object to be seen, her own subjectivity and perception work against her objectification. In Act II, only Winnie's head is visible. The complex experience of embodiment is presented by the distancing or disarticulation of the conventional body image, forging an aesthetic which operates at the interface of the corporeal, the cultural and the subjective. Beckett's late plays, in particular, while vocally gendered, present denaturalized, virtual bodies.

In *Not I* (1972), only a mouth is visible: '... whole body like gone...' (p. 382). While the gender of the voice is not specified, stage usage following Beckett's own practice is to cast a female performer: a male voice would produce a rather different interpretation of who is attempting to author Mouth's narrative. By removing the conventional body image, the stage space is interiorized, so that it becomes a skull/womb space, a matrix animated by the struggle to produce evidence of selfhood from fragmented, partial vocal, visual and textual bodies, and from fragments of recycled memory. In *Rockaby* (1981), the matrix is both the space of the stage and the rocking chair, the 'mother rocker', in which the *'prematurely aged'* W sits, and listens to her own voice lulling her into death: 'those arms at last' (p. 442). The matrix here is a space/mechanism of fusion, between daughter and mother, birth and death.

The relationship between daughter and mother, voice and body also structures the earlier play, *Footfalls* (1976). The daughter, May, a ghostly figure relentlessly pacing the stage, dialogues with the mother's voice (in her head or memory?) in Section I. In Section II, it is the mother's voice who directs the audience to look at May: V: 'But let us watch her move, in silence. (*M. paces. Towards end of second length.*) Watch how feat she wheels' (p. 401). In Section III, the mother's voice is silent, though it is resurrected within May's own monologue, where she recreates a dialogue between her fictional shadow self, Amy, and her mother: 'Amy. (*Pause. No louder.*) Amy. (*Pause.*) Yes, Mother. (*Pause.*) Will you never have done? (*Pause.*) Will you never have done... revolving it all?' (p. 403). Yet, the entire stage space functions as a womb/tomb/skull place, from which May fails to differentiate herself, but which also animates her insistence on performing the visual, vocal and aural traces of her existence: 'I must hear the feet, however faint they fall' (p. 401). On the one hand, Beckett confirms the masculine appropriation of the maternal reproductive function, transforming what Irigaray terms the '*sang rouge*' or red blood of the embodied fertile woman into the '*sang blanc*' ('*semblant*') of male aesthetic reproduction.[22] Yet the play also emphasizes an intersubjective production of self and other in which a woman (both 'character' and actress) determines to author her vocal and embodied performance of selfhood which includes the invisible, the remembered, the incorporeal.[23]

The representation of the maternal or matronly body therefore shifts in Beckett's theatre, from an emphasis on the facticity of gendered corporeal existence and social mores, to the very matrix of self and aesthetic production. This is achieved at the cost of erasing reproductive female corporeality and embodied difference. Yet there is also a recognition of the possibility of rearticulating the relationship between the imagined, corporeal and vocal bodies. In an Irish context, where the gender and function of the mother and the feminine has often been naturalized in national or post-national rhetoric, Beckett's theatrical presentation of gender as both ingrained and as performance, and the body as metamorphic matter where the virtual and the corporeal interface, and where the shapes of indomitable desire may take multiple gendered embodiments, may offer inspiration for the staging of alternative corporealities in contemporary Irish theatre.

Notes

1. See David Cairns and Shaun Richards, 'Tropes and Traps: Aspects of "Woman" and Nationality in Twentieth-Century Irish Drama', in Toni O'Brien Johnson and David Cairns (eds), *Gender in Irish Writing* (Milton Keynes and Philadelphia: Open University Press, 1991), pp. 128–37. Beckett's early fiction can be placed in the context of a demythologizing post-independence aesthetic, and includes in the novel *Murphy*, an ironic and highly sexualized version of Cathleen Ni Houlihan in Miss Counihan: 'Standing in profile against the blazing corridor, with her high buttocks and her low breasts, she looked not only queenly, but on for anything.' Samuel Beckett, *Murphy*, (London: Picador, 1973), p. 123.
2. Mary Bryden, *Women in Beckett's Prose & Drama* (Basingstoke: Macmillan, 1993).
3. Linda Ben-Zvi (ed.), *Women in Beckett: Performance and Critical Perspectives* (Chicago: University of Illinois Press, 1992).

4. Linda Ben-Zvi, 'Biographical, Textual and Historical Origins', in L. Oppenheim (ed.), *Palgrave Advances in Samuel Beckett Studies* (Basingstoke: Palgrave, 2004), pp. 133–53.
5. Ruby Cohn, *A Beckett Canon* (Ann Arbor: University of Michigan Press, 2001).
6. Fred N. Smith, *Beckett's Eighteenth Century* (Basingstoke and New York: Palgrave, 2002).
7. The text of 'Human Wishes' is published in *Disjecta: Miscellaneous Writings and a Dramatic Fragment by Samuel Beckett*, ed. R. Cohn (London: John Calder, 1983). All page references are to this edition.
8. Gerardine Meaney, *Sex and Nation: Women in Irish Culture and Politics* (Dublin: Attic Press, 1991), p. 19.
9. Peter Boxall, 'Freedom and Cultural Location in *Eleutheria*', *Samuel Beckett Today / Aujourdhui*, Vol. 7, 1998, p. 250.
10. All references are to *Eleutheria*, trans. Barbara Wright (London: Faber & Faber, 1996). Beckett withdrew performing rights to the play after the success of *En Attendant Godot* and the play was not published until after his death. It has never had a professional production. Beckett's French text was published reluctantly by *Edition de Minuit* in 1995, after an English translation by Michael Brodsky was published by Barney Rosset's Foxrock Inc. in New York that year. Beckett himself never translated the play into English.
11. Cited in Clas Zilliacus, *Beckett and Broadcasting: A Study of the Works of Samuel Beckett for and in Radio and Television* (Abo: Abo Akademi, 1976), p. 3.
12. Zilliacus, *Beckett and Broadcasting*, p. 3.
13. Everett Frost, 'A "Fresh Go" for the Skull: Directing *All That Fall*, Samuel Beckett's Play for Radio', in L. Oppenheim (ed.), *Directing Beckett* (Ann Arbor: University of Michigan Press, 1997), p. 200.
14. All references to Beckett's published plays, with the exception of *Eleutheria*, are to *The Complete Dramatic Works* (London: Faber & Faber, 1986).
15. See Helga Finter, 'The Body and its Doubles: On the (De)Construction of Femininity on Stage', trans. Matthew Griffin, *Women and Performance*, Vol. 9, No. 2, 1997, pp. 119–41, on the interrelationship of the vocal body, the visible body and the imaginary body-image.
16. A hinny is the offspring of a male horse and a female donkey. They are usually sterile.
17. Sarah Bryant-Bertail, 'The True-Real Woman: Maddy Rooney as *Picara* in *All That Fall*', *Assaph: Studies in the Theatre*, Vol. 11, 1995, p. 3.
18. Bryant-Bertail, in *Assaph: Studies in the Theatre*, Vol. 11, 1995, p. 10.
19. Sean Kennedy, ' "A Lingering Dissolution": *All That Fall* and Protestant Fears of Engulfment in the Irish Free State', in Linda Ben-Zvi (ed.), *Drawing on Beckett* (London: Assaph Books, 2004), pp. 247–62.
20. Linda Ben-Zvi (ed.), *Women in Beckett: Performance and Critical Perspectives* (Chicago: University of Illinois Press, 1992), p. xi.
21. Maurice Harmon (ed.), *No Author Better Served: The Correspondence of Samuel Beckett and Alan Schneider* (Boston, MA: Harvard University Press, 1998), p. 94.
22. Luce Irigaray, *Speculum of the Other Woman*, trans. Gillian C. Gill (Ithaca, NY: Cornell University Press, 1985), pp. 220–22.
23. See Peggy Phelan, *Unmarked: The Politics of Performance* (London and New York: Routledge, 1993).

6

Beyond the Pale: Neglected Northern Irish Women Playwrights, Alice Milligan, Helen Waddell and Patricia O'Connor[1]

Mark Phelan

> The dawning realization that women were almost wholly absent from historical records, bar the exceptions of a few isolated 'greats,' and the subsequent search to reclaim the history of all women – both the 'great' and the 'ordinary' – has presented a potentially revolutionary challenge to the teaching, research, and publishing of Irish History.[2]

This challenge, as laid out by Alan Hayes and Diane Urquhart, has yet fully to be taken up by Irish theatre historians as the experience of women playwrights, producers and actresses continues to be subordinate to the dominant National(ist) meta-narrative of Irish theatre historiography. This chapter argues the need for Irish theatre studies to move away from the singularity of 'nation' as the dominant conceptual and organizational category of historiography and criticism, as such a paradigm shift can replace this singularity with a plurality of histories, restore the histories of numerous neglected women playwrights, and in the process rejuvenate the wider field of Irish theatre history. This chapter attempts to recover the histories of three women playwrights written out of the Irish canon: Alice Milligan[3] (1866–1953), Helen Waddell[4] (1889–1965) and Patricia O'Connor[5] (1908–83).

Revival Women: Alice Milligan and Helen Waddell

Alice Milligan's extraordinary life and work is only recently receiving the critical attention it deserves as Catherine Morris's research has helped recuperate this marginalized figure from the footnotes of Irish history.[6] Milligan was a centrifugal figure of the 'Northern Revival' in which numerous women activists contributed as cultural revivalists, Nationalists, socialists and Suffragettes. Born into a Protestant family, Milligan became an indefatigable Suffragette and Nationalist, modelling her life and work on the civic, non-sectarian Nationalist ideals of the United Irishmen[7] and exercising a vociferous opposition to the sectarianism of Nationalist and Unionist Parties in Ulster through their affiliations with the Ancient Order of Hibernians and the Orange Order respectively.

Milligan was, in many ways, the Northern counterpart of Maud Gonne, not so much for her iconic beauty but for her galvanic energy and ubiquitous presence in all fields of Revivalist activity. She founded the Irish Women's Association (1894), the Henry Joy McCracken Literary Society (1895) and the Irish Women's Centenary Union (1897), so that 'the better half (numerically speaking, of course I mean) of the population'[8] could be involved in political activity where they may exercise a unifying influence. She taught, acted and published prolifically: her poems, pamphlets, articles, reviews, ballads and manifestos appearing in nearly all the leading papers and journals of the day, and she gave hundreds of lectures throughout Ireland. She wrote a number of patriotic plays;[9] the first of which was published in the *Shan Van Vocht* in 1898 to commemorate the centenary of the 1798 Rising.[10] She also pioneered a particularly effective form of political *tableaux vivants* which were staged throughout the country in big houses and parish halls, before audiences of aristocrats and artisans alike.

One of Milligan's most striking achievements was her co-editorship, along with Ethna Carbery,[11] of the *Northern Patriot*, as their radical approach led to the sacking of both women who defiantly went on to found a new publication, *The Shan Van Vocht*. In a golden age of Irish journalism, *The Shan Van Vocht* was one of the most influential and successful journals of the period, and a harbinger for advanced Nationalist thought. The paper radiated the redoubtable energy of both women and in its three-year life-span attracted work from every major public figure, politician and poet of the day. Milligan's biographer Sheila Johnston notes, '[i]n the pages of the *Shan Van Vocht* can be heard the first faint breaths of the infant Sinn Féin movement,'[12] and the poet, and husband of Carbery, Seamus McManus accurately, if patronizingly, opines:

[T]hese two girls, with their wonderful little magazine, patriotic, poetic, fiery, stimulating, revived Ireland's spirit when it seemed dead, and turned the tide of Ireland's fortune...With this revival of Ireland's poetry and Ireland's patriotism came the beginning of the Great Revival.[13]

The *Shan Van Vocht* was a milestone in political propaganda, winning many new converts (including Bulmer Hobson, co-founder of the Ulster Literary Theatre), and was one of the first literary outlets for the young James Connolly. It breathed new life into the asphyxiated voice of Northern Nationalism that had been stifled by the nineteenth century's industrialization, urbanization and evangelism which had consolidated Unionist hegemony. Even prominent Southern activists such as Maud Gonne saluted the North's efforts to 'lead the way':

[W]e were full of almost envious admiration of some numbers of the *Shan Van Vocht*, the daring little paper Anna and Alice were editing!...I thought Dublin would have to look to its laurels if it were not to be outdone in literary journalism by Belfast.[14]

It is an intriguing historical irony that contemporary scholars read the term 'the *Shan Van Vocht*' (the poor old woman) as a Nationalist literary-political trope and regard its significance – and signification – in relation to the social subordination and sexual sublimation of 'woman'. However, the denial of agency axiomatically associated with this particular 'masculinist' Nationalist construct is absolutely inimical with the empowering role this eponymous publication had in facilitating Milligan and Carbery to assume an active role in the public sphere of the Revival, where they promoted their Nationalist and Suffragette beliefs unhindered. It is also significant that although their Suffragette convictions were secondary to their Nationalist politics, the former fundamentally shaped the non-sectarian, egalitarian and secular nature of their Nationalism. Through their journal, they sought to engage more women in politics and, indeed, many *Shan Van Vocht* editorials appeal for solidarity in the face of bitter political division and call for the 'women of Ireland' to come forth so that political unity could be facilitated.

In addition to her extensive political work, Milligan was also active as a playwright, actress and choreographer. Her short plays, and *tableaux vivants* in particular, represent a vital, if neglected, dramaturgical contri-bution to the Irish Revival and are significant for the way in which they reflect and refract the dominant cultural Nationalist ideology of the period. These *tableaux* were produced throughout the country and had a profound affect on audiences North and South. Yeats was extremely taken with the stylized, imagistic and immobile form of acting pioneered in these productions and they undoubtedly influenced the development of his own aesthetic ideas on acting, scenography and performance. Maud Gonne also travelled to Belfast, where she was impressed by performances of Milligan's *tableaux*, so much so that she afterwards sought the assistance of her Ulster counterpart to help her *Inghinidhe na hÉireann* (Daughters of Erin) theatre company to stage similar work in Dublin. Maire Quinn wrote to Milligan on behalf of *Inghinidhe* and Gonne:

> Dear Miss Milligan, Miss Gonne has asked me to write to you with reference to the Gaelic *Tableaux*, which we are so anxious to have in Dublin. We were so pleased to hear...that you were interested in this project and had so kindly promised to give us the benefit of your experience and assistance in carrying them out...[15]

With Milligan's assistance, *Inghinidhe* soon developed a Nationalist 'mixumgatherum' theatrical programme, comprising performances of Irish music, dancing, singing and oral recitations, and with a series of *tableaux vivants* as the evening's political and theatrical centrepiece. The performative efficacy of this particular theatrical form is evident from contemporaneous reviews: one critic from the *Daily Express* wrote: 'If the aim of the Irish Literary Theatre is to create a national drama it is obvious that the development of Miss Milligan's method is the proper road to reach ultimate success.'[16]

Milligan not only choreographed and 'wrote' these *tableaux* but often acted in them and, indeed, performed in what was perhaps the 'first modern production in the Irish language'[17] in 1898. The same year, the *Feis Ceoil*, another crucially important movement of the Revival, was held in Belfast and featured a week-long festival of Irish music which concluded in the Exhibition Hall under the auspices of the Gaelic League, for whom Milligan choreographed her first series of *tableaux vivants*. These dramatized, 'scenes from the story of Cuchulain and the Flight of Diarmuid and Grainne'[18] and 'were loudly applauded'.[19] However, just to ensure the political import of these imagistic performances was not lost, they were accompanied by a lecture which located this triptych of *tableaux* within the larger political narrative of the Nationalist Revival.[20] Milligan wrote of her desire for these Gaelic *tableaux* to 'increase public interest in the National Literary Theatre';[21] and they certainly seemed to have the desired effect, as the following year, she was invited to Dublin to present plays and *tableaux* at Gaelic League meetings. Spurred on by the success of the Irish Literary Theatre (ILT), she wrote *The Last Feast of the Fianna* (1899) for the company who performed it in February 1900: a production singled out by some scholars as being especially important as it 'marks the first attempt to take Irish legend as the subject of national drama.'[22]

The simplicity of the *tableaux* form, however, belies the complexity of both its reception and its influence – dramaturgically and politically – on the later evolution of Irish drama. Its simplicity also reflects the limited resources at Milligan's disposal and the sophistication of her political thinking, as her constant travelling and lecturing at various political gatherings throughout Ireland brought home to her the need for a pragmatic propagandist form for promulgating the message of national revival. *Tableaux* provided a portable, flexible, fluid form: technically simple, short, adaptable, easy to rehearse, their minimalism made them mobile and they could be staged in non-theatrical venues like drawing rooms and church halls, as well as more established performance spaces. Often mounted behind gauze screens, their Celtic costumes, mythical subject matter and atmospheric music created an arresting visual and aesthetic effect, and their performances provided a creative platform for League meetings or political debate. These *tableaux* largely drew their *dramatis personae* from Irish legends; Cuchulain, Queen Maev, Oisin, Finn, but also featured more political and religious figures, like St Patrick, St. Brigid and the Shan Van Vocht. Contemporaneous reviews reveal that these *tableaux* had a remarkable effect on audiences as Irish mythology and Nationalist ideology were conflated in a visually compelling manner. Although simple in form, the embodied politics of these performances manifested a sophisticated kind of corporeal dramaturgy as the convoluted narratives of ancient myths were broken down into simple, imagistic snapshots. For example, scenes of violent combat were visually staged with actors 'standing still as statues in strained and difficult attitudes,'[23] whereas other *tableaux* featured voice-overs delivered outside the performance by an actor narrating the events depicted within. Milligan became increasingly skilful at manipulating this mode of performance, and the innovation of this form generated considerable interest with reviews consistently remarking on its vivid, visual appeal and its efficacy in engaging audiences.

The romantic imagistic appeal of this theatrical form was not only successful with 'sophisticated' audiences but also with working-class audiences, who frequented playhouses and music halls rather than the hired halls and private residences where much of the Revival's rarefied early drama was performed. Such audiences were familiar with *tableaux* through their experience of melodrama; a cognate pictorial, spectacular form wherein individual scenes often concluded with set *tableaux*. Thus, Milligan's modernist aesthetic was dependant on, rather than distanced by (in contradistinction to Yeats's dramaturgy), a plebeian theatrical tradition. Her nationalistic *tableaux* converged with the visual culture of the popular stage (whilst connecting with the high politics of the Revival), so that her political message was framed within the 'horizon of expectations' of popular audiences accustomed to the spectacular, 'moving picture' world of melodrama. The efficacy of this aesthetic form is particularly evident when one considers that many *tableaux* featured symbolic, personified images of Ireland, in the forms of Dark Rosaleen, and the Poor Old Woman. Consequently her plays partially paved the way, dramaturgically, visually and politically, for the most famous stage entrance in Irish theatre history: Maud Gonne's onstage embodiment of Kathleen ni Houlihan in Yeats's and Gregory's 1902 drama.

The medieval scholar, historian, translator, novelist, poet, playwright (and sister of the leading dramatist of the Ulster Literary Theatre, Rutherford Mayne), Helen Waddell occupies a very different position from Milligan, on the margins of both the Irish Revival and the male-dominated academy.[24] Although Waddell is better known both as a medieval historian and author in the mould of J. R. R. Tolkien and C. S. Lewis, her illustrious scholarly career got off to a slow start, stymied as it was by her sense of duty to her demanding, invalid step-mother, whom she looked after for a decade until her death in 1919. During this frustrating 'lost decade' in Belfast,[25] Waddell wrote numerous short stories, fairytales and legends, many of which were influenced by Japanese, Chinese, Indian and Persian sources, and it was also in this period that she wrote her first play, *The Spoiled Buddha*. Born in Japan, where her father worked as a missionary, Waddell's exotic oriental childhood and later occidental training as a classical scholar informed this unusual, esoteric play which was produced by the Ulster Literary Theatre in 1915.[26] Radically different in form from the staple kitchen comedies, realistic folk dramas and fantastic burlesques the ULT had hitherto produced, Waddell's play 'seemed to have been over the heads of the audience and the players'.[27]

The Spoiled Buddha's recondite nature baffled Belfast audiences who were unaccustomed to its eastern *dramatis personae* of Buddha and his disciples Binzuru and Daruma, and uncomprehending of its philosophical discussions of nirvana and 'Infinite Negation'.[28] Set in a holy Buddhist temple, the play's rarefied aesthetic, with its ritualized procession of chanting *Rakkan*, stylized speech and movement, and incense-infused staging, is reminiscent of Yeats's esoteric experimentation with Eastern mysticism and Noh drama. The play itself relates the eponymous fable of Binzuru, Buddha's disciple who falls from grace and the path to nirvana when he succumbs to the 'mortal sin' of falling for a beautiful woman. The play opens with Buddha dispensing his spiritual wisdom to his disciples, admonishing them to reject worldly desires of life, wine and women (vices regularly inveighed against every Sabbath day in Belfast, albeit from a different theological tradition). As Buddha teaches his *rakkan*, the alluring siren-like sound of women's voices, music and laughter is heard off-stage, prompting Buddha's retreat into a stony meditative trance to avoid the women, 'It is not good that the words of the Law should be spoken in the hearing of women.'[29] When they arrive on-stage, the women salaciously tease the silent, totemic figures of the meditating men, but after they leave, a curious Binzuru queries why the 'Law' forbids women, as Buddha decrees, for they also have souls. His master responds:

> Yea Binzuru. But it hath happened that in saving their souls a man hath lost his own. Hear, O Rakkan. There be three desires, and of them is she the deadliest. The Disturber of the Integrity is she, the Entangler of the Upright, the Snare of the World.[30]

Buddha's misogyny is rejected by Binzuru, as in his spiritual search to find the Infinite, he discovers it in the beauty of one of the women, an apostasy for which his fellow *rakkan* seek to expel him and for which he is punished by falling down the 'Scale of Virtue'. In the second half of the play, set two and a half millennia later, a lonely and bored Buddha has achieved Nirvana, but his shrine is empty and abandoned as young female worshippers buy incense sticks to burn to the female shrine of Kwannon, for Buddha 'maketh no account of women'.[31] Waddell's play is thus encoded with a fierce polemical attack against the institutional misogyny of organized religions – both Eastern and Western – which 'maketh no account of women', and the provenance of her feminist politics can be traced back to the research she undertook after completing her MA at Queen's University (1912), which focused on the 'feminine interest in drama'.[32] The topic of her research was:

'Woman as Dramatic Asset'; – in other words, the evaluation of US – the Eternal Feminine, in fact, from Noah's wife in the Miracle Plays...down through Portia and Cleopatra and the naughtiness of the Restoration, to Bernard Shaw's Candida.[33]

However, Waddell gradually moved away from an exclusive focus on dramatic misogyny in the Elizabethan and Restoration periods in favour of the medieval period in which she made her name. Jennifer Fitzgerald observes how the medieval period was more attractive to Waddell's feminist proclivities as, 'the ideology of medieval humanism was...attractive to the woman scholar: inspired by Neo-Platonism, it redeemed the body (especially the female body) which had been reviled by the Church as sinful flesh.'[34] From an early stage, Waddell's feminist convictions compelled her to challenge patriarchal misogyny wherever she found it; in ancient Chinese poetry, medieval morality plays, restoration comedy. However, as a student, and later as a struggling scholar, she was personally confronted with a manifestation of it in the male-dominated academy that she was unable to overcome, and which adversely circumscribed her career.

Thus, *The Spoiled Buddha* is not only informed by Waddell's childhood background, or her postgraduate feminist critique of clerical sexism and the patriarchal nature of the classical canon, but from her own bitter personal experience of being passed over three times for a lecturing post in the English department at Queen's University on the basis of her sex, and as such, the play caustically comments on the subordinated role of women in contemporaneous society. Although Waddell's childhood friend Monica Blackett recalls that Queen's proudly celebrated their distinguished past pupil as 'Ulster's Darling', and hailed her as 'the most distinguished woman of her generation',[35] her account occludes the fact that it was less conducive to the development of her early career.[36] On the other hand, Fitzgerald's superb essay exposes a different story, describing how the advent of World War One and the concomitant proliferation of opportunities for women[37] with the haemorrhaging of male academics for war work led to the 'opening up [of] posts to women' at Queen's, creating ideal conditions for a locally based, promising young scholar, like Waddell, to be appointed. However, in spite of being interviewed three times for vacant lectureships in the English Department at Queen's, she was sexually discriminated against on each occasion by her former supervisor, the Professor of English, Gregory Smith, whom she claimed, 'openly admits his prejudice against appointing women to academic posts'.[38] It is a measure of her deep frustration at these events that she left Belfast to pursue her doctorate at Oxford University almost immediately after the death of her step-mother, although, in spite of her prodigious talents and public acclaim as an innovative medieval scholar, she never obtained a permanent position in any of the numerous institutions she subsequently taught at.[39] A luminous, liminal figure, within and without the academy and the Irish Revival, operating on the thresholds of 'gender and nationality, religion and art, scholarship and creativity',[40] Waddell's life and career as proto-revisionist historian, feminist scholar and intercultural author is remarkable, and its reclamation can only enhance our understanding of women's experience of, and contribution to, a crucial period in Irish cultural history.

Post-1921: the ongoing struggle for independence: Patricia O'Connor

The partition of Ireland in 1921 led to further political polarization and reinforced the patriarchal nature of society both in the newly independent Free State in the South, and the British-ruled six counties of Northern Ireland. The quasi-theocratic nature of both states created a certain sectarian symmetry to the island and the subalterned position of women in these new political arrangements was shared by Protestant and Catholic women, North and South. Although implacably divided on the constitutional issue of partition, the patriarchal nature of Nationalism and Unionism meant they were ideologically in synch on social issues, most notably that women's position was in the home. This political consensus was reinforced by religious orthodoxy as the social teachings of the Protestant and Catholic Churches also converged in promoting 'women's primary duties as home-makers and mothers, focusing their interests and energies on the domestic sphere'.[41]

Following the dispersal of the Revival's cultural energies and the disillusionment of Nationalist hopes with the foundation of the new Northern Irish state and the political sundering of Ireland, the first woman playwright to emerge in Ulster after Waddell is the woefully neglected figure of Patricia O'Connor. In the male dominated, socially repressive, religious, ultra-conservative and censorious Northern state (itself a mirror of the Free State), O'Connor's plays critically interrogate the patriarchal hegemony of the 'Imperial Province' through her investigation of non-constitutional issues. Education, economic conditions, emigration and emancipation are consistently addressed in her work which frequently foregrounds issues that impact most upon women's lives: work, marriage, family life, religion and abortion. In this way, O'Connor's work complements that of Southern playwright Teresa Deevy, who tackled many of the same issues, although, the *mise-en-scène* of O'Connor's drama is a distinctly Ultonian one as it often portrays Protestant, (Unionist) families and the patriarchal nature of the Northern (Protestant) state.

Many of her plays deal with the education system or feature strong female characters who are teachers by profession, reflecting O'Connor's own background as a schoolteacher (one of the few careers open to women; see Figure 5). *Highly Efficient* (1942)[42] is particularly significant and was a notable popular success; its acerbic critique of the educational system struck a chord with critics and audiences and it presciently anticipated the wholesale reform introduced by the Butler Education Act (1944). The play is all the more interesting when one considers it in the context of the Irish theatre canon, constructed as it is from the extraordinary efflorescence of plays that self-consciously address the state of the nation, whilst ignoring the state of the State. *Highly Efficient* is perhaps the first play to critique the failure of a key structure of the new Northern state, and it is all the more significant that her attack is anti-patriarchal, not anti-partitionist in nature.

Figure 5 Patricia O'Connor (left). Photo: Courtesy of Lecale Historical Society.

O'Connor's play exposes the failure of the state's education system through her protagonist, Margaret Henderson. The conflict between the reformist and reactionary forces at the heart of the play is embodied in the opposition between the idealistic Henderson and her patrician, male inspectors, before whom she is requested to simply reply: 'Yes, Mr Andrews', 'Certainly, Mr Andrews', 'Whatever you say Mr Andrews.'[43] Only on the basis, as one female colleague reminds her, that 'you learn your lines and stick to them' will Henderson ever get on in her career.[44]

Contemporaneous reviews of O'Connor's play make interesting reading: its political message is not really recognized by most (male) reviewers, who prefer to extol its 'Ulster humour' instead of its exposure of the educational system itself.[45] Their failure to engage with the explicit political message of the play perhaps testifies to their unwillingness to bestow women with any political agency, and provides further insight into the insidious patriarchal process whereby female playwrights like O'Connor become buried in the theatrical past, imperceptibly erased from the critical and historiographical process of canon formation. Microcosmically, these reviews by male critics indicate the larger macro limitations of positivist methodologies of theatre historiography which collude in the occlusion of women playwrights from the theatrical canon.[46] Indeed, the patronizing nature of these reviews corresponds with the condescending tone of historian David Kennedy's high-handed evaluation of O'Connor as he highlights her 'moral earnestness' and adduces, 'she is too much the sociologist to be a successful dramatist.'[47] For a theatre historian to level the same criticism against any of the many male, canonical Irish, or even European, playwrights like O'Casey and Chekhov, is unthinkable.

Moreover, O'Connor's plays are never merely sociological, as within their ostensibly realist framework, there are often symbolic intertextual motifs that critically comment on the image of 'woman' as an idealized trope of the nation. *Voice Out of Rama* (1944) features a fascinating inversion of the Kathleen ni Houlihan narrative. Here, the malevolent figure of Aunt Rosie and her minatory invocations from the Bible prophesizing disaster, desecration and the sacrifice of children, manifest her as a Calvinistic counterpart to Kathleen ni Houlihan:

Rosie: Tis strangers as brings the trouble. I heard me father tell of the strange woman as came in out o' the sea, and her long wet hair around her, and she put a spell on a man from the land – a fine strong (*sic*) farming man, and he left the spade in the field and went after her, and he was never seen again till he was washed up on the shore and him strangled be her shining hair.

Betty: That's certainly a cheerful little tale... Perhaps the woman was Kathleen ni Houlihan.[48]

The female protagonists of O'Connor's plays are unafraid of confronting the patriarchal hegemony of their homes and workplaces. *Voice Out of Rama* dramatizes the fluctuating fortunes of the Orr family over a century and stages the unfolding clash of generational values, especially in relation to gender roles, as Ellen Orr remarks at the opening of the play, 'there's nothing so humiliating for a girl as to deprive her of an opportunity to be independent.'[49] Ellen, one of the youngest members of the Orr clan, has established her independence by leaving the family farm for the city where she works as a teacher, but she bitterly resents the humiliation her parsimonious father inflicts on her mother and the financial power he holds over the family:

Ellen: She works all the time and there's nothing in this house she can take any pride in. You'd buy machines for the farm but you'd nearly begrudge her a new coat. A woman wants something to think of besides work. It's not fair... You think of nothing but working and saving – and the price of cattle... You make me sick. No woman would want to come here or stay here, if she could go anywhere else. If I were mother I'd run away and leave you so I would. You stingy old devil.

Hugh: That'll do ye now Ellen, I've had enough o' yer sauce.

Ellen: There's no good in talking reasonably to you, you're stupid as well as stingy. I'll be jolly glad to get away from you anyway. I'd rather do anything, anything at all, than live on your rotten old farm.

HUGH: Quit girl you have me deeved.[50]

In another play, *The Farmer Wants A Wife* (1955),[51] the fiercely independent Margaret Wylie confronts her *paramour* John Bryson when she discovers his secret intention to emigrate to Australia. Frustrated by the passivity of the previous generation of women to their menfolk, and enraged by John's duplicity, she makes clear her resistance to the role of Kathleen ni Houlihan or any other masculinist constructs of sublimated, subordinate women that would undermine her own sense of selfhood:

John: I'll make good. I'll come back for you... You'll wait for me?

Margaret: Why?

John: I love you…You love me. (*Silence*) Margaret! Say something.

Margaret: (*slowly*) 'It may be for years, and it may be for ever, Then why art thou silent Oh voice of my heart?'… John?

John: Well?

Margaret: Do I look like Kathleen Mavoureen?

John: You're not a girl in a song!

Margaret: You're right! – I'm not any of the girls in any of the songs! 'I'll take you home again Kathleen.' 'The Country I'm leaving behind.' 'It's a long way to Tipperary.' 'The girl I left behind me.' 'Danny Boy.' 'The Mountains of Mourne' (*she reads the titles like a roll call working herself up as she goes on, until the last which she says softly and mockingly*) 'What will you do Love, when I am going…?'

John: DON'T

Margaret: No? Don't you like to remember the girls in the emigrant songs John?

John: It won't be long I promise you

Margaret: (*Blazing suddenly*) You promised! What's that worth now?…

John:…I'm going to Australia so that you and I won't be caught in the same old trap as Uncle Frank and old Uncle Davy

Margaret: I'm being caught in no trap, old or new.[52]

Margaret's extraordinary means of escape from this trap is to propose to John's elderly uncle Frank, the eponymous farmer who wants a wife, on the conditions that he renovates the house and removes his insufferable housekeeper. Her shock tactic works, prompting John to propose to prevent her marriage to his uncle, who is favourably disposed to her proposal, 'a fair enough offer'.[53] Although this situation is comically resolved, Margaret coldly observes that the same fate is 'far too common' for many young girls in the parish who are often forced to marry old men, a union that 'doesn't make anyone happy'.[54]

In O'Connor's virtually unknown one-act play *Canvassing Disqualifies* (1948), which attacks the corrupt and nepotistic nature of employment practices in the educational sector, Mrs Brent, a war widow and former principal schoolteacher, challenges the decision of the all-male School Committee conducting her job interview to appoint an inexperienced and unqualified male candidate instead of her. The Committee itself is divided; its chair has already promised the position to the son of a family friend currently studying for his teaching degree, but other Committee members begin to be swayed by the meritocratic logic of Mrs Brent's case:

Ferguson: [T]he committee have decided that we must appoint a man as the vacancy is for a principal teacher.

Smith: Mr Ferguson thinks that, I don't.

Ferguson: So you think, Davy that a woman is better suited for a position of responsibility than a man?

Smith: I don't ... it depends on what the job is and what the man's like. Is he better able to do the job? ...

Mrs Brent: [I]t would depend on qualifications and experience.[55]

Mrs Brent has a higher diploma in education, a BA, MA, and a decade of teaching experience, four years of which as principal of a large school, in sharp contrast to the preferred candidate who has yet to finish his qualifications and has no teaching experience whatsoever. After rationally questioning the wisdom, not to mention the justice, of their decision, Mrs Brent finds support and solidarity from an unexpected quarter as the wife of Committee member George Thompson, in whose home they have been convening, forcefully interjects:

Ferguson: Give the lad time. He hasn't learned how to teach yet.

Mrs Brent: And what happens to the school while you give ... the ... lad time to learn how to teach?

Cullen: There's one for you to answer, Mr Ferguson!

Ferguson: Mrs Brent doesn't expect an answer.

Mrs Brent: That is so. (*Looking around the company, and speaking with a slight husk in her voice.*) I used to expect so much. I wonder if I shall ever again be able to expect anything.

Mrs Thompson: (*Rising*) I couldn't listen to you men! You said David wasn't to be sentimental. Now every word you've heard shows her to be the best teacher. You're not thinking of the children or the school but your own obstinacy. 'I gave my word', say you. But will you say 'I made a mistake'? Oh, no. Men never make mistakes. The school can be ill-managed by a lad, the world can go to war, a man can give his word and those great wicked bombs destroy all the people and all the country. My son is dead. This woman's husband is dead because of the pride of men and their *word*. Do you think your word is the word of God?[56]

It is an extraordinary, explosive outburst; however, her attack on the logocentric power of patriarchy has little effect as Ferguson remains unmoved, feigns his regret and repeats that he cannot appoint Mrs

Brent. Her response is damning, but dignified: 'You choose the inexperienced and the less qualified not because you have anything against me, but because I had the ill fortune to be born a woman.'[57] The men's protests ring hollow, and indeed, after the next candidate is ushered in for interview, the real motives of some Committee members are revealed:

Cullen: I don't hold with women having a lot of letters after their names and taking responsible jobs that rightly belongs to men.
Miss Read: You don't hold with women being responsible for children?
(There is a general laugh)
Cullen: [I]t's against nature for women to be getting into power. Haven't men always run the world? Haven't they?
Mrs Thompson: Yes. And are you clapping yourself on the back for the grand way men ran it John Cullen?[58]

All of O'Connor's work is informed by her feminist politics and the political imperative of empowering and emancipating women. Some plays challenge male control of the educational system, which is in itself representative of larger patriarchal structures and values that shape the Northern state with regards to socio-economic, political and family life. Other works address sectarianism, familism, emigration and other social problems. Her little-known novel, *Mary Doherty*, set on the northern coast where 'religious and racial antagonisms are rife',[59] controversially raises the taboo subject of abortion.[60] Similarly, a collection of four one-act plays edited by O'Connor,[61] presents a diverse range of female roles and subject positions, creating a heterogeneous flux of female characters that undermines the fixed, traditional roles of women as wives, mothers and whores.[62] Significantly, this collection includes three women playwrights, (including O'Connor) and signals her desire to support and promote new work by women playwrights. In all three plays, women are never subordinate or of secondary importance, but active, engaged and centre-stage. O'Connor's work thus creates a coherent feminist position and perspective which contests the structural inequalities in Northern society. The transgressive plurality and transformative possibilities presented by her female characters challenge the normative cultural representations of women in Nationalist and Unionist discourse and dismantle the religious-politico forces which frame their reductive constructions of 'woman'. Recent scholarship has (partially) restored the neglected figure of Teresa Deevy to the Irish canon; a transformation that has largely been brought about by highlighting how her work critiques the patriarchal nature of the Church and State. I would contend that the same argument could be compellingly made for O'Connor's work *vis-à-vis* the Northern state, and this revisionist recuperation is long overdue, as her considerable body of work has been entirely effaced from the official narrative of Irish theatre historiography and from the feminist reconstruction of the Irish literary and dramatic canon.[63]

Milligan, Waddell and O'Connor are three women playwrights who expose the hidden lacunae of Irish theatre history and the limitations of the dominant methodology of Irish theatre historiography which has, until recently, prioritized texts over performance, high art over popular culture, professional theatre over amateur activity: a positivist, modernist engagement with the theatrical past that disadvantages particular theatrical forms such as *tableaux* and popular practices, and which *ergo*, disenfranchises many women playwrights. Moreover, this focus on literary theatre is further constricted, to use Joep Leerssen's phrase, by the 'auto-exoticism'[64] of Irish theatre historiography as it remains fixated on the 'nation' as the dominant conceptual and organizational category of theatre history and criticism. Finally, I would also contend that these Northern playwrights have been doubly occluded from the Irish canon, as geography, as well as gender, has placed them 'beyond the pale' of a meta-narrative of Irish theatre historiography that has been profoundly Dublincentric in nature.[65]

As the first study to investigate a tradition of Northern women playwrights in the pre-Troubles period, this chapter argues that these authors fundamentally rejected representations of 'woman' as a sublimated trope of nation, and resisted the dominant cultural ideologies of Nationalism *and* Unionism which sought to subordinate women by idealizing, or ignoring, their sexuality and subjectivity. Collectively considered, their work proves that silence does not equal absence and it goes a long way in unshackling the stereotype of voiceless women and in shattering the most invidious myth of all: that 'there are no Irish women playwrights.'[66]

Notes

1. Many thanks to Hugh Odling-Smee, curator of the Linen Hall Library's Theatre and Performing Arts Archives, for his invaluable assistance in reconstructing many biographical details of O'Connor's life, and for providing me with access to typescripts of O'Connor's work.
2. Alan Hayes and Diane Urquhart, *The Irish Women's History Reader* (London: Routledge, 2001), p. 2.

3. Alice Milligan, 1866–1953: [pseud. 'Iris Olkyrn' in *Northern Patriot*]; Born into a Methodist family in Omagh, Co. Tyrone, and daughter of Irish antiquarian Seaton F. Milligan (1836–1916); educated Methodist College, Belfast, Magee College, Derry, and King's Coll., London; introduced to Irish through great uncle Armour Alcorn, who spoke to farm labourers in Irish; went to Dublin to learn Irish; taught at women's college in Derry, moved to Belfast; contrib. *Sinn Féin, United Irishman* (from 1893), and *United Ireland*; collaborated with her father on *Glimpses of Erin* (1890); issued a novel, *A Royal Democrat* (1892); contrib. verse to *Belfast Naturalists' Field Club Report and Proceedings* (1894); published a life of Theobald Wolfe Tone (1898); *Beltaine* (Feb. 1900); *Ulad* (Feb. 1905); with Ethna Carbery founded and edited the *Northern Patriot*, organ of Henry Joy McCracken Literary Society in October 1895, later founded and edited with Ethna Carbery *The Shan Van Vocht*, (Jan. 1896–April 1899), admired by Bulmer Hobson and Roger Casement, George ('Æ') Russell, and J. F. Bigger; dismissed in Lady Gregory's diary as 'a tawdry little piece'; forced with her brother William to leave Ireland under 24-hour threat of execution by Loyalists, 1920; founding member of Ulster Anti-Partition Council; elected to Irish Academy of Letters; honorary degree of NUI, presented by Eamon de Valera, 1941; passed her final years disillusioned, isolated and lonely at home in Omagh.

4. Helen Jane Waddell (1889–1965): born in Tokyo, daughter of Hugh Waddell, a Presbyterian minister and orientalist; brother was Samuel Waddell (Rutherford Mayne); returned to Belfast, 1900; mother died of typhoid before return of father; educated Victoria Colleges, TCD, BA and MA; wrote bible stories for children while tending to her step-mother; entered Oxford 1919, (PhD in Medieval French); Cassell Lecturer, St Hilda's College, 1921; taught at Bedford Coll., 1922; freelance; first female member Royal Society for Literature (1931); honorary degrees from Durham, QUB and Columbia; encouraged Patrick Kavanagh to write *The Green Fool* (1938); asst. editor of *The Nineteenth-Century Journal*, 1938; retired 1945; suffered from a progressive neurological disorder; died from pneumonia, 1965. Published *Wandering Scholars* (1927); *Medieval Latin Lyrics* (1929); trans. Abbé Prévost's *Histoire de Chevalier des Grieux et de Manon Lescaut* (1931); *Book of Medieval Latin for Schools* (1931); *Beasts and Saints* (1934); *The Desert Fathers* (1936).

5. Patricia O'Connor (pseud.) Norah Ingram, 1908–1983: born Donegal; later moved to Killough, Co. Down. All her plays staged were performed by the Group Theatre including *Highly Efficient* (1942); *Voice Out of Rama* (1944); *Select Vestry* (1945), *Master Adams* (1949); *The Master* (194?); *The Farmer Wants a Wife* (1955); *Who Saw Her Die* (1957); *The Sparrows Fall* (1959). She also wrote two novels, *Mary Doherty* (London: Sands, n.d.[1938]); *The Mill in the North* (Dublin: Talbot Press, 1938).

6. See Catherine Morris, 'In the Enemy's Camp: Alice Milligan and *Fin-de Siècle* Belfast', in Nicholas Allen and Aaron Kelly (eds), *Cities of Belfast* (Dublin: Four Courts Press, 2003), pp. 62–71; 'Becoming Irish? Alice Milligan and the Revival', *Irish University Review*, Vol. 31, No.1, 2003, pp. 79–98.

7. Milligan published a life of Theobald Wolfe Tone (the leader of the United Irishmen) in 1898.

8. *The Shan Van Vocht*, September 1897, in Margaret Ward, *In Their Own Voice: Women and Irish Nationalism* (Dublin: Attic Press, 1995), p. 9.

9. *The Green Upon the Cape* (1898); *Oisín and Patraic* (1899); *Oisín in Tír na nÓg* (1900); *The Last Feast of the Fianna* (1900); *The Harp that Once* (1901); *The Deliverance of Red Hugh* (1901); *The Daughter of Donagh: A Cromwellian Drama in Four Acts* (1902).

10. *The Green Upon the Cape*, in *The Shan Van Vocht*, 4 April 1898.

11. Anna Johnston (1886–1911): daughter of the redoubtable Fenian Robert Johnston, married Donegal novelist and poet Seamus MacManus.

12. Sheila Turner Johnston, *Alice: A Life of Alice Milligan* (Omagh: Colourpoint Press, 1994), p. 80.

13. Seamus McManus (ed.), *The Four Winds of Éirinn* (Dublin: M. Gill & Son, 1918), p. 150.

14. Maud Gonne, *A Servant of the Queen* (Suffolk: Boydell Press, 1983), p. 176.

15. Cited in Robert Hogan and James Kilroy, *The Irish Literary Theatre, 1899–1901* (Dublin: The Dolmen Press, 1975), pp. 85–6.

16. Cited in Christopher Fitz-Simon, *The Irish Theatre* (London: Thames & Hudson, 1983), p. 137.

17. Hogan and Kilroy, *The Irish Literary Theatre, 1899–1901*, p. 52. The play in question was *The Passing of Conall* (anon.), published in *The Freeman's Journal* 21 November 1898 and performed in Letterkenny, Co. Donegal.

18. Alice Milligan, letter to *The Daily Express*, 21 January 1899, cited in Hogan and Kilroy, *The Irish Literary Theatre, 1899–1901*, p. 54.

19. 'The Gaelic League Festival', *The Irish News and Belfast Morning News*, 8 May 1898.

20. In many ways, this particular theatrical event constitutes the founding moment of Gaelic drama. See P. Ó Siadhail, *Istair Dhrámaíocht na Gaeilge, 1900–1970* (Conamara: Cló Iar-Chonnachta, 1993), p. 20.

21. Letter cited in Hogan and Kilroy, *The Irish Literary Theatre, 1899–1901*, p. 54.

22. P. J. Mathews, *Revival: The Abbey Theatre, Sinn Féin, The Gaelic League Movement and the Co-Operative Movement* (Cork: Cork University Press, 2003), p. 76.

23. 'The Gaelic League Festival', *The Irish News and Belfast Morning News*, 8 May 1898, cited in Hogan and Kilroy, *The Irish Literary Theatre, 1899–1901*, p. 57.

24. See Monica Blackett, *The Mark of The Maker* (London: Constable, 1973); David Burleigh (ed.), *Helen Waddell's Literary Writings from Japan* (Dublin: IAP, 2005); Dame Felicitas Corrigan, *Helen Waddell, A Biography* (London: Gollancz, 1986); Jennifer Fitzgerald, ' "Jazzing the Middle Ages": The Feminist Genesis of Helen Waddell's *The Wandering Scholars*', *Irish Studies Review*, Vol. 8, No. 1, 2000, pp. 5–22; Norman Vance, *Helen Waddell: Presbyterian Medievalist*, Robert Allen Memorial Lecture (Belfast: Presbyterian Historical Society of Ireland, l996).

25. Blackett refers to this period as the 'lost decade' in Waddell's life.

26. First performed on 1 February 1915, Grand Opera House, Belfast.

27. Sam Hanna Bell, *The Theatre in Ulster: A Survey of the Dramatic Movement in Ulster from 1902 until the Present Day* (Dublin: Gill & Macmillan, 1972), p. 44.

28. Helen Waddell, *The Spoiled Buddha* (Dublin: Talbot Press, 1919), p. 14.

29. Waddell, *The Spoiled Buddha*, p. 8.

30. Waddell, *The Spoiled Buddha*, p. 9.

31. Waddell, *The Spoiled Buddha*, p. 30.

32. Helen Waddell, Letter to George Taylor, 6 April 1919, cited in Jennifer Fitzgerald, ' "Jazzing the Middle Ages": The Feminist Genesis of Helen Waddell's *The Wandering Scholars'*, *Irish Studies Review*, 8:1 (2000), p. 12.

33. Letter to Margaret Martin, *c*.1912, cited Fitzgerald, ' "Jazzing the Middle Ages": The Feminist Genesis of Helen Waddell's *The Wandering Scholars'*, p. 11.

34. Fitzgerald, ' "Jazzing the Middle Ages": The Feminist Genesis of Helen Waddell's *The Wandering Scholars'*, pp. 10–11.

35. Blackett, *The Mark of the Maker: A Portrait of Helen Waddell*, pp. 85–6.

36. Although Queen's was the first college to allow women to enrol as students (it allowed its first female students in 1881 to attend Art classes and all other subjects soon afterwards), it did not appoint its first permanent woman lecturer until 1931.

37. Prior to World War One, female students at Queen's constituted less than a fifth of the total number of students, whilst immediately after the war they were nearly one-third.

38. As supervisor of Waddell's thesis, Smith was all too aware of his precocious student's feminist politics, which undoubtedly fortified his chauvinistic views: Fitzgerald, ' "Jazzing the Middle Ages": The Feminist Genesis of Helen Waddell's *The Wandering Scholars'*, p. 19.

39. Fitzgerald, ' "Jazzing the Middle Ages": The Feminist Genesis of Helen Waddell's *The Wandering Scholars'*, p. 5.

40. Fitzgerald, ' "Jazzing the Middle Ages": The Feminist Genesis of Helen Waddell's *The Wandering Scholars'*, p. 15.

41. Anna McMullan and Caroline Williams, 'Contemporary Women Playwrights', *Field Day Anthology*, *Vol. V* (Cork: Cork University Press, 2002), p. 1235.

42. First produced 21 September 1942 by the Ulster Group Theatre, at the Group Theatre, Belfast.

43. Patricia O'Connor, *Highly Efficient* (Belfast: The Quota Press, n.d.), p. 27.

44. O'Connor, *Highly Efficient*, p. 26.

45. See 'Theatre and Cinemas', *The Belfast Newsletter*, 22 September 1942, 6 October 1942, 13 October 1942; 'Stage, Variety, Screen', *Northern Whig*, 22 September 1942; 'The Group Theatre', *The Irish News*, 22 September 1942.

46. Various scholars have highlighted the limitations of positivist historiographical methods for feminist historians, See Tracy C. Davis, 'Questions for a Feminist Methodology in Theatre History', in Thomas Postlewait and Bruce McConachie (eds), *Interpreting the Theatrical Past: New Directions in the Historiography of Performance* (Iowa: University of Iowa Press, 1989), pp. 59–81.

47. David Kennedy, cited in Ophelia Byrne, *The State of Play: The Theatre and Cultural Identity in Twentieth Century Ulster* (Belfast: The Linen Hall Library, 2001), p. 34.

48. Patricia O'Connor, *Voice Out of Rama* (1944). The play's title refers to the Gospel of Matthew, 'A voice was heard in Rama, lamentation, weeping and great mourning, Rachel weeping for her children, and would not be comforted because they are not'. Chapter 2, verse 18. The play also references Abraham's attempts to sacrifice his own son according to God's decree, which helps Rosie justify her own attempts to have her nephew's daughter

killed. The figure of Aunt Rosie is very much the dramaturgical precursor of the ghost of Lily Matthews in Stewart Parker's Protestant alter-ego to Kathleen ni Houlihan in his play *Pentecost*. Typescript in Linenhall Library, p. 40.

49. O'Connor, *Voice Out of Rama*, p. 5.
50. O'Connor, *Voice Out of Rama*, pp. 34–5.
51. First produced 30 March 1955 by the Ulster Group Theatre, in the Group Theatre, Belfast.
52. Patricia O'Connor, *The Farmer Wants a Wife* (1955). Typescript in Linenhall Library, pp. 20–1.
53. O'Connor, *The Farmer Wants a Wife*, p. 23.
54. O'Connor, *The Farmer Wants a Wife*, p. 27.
55. Patricia O'Connor, *Canvassing Disqualifies*, in *Four New One Act Plays*, ed. Patricia O'Connor (Belfast: Quota Press, 1948), p. 80.
56. O'Connor, *Four New One Act Plays*, pp. 82–3.
57. O'Connor, *Four New One Act Plays*, p. 83.
58. O'Connor, *Four New One Act Plays*, p. 88.
59. Stephen J. Brown and Desmond Clarke, *Ireland in Fiction: A Guide to Irish Novels, Tales, Romances and Folklore*, Pt 2 (Cork: Royal Carbery 1985), p. 201.
60. The eponymous protagonist is seduced by a drunken suitor who later proposes marriage providing the children are reared as Protestants. Mary refuses to acquiesce to such demands but a 'timely operation' makes it impossible for her to have children and thus 'opens the way to marriage', Brown and Clarke, *Ireland in Fiction*, p. 68.
61. Includes *Witches in Eden* by Olga Fielden, *Dinsmore's Cash* by Anna McClure Warnock, *Canvassing Disqualifies* by O'Connor, and *You Never Know Your Luck* by Ruddick Miller.
62. See Bill Rolston, 'Mothers, Whores, and Villains: Images of Women in Novels of the Northern Ireland Conflict', *Race and Class*, Vol. 31, No. 1, 1989, pp. 219–36; Margaret Ward and Marie-Therese McGivern, 'Images of Women in Northern Ireland', *The Crane Bag*, Vol. 4, No. 1, 1980, pp. 66–72.
63. O'Connor is absent from all the major studies of twentieth century Irish theatre, Nicholas Grene, *The Politics of Irish Drama* (Cambridge University Press, 1999); Robert Hogan, *After the Irish Renaissance: A Critical History of Irish Drama Since the Plough and the Stars* (Minneapolis: University of Minnesota Press, 1967); D. E. S. Maxwell, *A Critical History of Modern Irish Drama, 1891–1980* (Cambridge University Press, 1984); Christopher Murray, *Twentieth-Century Irish Drama: Mirror up to Nation* (Manchester University Press, 1997); Lionel Pilkington, *Theatre and State in Twentieth Century Ireland: Cultivating the People* (London: Routledge, 2001); Shaun Richards (ed.), *The Cambridge Companion to Twentieth-Century Irish Drama* (Cambridge: Cambridge University Press, 2004). Surprisingly, she is also wholly absent from the *Dictionary of Ulster Biography*, ed. Kate Newman (Belfast: Institute of Irish Studies, 1993). In the various historical surveys of theatre in Ulster, O'Connor is only fleetingly referenced: she is allocated 5 lines in David Kennedy's survey of Northern theatre, and 5 and 31 lines respectively in Sam Hanna Bell's histories (Kennedy, 'The Drama in Ulster', in Sam Hanna Bell et al. (eds), *The Arts in Ulster: A Symposium* (London: George C. Harrap, 1951), p. 63; Bell, 'Theatre', in Michael Longley (ed.), *Causeway: The Arts in Ulster* (Belfast: Arts Council of Northern Ireland, 1971), p. 87; *The Theatre in*

Ulster (Dublin: Gill & Macmillan, 1972), pp. 88–9). Even the most recent Field Day anthologies of Irish women's writing provide little more than an inadequate and incomplete biographical entry (*The Field Day Anthology, Vol. IV*, pp. 1036–7). More recently, the Irish playography lists O'Connor's work, but again, its record of her plays is incomplete and her biographical details are brief in the extreme.

64. Joep Leerssen, *Remembrance and Imagination: Patterns in the Historical and Literary Representation of Ireland in the Nineteenth Century* (Cork: Cork University Press, 1996), pp. 35–8.

65. See Mark Phelan, 'The Critical "Gap of the North": Nationalism, National Theatre, and the North', *Modern Drama*, Vol. 47, No. 4, 2004, pp. 594–607.

66. This infamous quotation is attributed to an anonymous Dublin bookseller and was the ironic title of Glasshouse Theatre's mini-festivals of women playwrights in 1992–93.

7
Meta-Physicality: Women Characters in the Plays of Frank McGuinness

Eamonn Jordan

I

Patriarchy has both prescribed and fictionalized societal, gender, class and race relations, and it has also, to a considerable extent, fashioned and fabricated the dramaturgical practices of Irish theatre in terms of how plays are written, programmed, directed, produced, marketed and consumed. Moreover, the imaginations of Irish theatre practitioners, playwrights especially, have been seriously ideologically loaded, not only in the specific prioritization of primarily male values, references and aspirations, and in their general scrutiny of, and obsession with, masculinity, but also in their consistent subjugation, marginalization and objectification of the feminine.[1] Gendered relationships have been subjected to critical enquiry in terms of authority, agency, alienation, the body, space, transgression and execution of subjectivities, while post-colonial theory has expounded specific relationships between split subjectivities, patterns of imperial oppression and the dynamics of play.[2]

Since Frank McGuinness began writing in the 1980s, his plays have set considerable challenges for audiences, academics and theatre-makers alike, not only by the outstanding volume of work, but also by the range of forms he deploys and the creative and dramaturgical inspirations that he has both absorbed and intertextualized. In terms of gender, his dramas set very specific challenges, especially when it comes to his female characters. Of all the male playwrights writing today in Irish Theatre, McGuinness consistently confronts romanticized, conventionalized and stereotypical gendered roles and imperatives. Yet any writer, male or female, can find it hard to work outside the conventions, practices and aspirations of his/her predecessors.

Some recent critics offer substantial and decisive starting points in the interrogation of gender and Irish theatre in particular. I will mention four different interventions, by Lynda Henderson, Anne. F. Kelly (O'Reilly), Cathy Leeney and Anna McMullan, respectively. Henderson argues that women in Tom Murphy's dramas 'play supporting roles of literal catering, managing, conniving', but they have no access to the 'metaphysical debate'.[3] The notion of only male characters in Murphy's work having access to 'metaphysical debate' is more or less accurate. As a concept, the metaphysical dimension profitably destabilizes the connection between woman and the body, woman and emotion, as promoted by old binary stereotypes. Kelly argues that women in Murphy's plays are partly there to 'carry meanings that the male characters cannot reach. They are the necessary complement, the anima to the male animus – not subjects in their own right.'[4] Kelly's charge against Murphy stands up particularly in plays like *A Whistle in the Dark* (1961) and *Conversations on a Homecoming* (1985). *Bailegangaire* (1985) is of course the obvious exception to both critical appraisals. Leeney's analysis deals with the works of Teresa Deevy and Marina Carr. Leeney cogently argues that under patriarchy, alienation and exile are the lot of women, and these are absorbed often unconsciously and uncritically into Irish dramatic practices: 'The boundaries around Irish women's realities define containment as a form of exile; exile from self-expression, from self-determination.'[5] Alienation from self is one of the consistent qualities of McGuinness's characters, but it probably does not apply equally across genders. In her analysis of Tom Kilroy's *Double Cross* (1986), McMullan points out that in this play women 'by revealing or confronting duplicity, have the moral advantage', but 'the transformative potential of the mask eludes them. They are constant fall guys to the player princes.'[6] Where transformation is possible, McGuinness does not deny his female characters the transformative potential of the mask, but frames it within the fantastic, thus not so much refuting but postponing and/or destabilizing the comfort that such transformations generate within the frame of the real. Terry Eagleton in his discussions on Wilde, points to him 'adopting a performative rather than a representational epistemology'.[7] Such a distinction is essential to both the understanding of the Irish theatrical tradition in general and McGuinness's work in particular. This performative epistemology I denote in this instance as a meta-physicality, located in the possibilities, circumstances and the make-up of the mask, grounded in the sensibility of the body and its intuition, in the way that the carnivalized body celebrates and refutes.

Clearly, some characters do not wish for the 'transformative potential of the mask', for some the mask eludes them, but it is my contention that McGuinness generates enough energy and commitment for both a metaphysical consciousness and the illusionary and alienating potential for the mask or play to spring into being. McGuinness's women are perhaps at times morally superior to men, but seldom do they have a 'moral advantage'. The concept of play is problematic. McGuinness's work seems to facilitate recognition through acknowledgement, conspiracy, compromise and seldom transformation that is both internally and externally driven. The characters, both male and female equally, have access to a range of problematic emotions, resources, aspirations, and temptations, as they quest acceptance, forgiveness and the shadow of death. Through that process they embrace, often not easily, the unconscious darkness, the tenderness and terror of the body and the horror and sparkle of the imagination to generate and confuse. The sense of play is dark and frequently innocent, physical and metaphysical.

II

The Factory Girls (1982) was McGuinness's first major success and is set in a Buncrana shirt factory (Peacock Theatre, directed by Patrick Mason). The textile sector in Donegal in the 1980s had unusually high levels of women participating in the workforce. As part of an industrial dispute, five women, Ellen, Una, Vera, Rebecca and Rosemary lock themselves inside the factory, in the office of the company manager. The lock-in is a response to injustice, unfair work practices and increasing productivity demands, but it leaves all of the characters exposed in different ways. Their young male boss, Rohan, and their male union representative, Bonner, are the oppositional characters. The males serve as agents of a general masculine rule, whether it is Vera's husband who cannot manage sick children and tries to harass her into giving in, or the local priest who denies them their right to protest or to mass in the workplace. The women, despite the collective decision to occupy the building, are all very much individuals in their own right, ranging from the young Rosemary, to the elderly Ellen and Una. Vera has young children and Rebecca remains single. Rebecca's lesbianism is not made explicit but there are a number of references to it throughout.

Fundamentally, it is a play of protest by strong women with a range of emotions, responsibilities and desires. Ellen, by the play's end, sheds her position of dominance and is replaced by Rebecca as the group leader. There is no realist solution to the dilemma of work and the emergence of cheap international labour and materials. Having occupied the building and having seen the responses from the people around them, a crisis point emerges. Do they quit or not? As tempers fray and indecisiveness becomes more apparent, the 60-year-old Una makes a remarkable statement: 'I don't know what it's like not to be beaten. What it's like to win. I don't know what it's like even to fight to win. And I want to know what it's like to stand your own ground to the bitter end. I'm staying.'[8]

As the play ends, the women embrace defiance. The fact that it is a collective moment and not individualistic is notable, as is the realization that protest is not a long-term sustainable option. *The Factory Girls* begins a cycle of plays set in confined, exposed, excluded, private narrative or fantasy spaces, whether they are work spaces, graveyards, hostage cells, war trenches or bourgeois family spaces that have constituted the location of most of McGuinness's recent work. Within what seems like relative or extreme confinement, the imagination is key to the broadening of the parameters of space and in generating a counter-reality or alternative consciousness that does not lose sight of the real. The result is fantastic rather than mawkish, expressive rather than naïve and confrontational more than simple.

Baglady (1985) (Peacock Theatre, directed by Patrick Mason) is a one-woman piece written for Maureen Toal, who played Ellen in the original production of *The Factory Girls*. There was something hugely brave about McGuinness's attempt to deal with sexual abuse in Ireland at that time. The play opens with the character, Baglady, on stage, who is de-feminized, dressed to disguise her body outline and of course to keep warm – she lives on the streets, and the play maps her coming to terms with incestual sexual abuse and the drowning of a child, borne of that abusive relationship. She narrates a story that really is a collage of fact and displaced fantasy, truth and deception. While revelation might deliver truth, this provides no real cathartic qualities. On the one hand, she fleetingly deliberates on the fact that she remained unbelieved, while on the other, she asserts her own over-responsibility. Her father promised her a wedding celebration, a long white dress, cake to eat and lemonade to drink. The implications of the promise and the abuse which followed become inseparable.

Because of Baglady's gender in particular, McGuinness had to ensure that there was a fundamental grounding to the circumstances of rape. The body is challenged to dispense its story. On the work of Marina Carr, Melissa Sihra raises the important issue of the 'conflictual resonances of the body and the "non-body" where the representation of interior

narratives, memory narratives, imaginative realms and exterior landscapes, constantly compete for authority'.[9] The Baglady's battleground
is mind and body; the obligation to balance sense and non-sense and
the need to free up the thought processes so that the trauma can be
processed. Ultimately, it is the physicality of the body which articu-
lates – hands, gestures and the introduction of symbols and props free
up the voice to demarcate the trauma. The process of acceptance is
a striking mix of adoration, disbelief, self-censorship, repression and
socio/political collusion.

Anne F. O'Reilly (Kelly) argues that: 'In an attempt to bury her
[Baglady's] past she makes a ritual pile (like a cairn) of all the objects....
The burial ritual becomes her marriage, as she piles her wedding dress
and ring on the pile.'[10] So by the play's end, she gains a level of control,
however temporary, which she did not have previously – 'They're dead
now, dead and buried. I buried them. I married them.'[11] Here Baglady
re-enacts the ceremonial rite with the words 'with this ring, I thee wed.
This gold and silver, I thee give. With my body, I thee worship...'.[12]
Instead of a ring being placed on her finger for life, she removes
the ring from her finger, which symbolizes ultimately her perverse
loyalty to the oppressive violation of her father. Her final word as she
drops the ring is 'Drown'.[13] McGuinness creates a genuinely complex
female character, who uses ritual to engage and to disentangle, who
uses mask to disguise and misrepresent, and who uses language in a
profoundly complex repetitive way in order to fashion a type of realization. Her fragmentary understandings and her unsettling self-revelations
do not cohere into a complex and profound understanding. They are
mere stepping-stones that only more consistent deliberation and reflection can fuse. Moreover, he needed to capture the circuitous route
towards sophisticated admission, without generating any sense of easy
or vicarious reward for either the character or an audience.

In *Innocence* (1986) (Gate Theatre, directed by Patrick Mason) the
self-destructiveness and murderous instincts of the creative artist Caravaggio are altered not only by carnivalesque transgressions, but are also
transfigured by gender. By the end of the play, Lena, his partner of
sorts, has taken over the mantle of artist. The world is upside-down:
'*Lena*:...I knew then somehow we'd won, we turned the world upside-
down, the goat and the whore, the queer and his woman.'[14] Inspired,
she, who had served previously as a model for Caravaggio, sculpts an
image. I do not think that McGuinness is saying that she could not
create without him. It is their cross-connection or cross-fertilization
which is vital and urgent. Regardless, she is in part gender dependent

on a strained masculinity to generate the pathway. Lena is a model for him but also a mother figure. She nurtures and takes care of him, wipes his wounds, protects him from himself. Yet she is more than that. The spirit of transgression at the core of the artist's work is in a sense the shared reality between them, only that he is the one who constructs the images – of which she is part as she modelled for his paintings, while also being a force of renewal, sustenance and generation. Creativity can disinhibit. Their legacy is the eternity of his art and she is part of it. It is well known that Caravaggio used people within his own circles to model for him and he brought a groundness to religious paintings that unnerved his patrons.

Cast-wise, with *Carthaginian* there is for the first time, numerically, something approaching gender parity, that is, if we exclude the plays, *Borderlands* (1984) and *Gatherers* (1985) written for Team Theatre, the educational theatre company. In *Carthaginians* (1988) (Peacock Theatre, directed by Sarah Pia Anderson) the male and female characters are all locked into the grieving reflex that was brought about by Bloody Sunday, 30 January 1972, when British soldiers shot 14 people dead on the streets of Derry, during a civil rights protest march. The repressive sensibility and the inability to initiate the grieving process mean that almost all of the characters are locked into patterns of denial, repetition and self-destruction. Dido, a younger, exuberant homosexual male, so named after the classical figure from *The Aeneid* by a Lebanese sailor, has not undergone the same types of trauma. Meala, has lost her daughter to cancer, Greta has had a hysterectomy, Sarah has turned to drugs and prostitution in Amsterdam; their interactions with the world have a strong interpersonal dimension. For the male characters, activities seem more political first and personal second. The three women characters gather in a graveyard, believing that the dead will rise. The force which tentatively initiates recognition and change is the encounter that the characters experience while enacting Dido's playlet, *The Burning Balaclava*. On one level Dido's work is pathetically sentimental on many fronts, but because it confronts the events of Bloody Sunday through a carnivalesque framework, some mobility in thought, sensation and comprehension kicks in. Of course, their waiting has the intensity of pilgrimage, but the carnivalesque frame complements the ritual. Not only does such a playlet contain absolute requirements of cross-dressing and transformations in terms of gender, the doubling of characters and key symbolic images from the carnage of Bloody Sunday, but it is presented by Dido, under the pseudonym of Fionnuala McGonigle (F McG . . .).

Here then is an additional complication of gender roles and of the allocation of autonomy and authority. Dido's own name has overt echoes with the historic, mythic figure of Dido; second, within the play, it is a marker of Dido's sexual orientation; and third, it is about the transformation through gender and accent that can bring release. Fionnuala, who is notionally French, has written a play out of solidarity with the dispossessed. Dido's gender dexterity and its ambivalence offer a great deal of potency and disorientation. Ultimately, it is the transgender qualities that Dido brings which initiate change. Questions then, of course, need to be asked about the feminization of masculinity and the implications of it. Second, the mobility of Dido within the play's frame must also be considered, as must the fact that none of the female characters seem to have the same type of transformative possibility, locked as they are into patterns of self-justification and denial. Likewise, none of the women characters seem to have access to such misrule or *misalliance*.

From here, McGuinness's next major project was *Mary and Lizzie* (1989), (RSC, directed by Sarah Pia Anderson), a play about the two Burns sisters who lived with Frederick Engels, industrialist, writer, colleague and financial supporter of Karl Marx. Not only do the sisters hold their own in impressive company, but they aggressively contest gender and racial stereotypes and objectification. History had also expunged their presences from the great Marx/Engels narrative, and through the fantasia frame offered to McGuinness by his adaptation of Henrik Ibsen's *Peer Gynt*, he establishes multiple realities and lenses through which to interrogate class, gender and race relationships. The play deals with women across space and time, from the women of the camps in Ireland in the middle of the nineteenth century, awaiting the arrival of British soldiers to the women of the camps in Russia under communist rule, from the underworld where they encounter their dead mother to meetings with Queen Victoria (played by a man) by the seaside. That way, gender is mislocated across spatial and temporal continui, grounded both in the real and the fantastic, leading to multiple perspectives and a disorientation of coherence. The two sisters both have a sexual relationship with Engels, which becomes obvious when they perform a sexual act on him in the home of the Marx's. Fundamentally, the Burns sisters thrive on an aggressive stubborn streak, making them confrontational, caring, truthful, loyal and sincere, and bawdy, sexually predatorial and exhibitionistic. In this play the women have a full range of emotions and actions, within the given circumstances of their lives. It is the male characters who cannot access the higher metaphysical dimensions, locked in as they are to the material world, despite their historical importance.

The Bird Sanctuary (1994) (Abbey Theatre, directed by Robin Lefevre) continues on from *Mary and Lizzie* in that the female characters dominate the male ones, leaving them almost in silence. The play is set in Booterstown, Co. Dublin, in the Henryson family home, currently occupied by Eleanor, a painter and recluse. Eleanor is painting the Booterstown Bird Sanctuary, because if she does not, 'it will be lost' to global warming and to the planners who want to build a road through the sanctuary.[15] Ultimately, this play, like most dramas of Chekhov and Ibsen, builds towards symbolic resonance, in a way that justice, recognition or redemption is facilitated, leaving a quasi-realism in their wakes. McGuinness opts for the heightened symbolism of the Bird Sanctuary and how the characters invest in such symbolism as the governing consciousness, placing it beyond logic and beyond a simplistic moral grid. In the play, Eleanor's sister, Marianne, agrees not to sell the home, if Eleanor performs a destructive act. Marianne says: '...Kill her. You have the power. Witchcraft. Kill her, and you can keep this house. For life' – the 'her' being Marianne's husband's Tasmanian mistress.[16] Act Two opens with Eleanor dressed in black, dismembering a chicken carcass and wrapping the bones with thread and breaking bread and pouring wine over the bones, before combining the bones to make a cross.

Upon the announcement of the death of Marianne's husband's mistress, Handel's *Hallelujah Chorus* is played in celebration. As the play ends, the five characters re-enact the wedding ceremony of Stephen and Maria Regina, father and mother to Eleanor and her siblings. Eleanor asks Marianne to close her eyes and to imagine the finished painting of *The Bird Sanctuary*. The painting is conjured theatrically as the set opens to reveal its beauty. Marianne appropriates the symbolism temporarily, but it is left to Eleanor to elaborate upon it at a deeper level. A new beginning is there for the sisters to grasp, and the past must be left behind. Acceptance based on truth and frailty, evil and endurance is what matters. Here in this play, Eleanor, who is bi-sexual, wears not only the mantle of artist, but also that of performer. Through the imagination, she paves the way for difference and for hope for her family. Yet, she also, if we are to read the play on the level of realism, summons the darkness to kill. That is the ambivalence McGuinness is seeking, and women in this instance have both the capacity for dark and deviant play, as much as access to the existential debate. If Caravaggio can stir up ghosts in his nightmares, then Eleanor can bring death through black magic.[17]

Mutabilitie (1997) (Royal National Theatre, directed by Trevor Nunn) is formally indebted to the five-act Shakespearean form. Set in the late 1590s it tells the story of the wars of Munster and the relationship between two rival communities, the colonial English led by the renowned poet Edmund Spenser and his wife, Elizabeth, and the Irish ruled by the mythic Queen Maeve and her partner, King Sweeney. The wonderfully vibrant character 'File' or poetess (so well played by Aisling O'Sullivan in this first production) imagines that redemption will take the form of a man emerging from a river. When the playwright/poet character called William, and obviously Shakespeare (whom McGuinness creates as a closet Catholic), is found floating in a stream, he is cast as that figure. Neither he nor an uprising brings advantage.

Both File and her husband, Hugh, use disguise, theatricality and stealth to position themselves inside Spenser's fortress and from there, they hope to assist the rebellion. The play itself opens with two actors from William's company expressing comical misgivings about touring policy. However, as the play progresses the female characters possess a fundamentally more threatening and ambivalent response to performance. The daughter of the king, Annas, who also has an incestuous relationship with her brother, Niall, has a bond with one of the English prisoners of war, Richard, and only then, on the advice of File, betrays him and accuses him of an attack of which he is innocent. This leads directly to his death. Spenser's *The Faerie Queene* honours his virgin Queen, and in that fantasy and majesty, idolatry and projection conspire. However, his wife, who also shares the same name as his Queen, is beyond the stereotype of the notional feminine. Her rage is toward the Irish, who are in her words 'vermin', 'animals' and 'savages'.[18] Spenser's colonialism is propped up by the usual suspects, law, custom and religion: 'We must win this people to England's laws, to England's custom, to her religion. If we fail, then we abandon this people to the devil.'[19]

File, according to William, has the guile and 'the strength of a man'.[20] Further, she tells a story about how her child has died, which is contradicted by Hugh's account. He claims that she murdered her infant child with her bare hands in order to avoid detection from some passing soldiers, as they lay in hiding. Again, brutality is not gender specific. File is learned in law, languages, maths, astronomy and poetry, medicine and magic. Such magic is deemed evil by William. Revenge makes the heart brutal, as File acknowledges. File and Edmund fall under William's magic spell. William incites File to summon 'an ancient quarrel', the Fall of Troy. She summons from a dark space the Irish to perform it: 'Dreams ye dared of dark desires/ Forged in passion's funeral pyres.'[21]

The women's chorus challenges with: 'Chaos of change that none can flee/ This earth is *Mutabilitie*.'[22] Spenser has a vision of rebellion and carnage. By the play's end the Spenser household is burned down, not as the historical facts would have it, but by the hand of Spenser himself. Resolution of sorts comes out wandering from the woods. The Spensers' lost child is to be either hostaged or fostered. The latter results. The play concludes with File's invitation to the child to drink milk and eat.

Dolly West's Kitchen (1999) (Abbey Theatre, directed by Patrick Mason) is set in McGuinness's home town of Buncrana during World War Two, in the West household. A whole series of relationships develop and adjust over time, between Dolly West and Alec Redding, a British army officer; Esther Horgan (formerly West), and her husband Ned; Justin West, a member of the Irish army, and Marco Delavicario, an American soldier; and between Jamie O'Brien, another American soldier and Anna Owens, the West family maid. Rima West, the matriarch, leaves her mark on all of the relationships, provoking matters until issues are raised and dealt with. David Cregan argues that 'Rima functions as a catalyst for the disruption of sexual categories, as she forces a confrontation with desire in the personal lives of all three of her children.'[23] Cregan sees that as part of 'McGuinness's sexual identity project'.[24] Rima brings Marco home as a 'bit of badness', knowing that her son is hiding his sexual orientation.[25] Performativity takes the form of Marco's occasional high-camp sensibility and Rima's willingness to avoid all social decorums and manners. She says what she likes in whatever crude a fashion she desires. She challenges the conventions of her son's Nationalism. By the play's end, the war is over, Rima is dead. Dolly takes over Rima's role after her death, provoking Esther and Ned to conceive a child, in a way that her mother would have approved. Esther has relinquished the chance to be with Jamie, facing up to the pain of such a decision. Anna will go to America with Jamie, knowing of his greater interest in Esther, she needs to get away at all costs. She buys into that compromise. Justin and Marco wish to be with each other. Whilst sharing lamb, wine and bread the following exchange takes place:

Alec: Is the war over, Dolly?
(Justin, Marco, Anna and Jamie raise their glasses.)
Dolly: I hope so.
Justin: For richer or poorer – in sickness and in health – till death us do part.
Alec: Is the war over?
Dolly: I said I hope so.[26]

Not only has the breaking of bread and wine a strong Christian association, there is an attempt to merge this with matrimonial vows. Further,
Dolly can only offer closure through the expression of hope and not
certainty. Elizabeth Butler-Cullingford argues that McGuinness 'leaves
the outward structure of both the matrimonial and homosocial tropes
of union intact, but he radically transforms their content. Dolly is his
attempt to employ the marriage paradigm in the service of peace and
national reconciliation.'[27]

III

Across the body of McGuinness's work there is close to being as many
women as men in his plays. The plays are testimony to the ways
males and females relate, persuade, negotiate between genders and
across genders, the manner by which they exclude and how they might
conceive of and pursue connections. Ultimately, the gender of characters is a significant issue for audiences and an even more substantial
issue for scholarship. Across his work, not every male has access to the
transformative potential of the mask, nor every female, and characters
of both sexes have and have not access to the existential debate. The
misogyny of the males in *Observe the Sons of Ulster Marching Towards
the Somme* (1985) is countered elsewhere. What should be contested is
the notion that the playwright, unless he or she builds in some critical
framework that contests such failings, is condoning by duplicating the
prejudices of the greater First World order. Theatre has some relationship
to the Real, but reality is not its only characteristic. The imagination is
vital. As Edward Bond argues, the imagination is not free from ideological corruption as 'modern society does not own imagination, it only
exploits it'.[28]

In his 'Introduction' to *Plays 2*, McGuinness acknowledges that: 'At
the hearts' core these plays centre around rituals and the need to
disrupt ritual.'[29] The spirit of transgressive disruption is what McGuinness seeks, denying expectation, reversing genders, inverting truths.[30]
Indeed, many of his female characters, like his male homosexual characters, are best at doing it. They talk, they act, they accuse and they
pervert expectations and norms. But there are gender differences. What
the female characters, whether heterosexual, homosexual or bi-sexual,
seldom have, however, is access to the same levels of sexual desire. This
is perhaps a type of containment that Leeney talks about. Clearly, female
sexual desire is not as licensed, like that of Caravaggio in *Innocence*, and
only Mary and Lizzie Burns can be considered as sexually expressive or

assured. Also notable is the inclusion of many women that either have lost children or cannot have them. There are few women with living offspring, which taps into a different anxiety. Thus there is a dramaturgical unwillingness in this regard.

Those caveats aside, McGuinness's women characters express complex, ambitious and ambivalent deeds, needs, thoughts and emotions as much as his male characters. Grief, fear, regret, resolution, intensity, frivolity, madness and ambivalence can be seen across all of the plays. Love, hate, depth, insincerity, vengefulness, resignation, purposefulness, action and cowardice are also part of the emotional complexity of the dramas. As Mary in *Mary and Lizzie* states, 'You make it up as you go along.'[31] Greta in *Carthaginians* affirms that she is 'waiting for a miracle'. Later she adds: 'I want myself back.'[32] O'Reilly advises that 'The colonization of the female body either as a site for male meaning or carrier of repressed aspects of the cultural unconscious must be addressed by theatre audiences and practitioners.'[33] Like his male characters, his female ones, whether they are homosexual or heterosexual, working class or middle class, poetesses or bagladies, painters or shirt-makers, respond to the circumstances of their lives, to situations that are and are not of their own making. To these challenges there may well be solutions, but sometimes this is not the case. Then, subjectivity is a luxury, and agency is not so much about choices, but antagonism, resistance, the subversion of expectation and not giving in. In *The Factory Girls*, the women have, in terms of their work, everything to lose but collectively, the need to express their resistance through apparently doomed protest. By so doing, they raise the action of the play on to a higher level of consciousness, whereby their deeds are not about the immediate or the material, but about the collective and broader responsibilities of community.

In an interview, McGuinness acknowledges that his characters could not afford themselves the luxury of being victims.[34] That statement is a great insight into the mechanics of his characters. Agency is the ultimate luxury in a McGuinness play. More often than not, his endings are shaped by the collective rather than by individual journeys of the characters. In a way, when circumstances are not of the characters' own making, then it is easy to see why McGuinness finds solutions or endings that are not of their own doing themselves. That is the luxury he grants them. His disposition is to bring something else positive or not expected into the frame, some form of improvised consciousness, rooted in mutual and mutable desire, but not necessarily radiating from or anchored in the real. Thus he repositions his plays within colonized frameworks, and reasserts discourses of defiance, excess and objection.

Across McGuinness's work, subjectivity for either gender is never fixed or coherent, but split, fragmentary, provisional. More importantly, collectivity is of greater substance than subjectivity and functions as a counter to otherness. McGuinness's characters are not isolated and self-focused, but they play together. By so doing, they find solutions or resolutions, and it is the collective exuberance of play that delineates them as much as their gender; simultaneously, there is corporeality, desire and perversion in play, as well as an inauthenticity that embraces the immediate, disintegration, endurance and the vague and vagrant value of a ludic, free-floating nothingness – and if that is not metaphysical, nothingness is.

Notes

1. Mary Trotter argues that: 'Female characters provide the protagonist with emotional support, a source of conflict, or as sexual interest, but the real attention in the family memory drama centers on the patrilineal relationships.' See 'Translating Women into Irish Theatre History', in Stephen Watt, Eileen Morgan and Shakir Mustafa (eds), *A Century of Irish Drama: Widening the Stage* (Indiana: Indiana University Press, 2000), p. 165.
2. Anna McMullan argues that in Irish iconography, 'women have been associated both with the homeland, as Mother Ireland, and with the domestic space, particularly the kitchen. In the Irish theatrical canon women often figure a lost, damaged or barren home/land/womb – the Mother in Murphy's *Famine* or Sarah in Friel's *Translations*'. See 'Unhomely Stages: Women Taking (a) Place in Irish Theatre', in Dermot Bolger (ed.), *Druids, Dudes and Beauty Queens: The Changing Face of Irish Theatre* (Dublin: New Island, 2001), p. 72.
3. Lynda Henderson, 'Men, Women and the Life of the Spirit in Tom Murphy's Plays', in Jacqueline Genet and Wynne Hellegoarc'h (eds), *Irish Writers and Their Creative Process* (Gerrards Cross: Colin Smythe, 1996), pp. 88–90.
4. Anne F. Kelly, 'Bodies and Spirits in Tom Murphy's Theatre', in Eamonn Jordan (ed.), *Theatre Stuff: Critical Essays on Contemporary Irish Theatre* (Dublin: Carysfort Press, 2000), p. 160.
5. Cathy Leeney, 'Ireland's "Exiled" Women Playwrights: Teresa Deevy and Marina Carr', in Shaun Richards (ed.), *The Cambridge Companion to Twentieth-Century Irish Drama* (Cambridge: Cambridge University Press, 2004), pp. 150–63.
6. Anna McMullan, 'Masculinity and Masquerade in Thomas Kilroy's *Double Cross* and *The Secret Fall of Constance Wilde*', *Irish University Review: A Journal of Irish Studies*, Vol. 32, No. 1, Spring/Summer, 2002, p. 132.
7. Cited by Margaret Llewellyn Jones, *Contemporary Irish Drama and Cultural Identity* (Bristol: Intellect, 2002), p. 115.
8. Frank McGuinness, *Frank McGuinness: Plays One* (London: Faber & Faber, 1996), p. 84.

9. Melissa Sihra, 'Renegotiating Landscapes of the Female: Voices, Topographies and Corporealities of Alterity in Marina Carr's *Portia Coughlan*', in Brian Singleton and Anna McMullan (eds), *Performing Ireland: Australasian Drama Studies Special Issue*, Vol. 43, October 2003, p. 24.
10. Anne F., O'Reilly, *Sacred Play: Soul Journeys in Contemporary Irish Theatre* (Dublin, Carysfort Press, 2004), p. 30.
11. McGuinness, *Plays One*, p. 398.
12. McGuinness, *Plays One*, p. 399.
13. McGuinness, *Plays One*, p. 399.
14. McGuinness, *Plays One*, p. 284.
15. Frank McGuinness, *Frank McGuinness: Plays Two* (London: Faber & Faber, 2002), p. 293.
16. McGuinness, *Plays Two*, p. 289.
17. Helen Lojek distinguishes between McGuinness's female and male artists. See *Contexts for Frank McGuinness's Drama* (Washington: The Catholic University of America Press, 2004), pp. 135–6.
18. Frank McGuinness, *Mutabilitie*, (London: Faber & Faber, 1997), p. 8.
19. McGuinness, *Mutabilitie*, p. 10.
20. McGuinness, *Mutabilitie*, p. 4.
21. McGuinness, *Mutabilitie*, p. 75.
22. McGuinness, *Mutabilitie*, p. 78.
23. David Cregan, ' "There's Something Queer Here": Modern Ireland and the Plays of Frank McGuinness', *Performing Ireland: Australasian Drama Studies Special Issue*, Vol. 43, October 2003, p. 70.
24. Cregan, in *Performing Ireland: Australasian Drama Studies Special Issue*, p. 70.
25. McGuinness, *Plays Two*, p. 208.
26. McGuinness, *Plays Two*, p. 263.
27. Elizabeth Butler-Cullingford, *Ireland's Others: Gender and Ethnicity in Irish Literature and Popular Culture* (Cork: Cork University Press, 2001), p. 76.
28. Edward Bond, 'Modern and Postmodern Theatres', in an interview with Ulrich Koppen, *New Theatre Quarterly*, Vol. 50, May 1997, p. 103.
29. McGuinness, *Plays Two*, p. ix.
30. This is very close to Richard Schechner's work on the idea of dark play. See *The Future of Ritual: Writings on Culture and Performance* (London and New York: Routledge, 1993), p. 36.
31. McGuinness, *Plays Two*, p. 26.
32. McGuinness, *Plays One*, p. 350.
33. O'Reilly, *Sacred Play*, p. 313.
34. Quoted in Eamonn Jordan, *The Feast of Famine: The Plays of Frank McGuinness* (Bern: Peter Lang, 1997), p. ix.

8

Dead Women Walking: The Female Body as a Site for War in Stewart Parker's *Northern Star*

Rachel O'Riordan

> So when the big issues come to be decided, you see, we get cast in the same old roles again. Mothers, wives and mistresses. Goddesses, whores and sisters. Trophies and symbols. The Shan Van Vocht and Roisin Dubh.[1]

In the plays of Northern Irish dramatist Stewart Parker the female body becomes the medium through which issues of history, representation and loyalty are explored. Parker's dramaturgy plays with conventional realism, where women are almost shape-shifters. They can transcend boundaries of time and space, both physically – as with Lily in *Pentecost* (1987) and the Phantom Bride in *Northern Star* (1984), and metaphorically as with the fluid and inclusive thinking of Mary Bodle in *Northern Star*. Women characters in Parker's plays, whether alive or dead, ghostly or real, challenge the entanglements of sexuality, myth, heritage and politics. Stewart Parker was born in Belfast in 1941 and attended Queen's University where he was an integral part of a vibrant group of young writers which included Bernard McLaverty and Seamus Heaney. Parker wrote extensively for radio and television but it is as a playwright that he is most widely recognized. *Northern Star* was written in the later stages of a career beginning with *Spokesong* (1975) and culminating in *Pentecost*, which he wrote the year before his death in London in 1987. The first part of a triptych which includes *Heavenly Bodies* (1986) and *Pentecost*, *Northern Star* premiered at the Lyric Players' Theatre, Belfast in 1984, in a production directed by Peter Farago, featuring Gerard McSorley as Henry Joy McCracken and Emer Gillespie as Mary Bodle.

Parker's theatre continually examines the place and time of its construction. In the foreword of *Northern Star*, he writes: 'Plays and ghosts have a lot in common. The energy which flows from some intense moment of conflict in a particular time and place seems to activate them both.'[2] Actor and director Stephen Rea observes that Parker has 'an unavoidable preoccupation with the travails of Northern Ireland' which permeates the subject, narrative and construction of his work.[3] This preoccupation with place and history is explicit in *Northern Star*, which is set in '*Ireland, the continuous past. A farm labourer's cottage on the slopes of the Cavehill outside Belfast.*'[4] The action takes place after the 'botched birth' of the 1798 rebellion and centres upon the night before the leader of the United Irishmen, Henry Joy McCracken, is hanged. The action moves between 'present time' and McCracken's past with comrades such as Wolfe Tone, and the 'rebels' in Peggy Barclay's pub. Despite the fact that McCracken was a United Irishman, part of a band of men committed to social and political change, Parker emphasizes in this play how his primary relationships are with his lover, Mary Bodle, and his sister, Mary-Anne, both of whom are with him on this, his last night.

Northern Star is a seven-strophe pastiche of a history play, using real figures from Northern Ireland's past juxtaposed with imaginative theatrical devices such as the figure of the Phantom Bride and the ghost-widow of Mary Bodle's cousin, O'Keefe, a character who we never meet but who, it is suggested by Mary, angered the fairies who then punished him by death. These otherworldly figures provide a dramaturgical link between Ireland's mythic past and McCracken's present. Parker says of *Northern Star*: 'Ancestral voices prophesy and bicker, and the ghosts of your own time and birthplace wrestle and dance, in any play you choose to write – but most obviously when it actually is a history play.'[5] The three women who surround McCracken on his last night resonate on social, historical and imaginative levels and are corporeal sites for the war that is happening in Ireland; between past and present (Phantom Bride), between myth and logic (Mary Bodle) and between politics and the individual (Mary-Anne).

Parker begins *Northern Star* with an iconic image – Mary Bodle is singing and rocking a crib, bathed in moonlight. This is the archetype of romantic 'Mother Ireland', a cultural representation found in the earlier lyrical creation of *Róisín Dúbh* (Dark Rosaleen) and in W. B. Yeats's and Lady Gregory's *Kathleen ni Houlihan* (1902). The sexual politics of this iconic anthropomorphism of Ireland as woman are intimately connected to Nationalism and also to colonialism, where the British 'rape' of the island, the taking of it by force, results in an assumption of feminized victimhood and potential, frighteningly justifiable revenge. Edna Longley writes: 'While Virgin-Ireland gets raped and pitied, Mother Ireland translates pity into a call to arms and vengeance. ... Traditionally, it is her sons whom Mother Ireland recruits and whose *manhood* she tests.'[6] The female body that has become the recognized image for Ireland is surprisingly specific and consistent. She usually has long, dark hair, high cheekbones and blue eyes. This image of ideal beauty has so permeated the Nationalist consciousness as a marker of identity that it is frequently found on Republican murals in Belfast and Northern Ireland. This feminized corporeal ideal and its 'ancestral voice' is explored throughout *Northern Star* – transposed by Mary Bodle on to the male body of McCracken: 'The love of your family isn't enough. My love isn't enough. You want the love of the whole future world and heaven besides. All right, go ahead, let them love you to death, let them paint you in forty shades of green on some godforsaken gable-end!'[7]

Mary Bodle and Mary-Anne McCracken unify the thematic structure of *Northern Star*, where the similarity of the women's names interconnects Catholic and Protestant, as well as the roles of lover and sister. In Mary Bodle we see the visceral, earthly woman, in Mary-Anne, the cerebral mind, and in the Phantom Bride, the spirit. These women are all elements of the battle to unify past and present within Ireland, in turn represented by McCracken. Mary Bodle, the lover, is able to connect Ireland's traditional superstitions with the hard facts of her and McCracken's actual situation and says of the army: 'Brute men the like of that, imagine it – bloodshed and butchery every day of their lives – and the sight of O'Keefe's promised bride is enough to reduce them every one to whingeing like wee boys.'[8] In the presence of both the 'real' and ghostly female bodies in the play, the impossibility of escaping the 'ancestral voices' – for McCracken – is highlighted and explored. In the Phantom Bride, the dead woman walking, Parker presents a female figure who can transcend time itself; she is not bound by linear structure or by law. The Phantom Bride's power is such that: 'They say any man that looks her straight in the eye is a dead man.'[9] She is shown to be dangerous if directly confronted, but that confrontation is necessary. Parker negotiates a path through the seemingly contrasted energies of the two genders, and deploys the Phantom Bride to link them, dramatically and conceptually. Mary Bodle and Mary-Anne are more capable than McCracken of confronting both metaphorical and actual pain. McCracken says to Mary, after their rough love-making in Act One: 'I must have hurt you. I didn't mean to.' Mary replies: 'We don't hurt that easy. We're a lot tougher than men.'[10] Mary-Anne McCracken's resolutely forward-thinking attitude recasts mythic Ireland from a female perspective, and dismisses its poetic past more thoroughly than her brother. Mary Bodle is easy with myth and poetic thinking, with the 'Old Ireland' of warrior queens, fairy forts and devils. She is also pragmatically aware that without masculine presence the house is safer for McCracken, and it is in this female 'safe-house', with his lover, visited by his sister and protected by the Phantom Bride, that McCracken spends his last night. McCracken acquiesces to this: 'Protected by the Phantom Bride. So be it. For one last night. That's very quaint. A quaint way to go for the Man of Reason.'[11]

Northern Star is full of references to the female body, birth and land. McCracken tells Mary of the political efforts of the United Irishmen: 'We botched the birth, Mary. The womb may never come right again. Christ knows what hideous offspring it may bring forth from this day on.'[12] Here Parker distils the traditional emblematic image of Ireland as woman to the essence of the female, the womb. He also acknowledges the danger inherent in the romanticized female Ireland – she is presented as something almost sinister, spawning 'monsters' in a birth 'botched' by men. Here, McCracken is not assuming a misogynistic stance, but rather Parker gives the speech a guilty, culpable tone, showing the dangers of such associations.

McCracken is presented as an iconic figure in whom the traditional Catholic/Protestant contestation for land, power and control is located as he struggles to reconcile his political and social ideologies with his humanity and masculinity. McCracken speaks of the romantic Ireland which has been performed throughout history:

> Haven't we always been on a stage, in our own eyes? Playing to the Gods. History, posterity. A rough hard audience. Thundering out our appointed parts... A bunch of wet-lipped young buckos, plotting how to transform the world from Peggy Barclay's back room. Ballads and toasts, toasts and ballads. Speechifying. Pub talk. Declarations and resolutions of this, that and the other, I'd no patience with it all, I wanted to be up and doing.[13]

McCracken wants to be a part of the action, away from the feminized 'back room' of romantic history. His phrase 'up and doing' expresses urgency and attack. McCracken has no time for the songs and the stories of the old Ireland and wants to escape what he sees as the smothering womb of Ireland's mythic past. His description of 'wet-lipped young bucko's' is redolent of sexual desire – young men slavering and lusting over a plot from the motherly safety of Peggy Barclay's interior.

McCracken wants no part of this emasculatory dynamic, where talk replaces action.

Parker highlights the proximity of the sex/violence urge in the male by repeatedly juxtaposing images of McCracken's sexual activity and fertility with those of his impending death. In Act One McCracken asks of his and Mary's illegitimate daughter: 'Is the child asleep yet?' and Mary replies, 'She's dead to the world.'[14] Later McCracken says: 'One last night with you Mary, that's the gift I cherish...it's not sleep I want. It's your thighs around me.'[15] And after the army narrowly fails to arrest McCracken, Act Two opens with the couple having made aggressive love.[16] As McCracken's hanging comes ever closer, their relationship becomes more overtly sexual. The play contains many such juxtapositions suggesting that the sexual urge is close to the urge of violence (and death), and where politics and rebellion are continually channelled through the image of Ireland itself as a female body. Indeed, the 'male' action, the potential hanging, is set against the 'female' image of the crib from the very beginning of the play. Parker's stage directions read: *'There is a bed on one side of the loft, and a child's crib on the other. A length of rope is coiled round the massive main roof beam, just above the stair well.'*[17] The positioning of the rope between the bed, suggesting sex and procreation and the crib suggesting life, is deliberate. Death is imminent. The reality of McCracken's situation is always present in the minds of the audience as he cannot escape the facts of what he has done. The rope is a metaphor for law, order and discipline, shortly to be meted out by men.

McCracken's attempt to invent a new Ireland, one with a new simplicity of vision is stymied by the old order, the ancestral voices, the myth and magic and the old hurts and grief. In a highly imagistic speech, which shows Parker's subversive representation of a newly born nation, McCracken says:

Irish animals unite. Unite! Let the natural sons come into their inheritance. Catholic Protestant Dissenter, one big mongrel family, that was it. The new idea. And we were meant as its midwives...except that we botched the birth, you see, arse over tip, up to our oxters in bright red blood, the misshapen foetus scrabbling feebly away at the face of death, and the mother howling her entrails out, with the ring of logical faces round her, all concerned, all at a loss, mine amongst them, Henry Joy McCracken, fanfare please, Commander-in-Chief of the United Irish army of the North, brave croppy boys....[18]

The image of men 'logically' watching the woman/Ireland 'howling her entrails out' with the product of her labour a misshapen and feeble foetus, places the iconographical maternal body at the very centre of the play. Woman becomes a site for war and political battle, and is subject to the penetrative male voice and gaze. Indeed, the image Parker draws here is redolent of rape – a united group of men stand around watching a woman in extremis; they are passive, cold and distant, voyeuristically observing the pain that they have caused.

Confrontation occurs in the play when, with Mary Bodle singing in a kind of accompaniment, the Phantom Bride physically forces McCracken to acknowledge the past that he has, through politics and reason, tried to move away from by forcing her body on to his: '*She kisses him, and then, with a predatory leap, clamps her bare legs around his waist and her arms around his neck.*'[19] Here sex and death, past and present, myth and logic, and male and female are manifestly entwined, and the Phantom's aggressive sexual agency forces McCracken to both connect with the mythic past and confront his impending 'logical' death. Here, too, we see the male fear of woman/Ireland's potential vengeance that Parker acknowledges throughout the play. The Phantom's revenge is upon all men, any man, for the wrongs done to her – as will Ireland herself's be. As McCracken says: 'We never made a nation. Our brainchild. Stillborn. Our own fault. We botched the birth. So what if the English do bequeath us to one another some day? What then? When there's nobody to blame except ourselves?' [20]

The women in *Northern Star* are presented as sites for the destabilization of the conflicts and energies of Ireland's historical past. Parker's female characters frequently subvert emblematic images of Irish womanhood and Irish mythology, being fundamental to the conflict resolution which so permeates his work. Indeed, Parker's understanding of the importance of the positioning of the female voice and body on stage is vital to the re-examining of old arguments that his plays demand. In *Pentecost*, 74-year-old Lily, the Protestant matriarch, says: 'At least I never let myself down – never cracked. Never surrendered. Not one inch. I went to my grave a respectable woman … never betrayed him.'[21] Lily's self-sacrifice and sublimation of her own sexual desire for an English airman into a 'loyal' marriage becomes a medium for the sometimes embattled position of the male Loyalist voice. Like the Phantom Bride, Lily is a ghost, an 'ancestral voice' and she too occupies the transitional space between past and present. In Parker's plays women's bodies are shown to be fluid, free and are able to incorporate and absorb more than one time, place or concept. They are ghosting the island and the men – dead women walking, like the Bride and Lily; lovers, sisters, mothers and whores. Parker fills his plays with these 'spirits', their actual live-ness, or otherwise, less relevant than their resonances and voices.

Notes

1. Stewart Parker, *Northern Star*, *Plays: 2* (London: Methuen, 2000), p. 34.
2. Parker, *Plays: 2*, p. xii.
3. Stephen Rea, 'Introduction', *Plays: 2*, p. x.
4. Parker, *Plays: 2*, p. 3.
5. Parker, *Plays: 2*, p. xii.
6. Edna Longley, 'From Cathleen to Anorexia: The Breakdown of Ireland', in Angela Bourke et al. (eds), *The Field Day Anthology of Irish Writing, Volume V: Irish Women's Writing and Traditions* (Cork: Cork University Press in Association with Field Day, 2002), p. 404.
7. Parker, *Plays: 2*, p. 55.
8. Parker, *Plays: 2*, p. 51.
9. Parker, *Plays: 2*, p. 6.
10. Parker, *Plays: 2*, p. 51.
11. Parker, *Plays: 2*, p. 7.
12. Parker, *Plays: 2*, p. 8.
13. Parker, *Plays: 2*, p. 9.
14. Parker, *Plays: 2*, p. 5.
15. Parker, *Plays: 2*, p. 22.
16. Parker, *Plays: 2*, p. 51.
17. Parker, *Plays: 2*, p. 3.
18. Parker, *Plays: 2*, p. 8.
19. Parker, *Plays: 2*, p. 50.
20. Parker, *Plays: 2*, p. 81.
21. Parker, *Plays: 2*, p. 231.

INTERCHAPTER III: 1970–2005

Melissa Sihra

Since the 1970s immense social and cultural changes have taken place for women in Ireland, North and South. While a new energy emerged with the next generation of women who began directing, writing and acting in their own companies in the 1980s and 1990s, Irish theatre was undoubtedly dominated by men throughout the 1970s and 1980s. The period saw a significant consolidation of talent with the work of Brian Friel, Tom Murphy and Frank McGuinness. Derry-based Field Day Theatre Company, co-founded by Friel and Stephen Rea in 1980, aimed at creating a hypothetical 'fifth province' and was committed to exploring history, language and identity from both north and south of the border. With its exclusively male directorate, the company lasted for over ten years producing one (male-authored) play per year and touring the island. Under the general editorship of Seamus Deane, the company published the three-volume *Field Day Anthology of Irish Writing* in 1991, as well as pamphlets and plays. The elision of the traditions of women's writing in the anthology became immediately apparent. Nuala O'Faoláin states, 'while this book was demolishing the patriarchy of Britain on a grand front, its own native patriarchy was sitting there as smug as ever.'[1] As a result of this exclusion, fourth and fifth volumes, dedicated solely to women writers and edited by female scholars and writers, were published in 2002 – enabling the actual 'missing province' to finally manifest. While certainly going some way towards redressing the shocking lack of women writers from the first three volumes, the sense of tokenism remains and is synonymous with the broader marginalization of women in Irish political and cultural discourses.

The Irish Women's Liberation Movement (IWLM) and the inauguration of the First Commission on the Status of Women took up the fight for equal rights which had been begun by women in the earlier decades of the twentieth century. Women now vociferously challenged legislative restrictions on birth control, abortion and divorce, as well as demanding equal pay and education and the lifting of the marriage bar.

While the hierarchy of the Catholic Church began to be questioned in the Republic in the 1970s, at the same time north of the border political conflict erupted in what would turn out to be almost 30 relentless years of bloody violence between Protestant and Catholic communities. Feminism and women's rights were subsumed in Northern Ireland beneath the more immediate and visible realities of sectarian conflict. Bríd Rogers, who led the SDLP talks team during the Good Friday negotiations of 1997 acknowledged that 'the struggle for women's rights is in many ways comparable to the struggle for equality of rights between Nationalist and Unionist in Northern Ireland. The essential and often most difficult first step is to get society to recognize that there is a problem.'[2]

Senator David Norris, a key figure of the Gay Rights Movement in the Republic observes that, at this time, 'If you were not heterosexual, Roman Catholic and Republican, you were out of it, [and] women were ignored, as usual.'[3] Norris challenged the state in the European Court of Human Rights during the 1980s, resulting in the decriminalization of homosexuality in 1993. The first gay marriage on the island took place between two women in Belfast in 2006 and the Irish constitution is currently under review in order to accommodate gay civil union. The issue of contraception was hotly debated in the 1970s. According to the Papal encyclical *Humanae Vitae* (1968), birth control was strictly prohibited. Lobbying groups of women went to Belfast from Dublin on the 'contraception train' in the early 1970s, carrying back condoms and waving them at Gardaí. Major conflicts also occurred outside the *Dáil* (parliament) between liberal pro-choice activists and conservative forces such as the Society for the Protection of the Unborn Child (SPUC). Charles Haughey's Fianna Fáil administration was the first to approve legalized contraception with The Family Planning Act of 1979. This bill allowed married couples only to access contraception by prescription. While the restrictiveness of the bill was widely contested, the seeds of change were finally being sown even if in a limited capacity.

The authority of the Catholic Church began to recede in the 1970s. Pope John Paul II's visit to the Republic in 1979 can be seen as the last major flourish of Catholicism in Ireland in the twentieth century. 'Well-Woman Centres' were being set up to educate and provide services for women regarding their sexual health, and in 1985 contraception became available for the first time to over 18s after a referendum was passed by two votes to one. In 1986, the first divorce referendum took place, where a demographic split could easily be discerned between a minority pro-divorce urban population and a majority anti-divorce rural population. While issues of morality played a part in this outcome, the more pressing factor of land ownership was what swayed the rural population to vote against the bill. Divorce was finally legalized in the Republic after a less than one per cent majority in 1995, and abortion remains illegal despite the continued plea of younger Irish women to 'keep your rosaries off our ovaries'.[4]

Factors which contributed to the diminished power of the Catholic Church in the final decade of the millennium include the revelation in 1992 that the revered former Bishop of Galway, Eamonn Casey, fathered a son with an American woman. Once payments into her account from Church funds were proven, Casey escaped to South America, leaving the Republic reeling in his wake.[5] Similarly, the exposure of Fr Michael Cleary's violation of the vow of celibacy with his fathering of a child added to the break-down of faith. Conor Brady, former editor of *The Irish Times,* comments:

> The fall of Bishop Casey was a monumental event in Ireland. By comparison with what was later to emerge during the 1990s about clerical sex abuse of children, his offence was perhaps a venial one, and came to be regarded as such. But in its time and circumstances it was seen as a shocking revelation of the gap between what the Catholic Church preached and what some of its leading figures practised.[6]

The torrent of revelations and public tribunals relating to child sex abuse by members of the clergy in the 1990s certainly heralded an end of the Church's hierarchical control. In 1999 the State issued a formal public apology to all victims of clerical and institutional abuse and a Redress Board was set up to offer compensation with an overall estimated cost of 850 million euro.

By the close of the twentieth century Ireland had the fastest growing economy in the world. In November 1990 the liberal Labour academic and lawyer Mary Robinson was elected as the first female president in the history of the state. Robinson's election would have been unimaginable in the 1970s, and while this is more of a ceremonial than actively political office, her presence afforded a new focus on women's rights and roles within society. Robinson's passionate inaugural speech at Dublin Castle on 3 December 1990 famously addressed '*Mná na hÉireann* – women of Ireland', who, 'instead of rocking the cradle, rocked the system', marking a new atmosphere of confidence, visibility and energy for women in Ireland. In her first address as President, she stated: 'I want women who have felt themselves outside history to be written back into history.'[7] Extraordinarily popular, Robinson served two terms and then became

United Nations High Commissioner for Human Rights. She was succeeded in 1997 by Northern Irish Catholic Mary McAleese – another brilliant and articulate woman also with a legal and academic background.

In 1983, the year that Northern Irish playwright Patricia O'Connor died, Belfast-based Charabanc Theatre Company was co-founded by five out of work actresses – Brenda Winter, Carol Moore, Eleanor Methven, Marie Jones and Maureen McCauley. In a recent interview, Methven says: 'We were angry. We were very, very angry. . . . When I was eighteen and joined the profession I remember thinking, "At least I'll never be sexually discriminated against, because no man can ever take my job." What I didn't realize for about a year was that there just weren't any jobs for women.'[8] The company produced new plays between 1983 and 1995, in response to the lack of challenging central roles for women in Irish theatre. While initially enlisting the guidance of playwright Martin Lynch, the women soon tapped into their own writing abilities, producing some of the most exciting and vibrant theatre of the time. Charabanc's first play, *Lay Up Your Ends* (see Figure 6), looked at the

Figure 6   Brenda Winter, Eleanor Methven and Marie Jones in the 1983 Charabanc Theatre Company production of *Lay Up Your Ends*, Arts Theatre Belfast. Photo: Courtesy of Chris Hill Photography.

Belfast linen-mill workers strike of 1911. Mark Phelan points out that, '*Lay Up Your Ends* emerged from an innovative process of collective research conducted by all five actresses, which sought to restore the silenced voices of Belfast mill girls as a direct challenge to the patriarchal historiography that had subalterned them on the basis of their class and gender.'[9] The production was ground-breaking, not only in terms of the collaborative process that underpinned it, but in the way it merged the personal and the political from women's perspectives. Phelan observes, 'The bawdy badinage of the millworkers in *Lay Up Your Ends* explicitly connects the sexual and industrial economies as the women mock the way in which sexual reproduction and child rearing are conducted on the same principles of mass production that operate in the mills.'[10] In a scene between two mill girls, sexuality, commodification and reproduction are interwoven with the world of labour:

Florrie: Accordin' to Mary Galway, the mill trade's been fallin' off. They say there's too much pilin' up in the warehouse and they have to cut back on production.
Belle: (*Entering, having heard what the others were saying.*) That's what you should tell your Alfie, Ethna, next time he's lukin' his way w'ye – 'hey Alfie, the house's full, I'm cuttin' production!'[11]

Methven remembers how, on opening night, 'the audience queued from the door of the Belfast Arts Theatre down Botanic Avenue and around the corner to Lavery's Pub.'[12] With Marie Jones as Writer-in-Residence until 1990 the company produced 24 shows, playing in venues across the sectarian divide, touring all over the island, as well as performing in the United States and Russia to huge acclaim. Unlike Field Day, however, most of Charabanc's plays remain unpublished.[13] Christina Reid and Anne Devlin also began to write for the stage in the 1980s, but both women left Northern Ireland to pursue careers in England. Brought up in Protestant working-class Belfast, Reid's plays, *Tea in a China Cup* (1983), *Joyriders* (1986) and *The Belle of Belfast City* (1989), have won many awards and are critically and popularly acclaimed. Reid has been Writer-in-Residence at the Lyric Theatre, Belfast, and the Young Vic and her work has been produced for radio and television and her plays are published by Methuen.

In the 1970s feminist political activist Margaretta D'Arcy (1934–) co-authored, with John Arden, a number of plays which explore issues relating to Irish politics and colonialism, such as *The Ballygombeen Bequest* (1972), *The Non-Stop Connolly Show* (1975) and *Vandaleur's Folly*

(1978). D'Arcy began her career as an actress in Dublin and now lives in Galway. As well as conventional theatre, D'Arcy is interested in the subversive potential of public performance, such as street marches and other happenings, as alternative ways of instigating political intervention.[14] In Dublin, Glasshouse Theatre Company was co-founded in 1990 by producer Caroline Williams, director Katy Hayes, actor Siân Quill and writer Clare Dowling and produced ten shows up until 1996. The collaborative company was set up with an explicitly feminist agenda to explore issues relating to women's experience which, the founders felt, was unrepresented in Irish theatre. They observe:

> Ireland has never had an easy relationship with the feminist movement, and Irish theatre even less.... The lack of women playwrights meant that women's stories didn't get told.... And the scarcity of women producers and directors meant the decision-making process was overwhelmingly male dominated.[15]

As well as producing new plays by women (Emma Donoghue, Trudy Hayes, Clare Dowling), Glasshouse developed an archive project *There Are No Irish Women Playwrights! 1* and *2*, at the Project Arts Centre, 1992–93, which identified new playwrights and celebrated old. The first of these events presented extracts from works by contemporary playwrights such as Deirdre Hines, Geraldine Aron, Marina Carr and Anne Devlin, while the second focused on the period of 1920–70, 'from Kate O'Brien to Edna O'Brien'. A lack of funding and other commitments finally caused the company to call it a day.

Garry Hynes co-founded the Galway-based Druid Theatre Company in 1975, with actors Marie Mullen and Mick Lally. Hynes's talent for working with new writing and her ability to unlock the visceral energies of the stage-worlds of playwrights such as J. M. Synge and Tom Murphy soon emerged. Her production of Murphy's remarkable play *Bailegangaire* in 1985, a poignant expression of women's abandonment and marginalization on the cusp of modernity, remains a landmark moment in Irish theatre history. Hynes held the post of Artistic Director of the Abbey Theatre from 1991–94 and in 1998 she became the first woman in Broadway history to win a Tony Award for directing. During her tenure at the Abbey, Hynes programmed the work of then emergent playwright Marina Carr and subsequently directed the award-winning premiere of Carr's *Portia Coughlan* (Peacock, 1996) and *On Raftery's Hill* in 2000 (Druid/Gate). In 1984 director Lynne Parker co-founded the prolific Rough Magic Theatre Company. Funded by the

Figure 7 Olwen Fouéré in *Chair* by Operating Theatre Company in 2001. Peacock Stage. Photo: by kind permission of Amelia Stein.

Arts Council, the award-winning company focuses on the production of new work and a Literary Department was established in 2001. In 1995 Annie Ryan founded the highly successful Corn Exchange Theatre Company. Award-winning Actor Olwen Fouéré co-founded Operating Theatre, with Roger Doyle, in 1980 and continues to devise and perform ground-breaking physical and music-based theatre in works such as *Chair* (2001; see Figure 7). She also serves on the board of directors of the Abbey Theatre.

Teresa Deevy's 1936 drama *Katie Roche* was produced again in 1994, this time in the Peacock theatre, directed by Judy Friel, with Derbhle Crotty playing the eponymous character. Friel comments: 'When Patrick Mason, the Artistic Director of the Abbey Theatre, gave me the plays of Teresa Deevy to read I was surprised simply by the existence of another female Irish playwright in the first half of the century apart from Augusta Gregory. ... I found no published letters, no biographies.'[16] The performance genealogy of Deevy's play highlights issues of women's absence from main stages in recent history. Anthony Roche observes that the 1975 Abbey production of *Katie Roche* is 'an isolated incident, since there were virtually no concurrent production of plays by Irish women playwrights at the time. The context had not changed utterly by 1994 when Irish women playwrights were (and are) still the exception.'[17] In the centenary celebrations of the Abbey Theatre (2004) the work of female playwrights was completely absent from the main-stage. While Marina Carr's visual image was central in the publicity brochure, surrounded by a halo of male playwrights and Lady Gregory, *Portia Coughlan* was relegated to the smaller Peacock stage. It is astounding that Lady Gregory, author of over 40 plays and co-founder of the theatre, was not represented in any way during the centenary. Despite this, there are more women than ever before creating theatre on the island. Along with the proliferation of predominantly female students in the growing number of university Drama Departments, women are continuing to found companies in which they are Artistic Directors, serving on new and established boards, being appointed to senior artistic and executive roles in funded companies, working in senior positions in the academy, getting their plays published and produced, and designing and directing for the stage. There is still a long way to go, but much has been achieved, and the twenty-first century is an exciting time of possibility for women in Irish drama.

Notes

1. Nuala O'Faoláin cited in Diarmaid Ferriter, *The Transformation of Ireland, 1900–2000* (London: Profile Books, 2004), p. 26.
2. Ferriter, *The Transformation of Ireland, 1900–2000*, p. 657.
3. *Altered States (Part I): 'So Long Holy Ireland'*, RTÉ 1, 4 October 2005.
4. *Altered States (Part III): 'A Bitter Divorce'*, RTÉ 1, 25 October 2005.
5. Casey returned to Ireland for the first time since his disgrace in 2006 and has now retired.
6. Conor Brady, 'If you're wrong . . . the church will destroy *The Irish Times*', *The Irish Times*, Weekend Review, 8 October 2005, p. 1.
7. Kit O'Céirín and Cyril O'Céirín, *Women of Ireland: A Biographic Dictionary* (Galway: Tír Eolas, 1996), p. 5.
8. 'Eleanor Methven and Carol Moore (Scanlan) in Conversation with Helen Lojek', in Lilian Chambers, Eamonn Jordan and Ger Fitzgibbon (eds), *Theatre Talk: Voices of Irish Theatre Practitioners* (Dublin: Carysfort Press, 2001), p. 343.
9. Mark Phelan, 'Later Stages: Charabanc Theatre Company', Unpublished Lecture, Queen's University Belfast, 13 March 2006.
10. Phelan, 'Later Stages: Charabanc Theatre Company', Unpublished lecture.
11. Martin Lynch and Charabanc Theatre Company, *Lay Up Your Ends* (1983), Manuscript, Linen Hall Library, p. 15.
12. Chambers et al., *Theatre Talk: Voices of Irish Theatre Practitioners*, p. 343.

13. Many of Charabanc's plays are held in the Performing Arts Archive of the Linen Hall Library, Belfast. In Autumn 2006 Colin Smythe Ltd. Published *Four Plays by Charabanc Theatre Company: Reinventing Women's Work*, edited by Claudia Harris. The collection contains four plays, *Now You're Talking* (1985), *Gold in the Streets* (1986), *The Girls in the Big Picture* (1986) and *Somewhere Over the Balcony* (1987).
14. John Arden and Margaretta D'Arcy, *Arden/D'Arcy Plays One* (London: Methuen, 1991).
15. Caroline Williams, Katy Hayes, Siân Quill and Clare Dowling, 'People in Glasshouses: An Anecdotal History of an Independent Theatre Company', in Dermot Bolger (ed.), *Druids, Dudes and Beauty Queens: The Changing Face of Irish Theatre* (Dublin: New Island Press, 2001), pp. 134, 135.
16. Judy Friel, 'Rehearsing *Katie Roche*', *Irish University Review*, Vol. 25, No.1, Spring/Summer, p. 117.
17. Anthony Roche, 'Women on the Threshold: J. M. Synge's *The Shadow of the Glen*, Teresa Deevy's *Katie Roche* and Marina Carr's *The Mai*', *Irish University Review*, Vol. 25, No.1, Spring/Summer 1995, p. 143.

9
Women in Rooms: Landscapes of the Missing in Anne Devlin's *Ourselves Alone*[1]

Enrica Cerquoni

> Landscape is 'intrinsically *anexact*' for it escapes measurement; whatever escapes measurement must escape a quick and single definition as well.[2]

> Instead of writing what we remember, I'd like to write about what is missing. This writing [ha]s to do with being separated for the first time from the sounds of speech that made sense.[3]

I

Given the focus of this volume on the questions of women's authorship and representation in Irish drama since the beginning of the twentieth century, I intend to focus on the theatrical contribution of playwright Anne Devlin to the redressing of what Melissa Sihra refers to as the 'symbolic centrality and subjective disavowal' of women's place in Ireland.[4] The controversial theatrical project of identity-formation in early twentieth-century Ireland infringed upon notions of femininity and womanhood, masculinity and manhood. One legacy of this project is what Medb Ruane terms, 'The Cathleen principle', a gender heritage that has impinged on Irish theatrical expression ever since.[5] As Mary Trotter remarks, from Gregory's and Yeats's *Kathleen ni Houlihan* 'to McDonagh's virgin/whore "Girleen" in *The Lonesome West* (1997), Irish female characters have embodied the nation, the land, the desires or responsibilities of male characters, but rarely have they been authentic, complex, autonomous women'.[6] Devlin's play-writing exposes the omissions of such a theatrical cartography – in her plays 'the disappeared are the key'.[7] This exploration of Devlin's aesthetic of the disappeared concentrates on her first play *Ourselves Alone* (1985) and, more specifically, on two aspects of the play's dramaturgical topography: the contentious onto-ideological site of the room, and the women char- acters' positions of visibility and invisibility, outsideness and insideness within this ambivalent hosting structure.

The notion of the 'room', the signpost of theatrical realism, is central in Devlin's dramaturgy in both *Ourselves Alone* and *After Easter* (1994).[8] In *Ourselves Alone* women are confined within physical and ideological rooms, but carve out more permeable rooms of inner existence. The inner spaces of the female protagonist of *After Easter* form the play's dramaturgical constituency; yet the room is still Greta's point of depar- ture. Before starting the play's quest, Greta touches the walls of the room she is in and, significantly, says: 'Goodbye, room'.[9] The dramat- urgical status of the room, and its ideological significance in relation to women's subjectivity in *Ourselves Alone*, is what this chapter seeks to explore.

II

Anne Devlin was born in 1951 on the Grosvener Road beside the Falls Road in Belfast to a socialist father and a Catholic mother, and when she was 12 the family moved to Andersonstown. Devlin has lived in England since 1976 and now lives in London. She writes:

> I feel that I'm not at home in Ireland and I'm not at home in England, in the sense of where I should be and who I'm writing for. I have this feeling that I go to places for a while and then I move on.... What I'm saying is that I have to keep moving – it's as if I can't put down roots, history won't let me. I do have a sense of a real absence of roots, but I think that's not just my experience.[10]

The importance of place, of departures and returns, of journeys away, marks all her work. *Ourselves Alone* was written after she had left Ireland and moved to England, yet, as Devlin admits, 'in my head I was still there, and so I was creating the sounds that I needed to hear, and they were women's voices.'[11] In between *Ourselves Alone* and *After Easter*, in 1989, Devlin co-wrote *Heartlanders* with Stephen Bill and David Edgar. This community play, which was commissioned by the Birmingham Repertory Theatre to celebrate Birmingham's centenary, was produced with a cast of over 100 performers under the direction of Chris Parr. In *Heartlanders* the notion of being an outsider shapes the process of play-writing, as each main character is a particular outsider within the city of Birmingham. This proliferation of passages, this being in-between places finds a correspondence in the multimediality which features in Devlin's play-writing; she has extensively written and adapted pieces for different artistic media, such as theatre, television, radio and cinema. In 1986 she published a collection of short stories, *The Way-Paver* (Faber), some of which have been adapted for television. Devlin has won several awards, among which are the Hennessy Literary Award for her short story *Passage* (1982) and the Samuel Beckett Award (1984), and in 2004 she was Writer-in-Residence at Trinity College Dublin.

III

Devlin remarks: 'When I first came to England I found myself completely removed from the sounds, from the voices that I had been used to hearing....'[12] In her imagination and in her dreams, however, she has taken them with her: 'I am continually trying to leave Ireland and longing to go back. It is both a tyranny and a privilege.'[13] Writing a play becomes a way of dramatizing that metaphysical loss, that absence, that which she is missing, diasporically and ontologically. *Ourselves Alone* is 'an acoustic landscape' and hearing familiar sounds is part of her attempt to reclaim and repossess.[14] Devlin's complex act of play-writing is, borrowing from Peggy Phelan's definition, 'toward disappearance, rather than ...toward preservation'.[15] By placing ghostly moments of memory, moments of absences, moments of hearing instead of seeing, Devlin points to what is left out of the frame of theatrical representation, to its blind spots, and uses that absence to generate the ontology of lost aspects of subjectivity, that which 'becomes itself through disappearance'.[16]

Devlin's ephemeral dramatization of disappearance, of an invisible yet audible consciousness, starts paradoxically within rooms, the most traditionally concrete structures of containment in theatrical representation. The room has been central in the gender history of European theatrical expression, especially since the latter part of the nineteenth century. In the Irish theatrical context, this ambiguous three-walled space, be it a cottage kitchen, a living room or a bedroom, is a contentious metonym for the gendered nation. This fictional construct has been seminal in enabling and upholding the unbalanced gender architecture at the basis of the notion of theatrical nationhood and in projecting on to its female occupants a non-constituent subjectivity, a curtailed and enforced identity of enclosure and regulatory domesticity. If the silent ghost of woman's subjectivity haunts the room, so does the mute spectre of woman's consciousness. In order to search for those sound-less blanks of disappearance, Devlin's theatrical imagination journeys through the uncomfortable, painful space of the room, and goes beyond the limitations of its representational reality and realist legacy.

The room, as textual trope and visual image, is complicated in *Ourselves Alone*. Actual mimetic locations – the club, Donna's house, John McDermott's flat, a Dublin hotel room, the Botanic Gardens in Belfast – are interspersed with nocturnal worlds, through verbal *tableaux* and dreamscapes, which juxtapose parallel life stories of woman's inter-iority. If stage directions set the play in physical rooms, word-scapes and dreamscapes elude them and disclose different scenic possibilities. Because of this intersected matrix of outward and inward spaces, the play's spatial core is unlocatable and in perpetual motion, floating in an unmarked space between box rooms and fluid, excessive sketches of memory and streams of consciousness. Within realistic rooms of invis-ibility and oppressiveness, poetic rooms of the soul lie concealed.

IV

Ourselves Alone developed out of the lack of women's voices and presences within the rooms of the English theatrical landscape. Co-premiered in 1985 at the Liverpool Playhouse and at the Royal Court in London, *Ourselves Alone* was commissioned by the then artistic director of Liverpool Playhouse, Bill Morrison, in order to create parts for women performers. The play addresses a further absence by focusing on the forgotten world of women in post-hunger-strike Northern Ireland. The co-production was directed by Simon Curtis and designed by Paul Brown, with Hilary Reynolds as Frieda, Bríd Brennan as Josie and Lise-Ann McLaughlin as Donna. The seven male roles were interestingly divided among four male performers; Mark Lambert played Gabriel and Liam and Adrian Dunbar performed John McDermott and Cathal O'Donnell, while John Hewitt played Malachy and Liam de Staic was in the role of Danny. The doubling of performers in the male roles in this production prompts a reflection on the interchangeability of male char-acters in their exertion of patriarchal authority, notwithstanding their different ideological affiliations. The following year this co-production toured to Ireland and played at the John Players Theatre as part of the Dublin Theatre Festival. *Ourselves Alone* was published in 1985 by Faber & Faber and won the Susan Smyth Blackburn Prize and the George Devine Award, both in 1985. The play has been widely produced in the United Sates (Washington, Chicago, Los Angeles) and in Europe

(Germany and The Netherlands).[17] Notwithstanding the achievements of *Ourselves Alone* in England, Ireland, the United States and Europe in the mid-eighties and in the early nineties, the play is still a blind spot of invisibility and inaudibility in Belfast, and also at the Abbey Theatre in Dublin, the National Theatre of Ireland, where none of Devlin's stage plays have ever been produced.

The 'ourselves alone' of the title translates literally into English the Irish 'Sinn Féin', title and political project of the Nationalist Party in Ireland, connected to the Irish Republican Army. The play reveals the political meaningfulness and gender-inflection of the phrase, pointing toward that which is missing and redressing it in women's terms, as the play focuses on the controlled lives of three women in Northern Ireland's Catholic West Belfast during the early 1980s. Thus, as Alisa Solomon argues, 'the play inverts the militant mantra, not only by using it to describe three women, but three women who are constrained, dismissed, left behind, even beaten by male heroes of the cause.'[18] If the play is set mainly in 'rooms' in Andersonstown, it also expands its national geography, as it spaces out to other rooms in Dublin, in South Belfast, in the Botanic Park. England is also indirectly on the play's map through the character of Joe Conran, a British agent disguised as Republican activist, and through Frieda's intention to move there at the play's close. The three women's voices in the play belong to Frieda and Josie, who are sisters, and to Donna, who lives with Liam, Frieda's and Josie's paramilitary brother, who is in and out of prison. Frieda, the 'funny' voice in the play, is a singer and song-writer who rejects any political activity; Josie, the 'serious' voice, is involved in the Republican movement; Donna, the 'voice of a woman listening'[19], incarnates the domestic centre of the play, offering tenancy and support to Frieda's and Josie's more nomadic lives. The play explores the stifled existences of these three female protagonists under the pervasiveness of patriarchy and points to 'how finally and intimately *alone* the women are'.[20] In this lack of expression and freedom, the women characters' 'small daily acts are the mode of resistance'.[21]

V

A layered aural texture counterpoints the exposed lives of the three women; cacophonic sounds such as dustbin lids, intermittently signalling internment, Frieda's scared footsteps, Donna's baby crying and the Chinese New Year celebrations can all be heard within the women's landscape. This complex grammar of off-stage sounds interjects with the grammar of on-stage images: it signposts displacement and alienation and 'is suggestive of equivalent presences: political-military, family domestic or merely contingent'.[22] The play's polyphonic composition incorporates mostly women's voices, striving to appear within the binding contours of the rooms which contain them. Frieda's first appearance, within the room of the Belfast Republican club, has to do with disappearance and invisibility, with the misuse of her singing practice, which performs phantom sounds and enacts a spectacle of pain, as her body's tempo is not tuned to the content of the Nationalist song. To be in line with the Nationalist, all-male subject-matter of the song *The Men Behind the Wire*, Frieda, as she is being told, has to 'work hard'.[23] The tempo moves against her body, as she attempts to incarnate ideologically determined lines from the musical canon available to her; such songs which completely 'eulogize men' and exclude women and their experiences.[24] Her female presence within the markedly male power structures of the dimly lit Republican club is one of 'outside-ness', of isolation, of controlled visibility. Although *'the surroundings are not so visible'*, the coordinates of hegemony are clearly perceivable; hanging on the walls are the black and white portrait-photographs of the ten – recently dead at the time of premiere – Republican hunger-strikers.[25] The 'masculinity' of history, authority and sacrifice is pitted against Frieda's resisting body. The sense of Frieda being occluded at a visual, emotional and expressive level is also actualized by her gradual loss of physical space in this scene as the club gets suddenly crowded with men, anticipating the physical and verbal violence she later experiences at her father Malachy's hands. Woman's fragile existence is constantly under patriarchal surveillance and the scene registers 'the effacement of the subject within a linguistic and visual field which requires her to be either the Same or the containable, ever fixed, Other'.[26]

A disciplining 'room' of invisibility and inaudibility imposed upon women in *Ourselves Alone* within their own community and culture takes different forms. When the father Malachy and his son Liam return to Donna's house, he completely ignores Frieda:

Liam: *(Starts suddenly at the sight of Frieda.)* What's she doing here?
Malachy: Who?
Liam: Frieda! She's standing right behind you!
Malachy: I don't see anyone.[27]

Frieda's lack of visibility within visibility, her being pushed off-stage on-stage, lays bare how the women become 'living contradictions to the political agenda and are frequently silenced, either by being shouted down, ignored or physically struck in the face'.[28] This scene is crucial in understanding the women's state of internal exile. Frieda's status of invisibility is not the only visual effacement within the gender economy of the room. Malachy's and Liam's return to Donna's house sets the scene for an altercation between them over Josie's impending mother-hood. Josie's pregnancy to Joe Conran, the revealed British agent who has betrayed the Republican organization, raises the spectre of mixed identity, and the loss of singularity emerges. Josie's split body, 'her two hearts'[29], reveals a rift between two generations of patriarchal ways of seeing within the Nationalist ideology; older Malachy, who wants to father Josie's child, and younger Liam, who wants Josie to have an abor-tion. The body of the mother, crossing threshold boundaries of iden-tities, '*breaks* the smooth symmetry of paternal linearity and inheritance, the myth of historical determinism and progression, and the consolation of a coherent nonfluctuating time...'.[30] At the end of the scene Josie metaphorically disappears; she goes acoustically missing once Liam's and Malachy's power struggle over the destiny of her unborn child is over. Josie, as the mother-to-be, as 'the traditionally mute body',[31] plays no part in the dispute over the patrolling of her own 'waiting' body. Josie's silent shadow circulates within the room from her brother Liam to her father Malachy, who claim the ownership of her body's past and future and ensure the continuity of it within family walls. Stage directions see Josie's verbal expression shifting from being '*in terror*' to '*hesitant*' before she finally withdraws into silence; then she is led away off-stage by her winner father-master, '*who begins to move through the room to the door*'.[32] When Donna calls her name, before she leaves, Josie does not answer, '*she does not turn around*'.[33] She remains eloquently silent: there is ambivalence in her mute body. According to Brendan MacGurk, 'Josie permits herself to be imprisoned within the patriarchal system she understands and despises.'[34] Her absence from the logos recalls surveillance; yet it could also be seen as, borrowing from Elin Diamond, 'the sound of historical pain, of contestation, of resistance'.[35] Josie has retreated, in that moment of absence, into the inner rooms of sleepwalking and fragments of memory, through which she moves back and forth throughout the play. Whether Josie will ever be back from these moments of gap between thoughts and words remains unknown.

On the surface, the play is set in physical rooms, but at a deeper level, it happens in subversive rooms of female existence, hidden from view. Frieda's poetic reminiscence in the play's concluding moment is one example of this deeper structure:

We three slipped off from the campfire to swim leaving the men arguing on the beach...and we sank down in the calm water and tried to catch the phosphorescence on the surface of waves...It was as though we swam in the night sky and cupped the stars between our cool fingers.[36]

The metaphysical realm of the sea, as a boundless room of the spirit, embodies for the three women a releasing space of physical and spiritual nakedness, which binds them together regardless of their disappointing experiences. Frieda's leap of poetic language moves the play to another level of experience, to a 'heterotopic'[37] realm, which, as Devlin remarks, is also 'the progress of the journey in *Ourselves Alone*'.[38] This quest towards the transcendence of experience as an absence from the representational real, from the restrictions of literal languages and actual spaces, is achieved in *Ourselves Alone* through the complexity and straining of the verbal forms of expression towards what Devlin defines as 'the elements of possibility'.[39] The disciplinary intrusion of male presence darkens the radiance of the scene:

And then they saw us. First Liam and then John, and my father in a temper because we'd left our swimsuits on the beach. And the shouting and the slapping and the waves breaking over us. We raced for cover to another part of the shore. We escaped into the shadows and were clothed again before they reached us.[40]

Frieda's inner life of phosphorescence is a moment of possibility which can just be lived through memory, 'the memory of it is all they have got to stay in them, they could not get there yet'.[41]

Word-scapes are also combined with shock tactics in a defamiliarizing Brechtian effect in order to convey ontological spaces of female absence. This is evident in the scene in which Frieda talks about Cora, Frieda's and Josie's disabled aunt:

Cora is blind and deaf and she has no hands, and she's been like that since she was eighteen. And Bridget, the other one, is a maid because she stayed to look after Cora. And I'm still a maid because I'm looking after both of them...she was storing ammunition for her wee brother Malachy – my father, God love him – who was in the IRA even then. He asked her to move it. Unfortunately it was in poor condition, technically what they call weeping. So when she pulled up the floorboards in her bedroom – whoosh! It took the skin

off her face. Her hair's never really grown properly since and look –
no hands! (*She demonstrates by pulling her fists up into her sleeves*).[42]

The use of wry humour functions as a subversive political tool in
performance to bring in the 'unrepresentable', the unseen, and destabilizes the sacredness of the image, while also facilitating the communication of the bleak and tragic subject-matter. Cora's reported symbolic
exposure at the head of public parades and marches, as a 'ghost that is
the phantom of no flesh',[43] powerfully evokes the discrepancy between
masculinist ideology and women's (un)reality. Theatrical presentation
here succeeds in laying bare the operations of power, and the omissions
and divisions involved in the construction of womanhood within an
Irish historical and cultural context.

The inner 'langscapes' are first introduced in the text through Josie's
stage persona. The physical absence of her lover Cathal O'Donnell, a
member of the Republican organization, is metonymically replaced by
the image of shared intimacy between them, in which the bed 'is like
a raft and that room is all the world to us'.[44] The incorporeal room of
the bed allows for body-swapping and for the emergence of withheld
identities. Against the oppression of history and tradition, Josie can be
totally herself, but she can also cross her bodily subjectivity and become
somebody else: 'sometimes I am not even a woman. Sometimes I'm a
man, his warrior lover.'[45]

If the bed is a transformative space in Josie's account, it becomes a
haunting and haunted site in Donna's disturbing soliloquy about the
ghostly visions of the devil in her bed: 'The devil's back. He was lying
with his head on my pillow this morning.... I felt so sick at the sight of
him because I knew I didn't have the strength to struggle anymore.'[46]
Donna's verbal fragment of memory suggests that trauma 'is stored
in the body'.[47] This echoes Josie's fearful visions of a black figure –
a priest or a policeman and thus a force of masculine authority and
subjection – looming over her bed and recalls the watchful presence
of the two men in the interrogation scene. Devlin's manipulations of
visible and invisible rooms put forward the at once overt and hidden
state of surveillance of women, and the alienation and exclusion of
the female subject within dominant structures of self, language and
representation.

It is no coincidence that the role of somnambulist is assigned to Josie.
Sleepwalking is a liminal activity; the mundane world is invisible to the
somnambulist, whose body withdraws into an inward act of looking
which crosses thresholds of perception. In this borderline state, Josie's

trace of being, '*silhouetted in the doorway*' from another level of experience, is 'looking through her life for us. She'll be back in a minute.'[48]
Josie's nightly absences reflect the inability of her skin 'to house her
spirit';[49] however, they also envision moments of freedom and possibility, in which, to paraphrase Bert O. States, the being within Josie's
being is unlocked and the room marked 'subject' can be entered.[50] As
the control exerted on Josie's persona extends to the inside and outside
of her body, sleepwalking offers a fissure of absence, a liminal point,
'a space in which there is no ground, a space in which the (bare) feet
cannot touch the ground'.[51]

Indefinite realms of representational existence are epitomized in the
scene between Frieda and John McDermott in Belfast's Botanic Park,
with Frieda repeatedly '*looking skyward*' and '*running with her hands
outstretched...hands cupped*',[52] in an upward attempt to count and
catch leaves. This surreal atmosphere of intangibility, playfulness and
emotional intensity, which the image of the falling leaves engenders,
contrasts with the materiality and immanency of external interruptions
(police). Even though the scene is set outdoors, that outside space is
revealed as completely closed. As in the final monologue of the play,
Frieda's metaphysical flight of subjectivity outside confining rooms in
order to chase happiness – for every leaf 'you catch you have one happy
day next year'[53] – gets curtailed by sudden interferences. Imelda Foley
indicates how 'the innocence of any free female activity is obstructed
and pronounced aberrant, whether it be hair dyeing, catching falling
leaves, drinking wine or nude bathing.'[54] The scene epitomizes the inability of structures of representation and of society to house woman's
permeability of experience, 'her walking with The Invisible'.[55] It also
visualizes the play's journey to counter that impossibility. The scene
stages the condition of woman's being 'caught between her body and
her spirit' and of remaining exiled to both.[56]

Theatre practitioners stress the importance of this scene to their
concepts of the play. Mary Howard, who directed *Ourselves Alone* for
Strand Players in 1993 in Dublin, emphasizes how subtle changes in
lighting and the performers' bodies convey the metaphysics of the scene
and 'make present what is absent'.[57] She saw the scene 'not so much
as a fantasy, but as an interlude',[58] and decided to set it on a bare
stage, emptied of any naturalistic prop. The scene's movement towards
subversive dimensions of existence and of representation was captured
by other productions of the play, for instance in a Dutch-language
version by the Dutch company Theatre van het Oosten under the direction of Garry Hynes.[59] The production opened on St Patrick's Day at the

Theater aan de Rijn in Arnhem for the Irish Festival in The Netherlands in 1990. The symbolic visual texture of this scene significantly provided the conceptual image for the whole set of the play. The production maintained some realist elements; Jackie Fletcher, dramaturg and producer of this production, remarks how both she and director Hynes saw the play as essentially a realist piece; however, Hynes's visionary *mise-en-scène* broke the classical notion associated with realist interiors and rooms insofar as the whole stage floor rested not on a concrete ground but on 'a bed of leaves'.[60] Despite this key visual factor, the critical response, while expressing overall positive comments about Devlin's play, criticized the production for being too cautious with the play-text – 'for its realist *mise-en-scène*, reminiscent of the 1970s...'.[61] Fletcher's point deserves attention as it emphasises the diverse ways of seeing and perceiving inherent in different theatrical contexts and traditions: 'it is interesting that Anne Devlin has said that this production was the least realist in style. The production was criticized severely in the Netherlands because it was too realist. Realism has been rejected as thoroughly "old fashioned" in the very postmodern realm of Dutch theatre.'[62] Hynes's carpet of leaves removes the play from the visual entrapments and risks of strict realism, and the power of its subtextual surrealism emerges. The scenic presentation reveals the permeability of the bounded room; if the play happens in rooms, it also travels very much out of them.

Critics who have concentrated on the ostensibly realist 'limits' of Devlin's early play have failed to recognize the disruptive, surreal incisions mining the play's more external realist cartography. Insightful analysts such as Imelda Foley, Helen Lojek and Anthony Roche,[63] have acknowledged the play's contribution in foregrounding women's experiences and values, but detect a certain absolutism and separatism in the thematic and formal development of that subject-matter, which maintain gender categories as rigidly dichotomized. Foley, among them, identifies 'moments of *écriture feminine*...a submerged potential [which is] stifled and asphyxiated by patriarchy'.[64] Addressing the question – can a realist play be a feminist play? – their interpretations fail to see how the vital challenge of the play lies in its articulation of loss and in its reaching out to the 'other', to the erased from the apparatus of representation.

Phelan's and Diamond's illuminating studies prove that realist and feminist practices in theatrical representation are not mutually exclusive.[65] Late nineteenth-century realism, the patriarchal form *par excellence* of theatrical expression, can be dismantled from within. What Diamond defines as 'the drama of "ourselves in our situation"' exists only by repressing other selves, other situations.[66] Devlin's 'inner rooms' envisage an alternative kind of dramaturgical composition, within the bending bones of realism, yet are resistant to it. The verbal memorials, nightmares and trance-states in *Ourselves Alone* embody an aesthetic quest for opening up realist practices so as to accommodate and express the multi-dimensional visions of women playwrights and the complexities of their female characters in theatrical representation.

In *Ourselves Alone*, women characters as hearers and seers traverse walled rooms and dimensions of experience. Positioned between dreamscapes and reality, between an inner free zone and an outer zone of surveillance, the liminality of their consciousness calls forth an ambiguous invocation of representational mimesis. Here the realist frame of the room of existence is *anexact* and begins to lose recognizable boundaries, in which 'we may begin to inhabit the blank without forcing the other to fill it.'[67] *Ourselves Alone*'s innovative vision develops two plays in one; a play 'without', whose surface designs of visibility take place in the inherited rooms of theatrical realism and naturalism, and a play 'within', whose deeper textures of invisibility rupture the more external framework and occur in the boundless rooms of woman's absence and loss, of her inner existence, of her disappeared realms of the self, of her imagery. Devlin's border aesthetic of rooms and female ontology, deploying a complex, expanded and hybrid notion of realism disrupts the seams of conventional realism and demonstrates that there can be many forms of realism. Her transgressive, radical refigured realism of discontinuity is a form in flux, which can break the certainties of a saturated, outmoded realism and question its ideologies, thus opening up wider and transformable rooms of history, identity and experience.

Notes

1. For this chapter I wish to express my deepest gratitude to Anne Devlin for her generosity, inspiration, kindness and patience. I also wish to thank Jackie Fletcher for kindly communicating with me about aspects of her work as dramaturg and producer in a Dutch production of *Ourselves Alone* directed by Garry Hynes for the 1990 Irish Festival in Arnhem, The Netherlands. My thanks to Mary Howard, who directed *Ourselves Alone* for Strand Players in Dublin, 1993, for patiently discussing with me her directorial choices. I also wish to thank Cathy Leeney and Eric Alexander for providing me with information and translations of Dutch reviews of the above production. My thanks also to Jennifer Armstrong and Mike Wilcock for their comments on an early draft of this chapter.
2. Edward Casey, quoted in Una Chaudhuri and Elinor Fuchs (eds), *Land/Scape/Theater* (Ann Arbor: The University of Michigan Press, 2002), p. 2.

3. Anne Devlin, 'Writing the Troubles: Talks by Glenn Patterson, Anne Devlin and Colm Tóibín', in Brian Cliff and Éibhear Walshe (eds), *Representing the Troubles: Texts and Image, 1970–2000* (Dublin: Four Court Press, 2004), pp. 15–27 (pp. 19–21).

4. Melissa Sihra, 'Renegotiating Landscapes of the Female: Voices, Topographies and Corporealities of Alterity in Marina Carr's *Portia Coughlan*', *Australasian Journal of Drama Studies*, Vol. 43, 2003, p. 19.

5. Medb Ruane, 'Re/Dressing Cathleen: A Local Perspective', in Jennifer Grinnell and Alston Conley (eds), *Redressing Cathleen: Contemporary Works from Irish Women Artists* (Chestnut Hill, MA: McMullan Museum of Art, Boston College, 1997), pp. 11–17 (p. 11).

6. Mary Trotter, 'Translating Women into Irish Theatre History', in Stephen Watt (ed.), *A Century of Irish Drama: Widening the Stage* (Bloomington: Indiana University Press, 2000), pp. 163–78, p. 164.

7. Anne Devlin, '*After Easter*', Unpublished Lecture, 8 April 2004, University College Dublin.

8. *After Easter* was first produced by the RSC at The Other Place in Stratford-Upon-Avon, directed by Michael Attenborough with stage design by Francis O'Connor, with Stella Gonet in the lead role as Greta. It was first staged in Northern Ireland at the Lyric Players Theatre in Belfast in November 1994, directed by Bill Alexander, designed by Stuart Marshall with Jeananne Crowley as Greta.

9. Anne Devlin, *After Easter* (London: Faber, 1994), p. 8.

10. Anne Devlin, 'About That: Irish Plays, Bill Morrison, Anne Devlin, Conor McPherson', in *State of Play I: Playwrights on Playwriting*, ed. David Edgar (London: Faber, 1999), pp. 96–9, (p. 96).

11. Devlin, in *State of Play I: Playwrights on Playwriting*, p. 97.

12. Devlin, in *State of Play I: Playwrights on Playwriting*, p. 97.

13. Catherine Walsh, 'Eulogy to a Lost Generation', *The Irish Times*, 25 September 1986, p. 12.

14. Devlin, in *State of Play I: Playwrights on Playwriting*, p. 97.

15. Peggy Phelan, *Unmarked: The Politics of Performance* (London: Routledge, 1993), p. 148.

16. Phelan, *Unmarked: The Politics of Performance*, p. 146.

17. USA premiere in Washington at the Arena Theatre in 1987, directed by Les Walters. In Chicago it played at the Bailiwick Theatre in 1988, under the direction of Kyle Donnelly. In Los Angeles the play was produced at the Tiffany Theatre, Sunset Boulevard, in 1989, and was directed by Donna Deitch. The German production at the Schauspielhaus in Hamburg in 1987 was directed by the Brechtian theatre director Peter Palitzsch.

18. Alisa Solomon, 'Challenging Rhetoric', *Village Voice*, Vol. 42, 1992, p. 92.

19. Anne Devlin, 'Author's Note', *Ourselves Alone* (London: Faber, 1985).

20. Brendan MacGurk, 'Commitment and Risk in Anne Devlin's *Ourselves Alone* and *After Easter*', in Eberhard Bort (ed.), *The State of Play: Irish Theatre in the Nineties* (Trier: Wissenschaftlicher Verlag Trier, 1996), pp. 50–64 (p. 51).

21. Esther Beth Sullivan, 'What is "Left to a Woman of the House" When the Irish Situation Is Staged', in Jeanne Colleran and Jenny S. Spencer, (eds.), *Staging Resistance: Essays on Political Theatre* (Ann Arbor: The University of Michigan Press, 1998), pp. 213–28 (p. 221).

22. Peter Denman, 'The Complexities of Being Irish', *Irish Literary Supplement*, Vol. 6, 1987, p. 18.
23. Imelda Foley, *The Girls in the Big Picture: Gender in Contemporary Ulster Theatre* (Belfast: The Blackstaff Press, 2003), p. 76.
24. Foley, *The Girls in the Big Picture*, p. 77.
25. Devlin, *Ourselves Alone*, p. 13.
26. Phelan, *Unmarked: The Politics of Performance*, p. 158.
27. Devlin, *Ourselves Alone*, p. 86.
28. Anthony Roche, *Contemporary Irish Drama: From Beckett to McGuinness* (Dublin: Gill and Macmillan, 1994), p. 237.
29. Roche, *Contemporary Irish Drama: From Beckett to McGuinness*, p. 79.
30. Phelan, *Unmarked: The Politics of Performance*, p. 128.
31. Tania Modleski, 'Some Functions of Feminist Criticism, or the Scandal of the Mute Body', *October*, Vol. 49, 1989, 3–24 (p. 15).
32. Devlin, *Ourselves Alone*, p. 88.
33. Devlin, *Ourselves Alone*, p. 88.
34. MacGurk, in *The State of Play: Irish Theatre in the Nineties*, p. 59.
35. Elin Diamond, *Unmaking Mimesis* (London and New York: Routledge, 1997), p. xiii.
36. Devlin, *Ourselves Alone*, p. 90.
37. For the notion of 'heterotopia', see Michel Foucault, 'Of Other Spaces', *Diacritics*, Vol. 16, 1986, 22–7.
38. 'Anne Devlin in Conversation with Enrica Cerquoni', in Eamonn Jordan, Lillian Chambers and Ger Fitzgibbon (eds), *Theatre Talk: Voices of Irish Theatre Practitioners* (Dublin: Carysfort Press, 2001), p. 109.
39. Jordan et al., *Theatre Talk: Voices of Irish Theatre Practitioners*, p. 109.
40. Devlin, *Ourselves Alone*, p. 90.
41. Anne Devlin, Personal Interview, Dublin, 15 February 2001.
42. Anne Devlin, Personal Interview, Dublin, 15 February 2001.
43. Jacques Derrida, 'The Double Session', in *Disseminations*, trans. Barbara Johnson, (Chicago: University of Chicago Press, 1981), pp. 173–226 (p. 206).
44. Devlin, *Ourselves Alone*, p. 16.
45. Devlin, *Ourselves Alone*, p. 17.
46. Devlin, *Ourselves Alone*, p. 53.
47. Roberta Curlberston, 'Embodied Memory, Transcendence and Telling: Recounting Trauma, Reestablishing the Self', *New Literary History*, Vol. 26, 1995, pp. 169–95 (p. 180).
48. Devlin, *Ourselves Alone*, p. 35.
49. Phelan, *Unmarked: The Politics of Performance*, p. 10.
50. Bert O. States, 'The Phenomenological Attitude', in Janelle G. Reinelt and Joseph R. Roach (eds), *Critical Theory and Performance* (Ann Arbor: The University of Michigan Press, 1992), pp. 369–80 (p. 370).
51. Phelan, *Unmarked: The Politics of Performance*, p. 153.
52. Devlin, *Ourselves Alone*, pp. 64, 66.
53. Devlin, *Ourselves Alone*, p. 67.
54. Foley, *The Girls in the Big Picture: Gender in Contemporary Ulster Theatre*, p. 89.
55. Phelan, *Unmarked: The Politics of Performance*, p. 10.
56. Phelan, *Unmarked: The Politics of Performance*, p. 10.
57. Mary Howard, Personal Interview, Dublin, 19 May 2005.

58. Mary Howard, Personal Interview, Dublin, 19 May 2005.
59. The theatre group Theatre van het Oosten is now called Toneelgroep Oost-pool.
60. Anne Devlin, Unpublished Interview, Dublin, 15 February 2001.
61. Dirkje Houtman, 'In Irish Political Plays People Suffer, Weep and Scream', *Trouw*, 23 September 1990, p. 8. See also Marian Buijs, 'Suffering Women in Irish Tribal Wars', *Volksant*, 20 March 1990 and an anonymous review, 'Solid Play by Devlin on Feeling and War', *Gelderlander*, 19 March 1990.
62. Jackie Fletcher, email, 23 March, 2005.
63. See Foley, *The Girls in the Big Picture: Gender in Contemporary Ulster Theatre*; Lojek, 'Difference Without Indifference'; Roche, *Contemporary Irish Drama: From Beckett to McGuinness*.
64. Foley, *The Girls in the Big Picture: Gender in Contemporary Ulster Theatre*, p. 89.
65. See Phelan, *Unmarked: The Politics of Performance*; and Diamond, *Unmaking Mimesis*.
66. Diamond, *Unmaking Mimesis*, p. 7.
67. Phelan, *Unmarked: The Politics of Performance*, p. 33.

10

Staging the Liminal in Éilís Ní Dhuibhne's *Dún na mBan Trí Thine* (The Fort of the Fairy Women is On Fire)

Anthony Roche

Critical discussion on the place of women in Irish drama has increasingly found value in the concept of the liminal as an in-between space, as neither here nor there. The most obvious reason is that the accepted canon of Irish theatre in the past century has been virtually an all-male preserve. Even when a woman is an active (and produced) playwright, as was Lady Gregory, critics often sideline this activity in favour of her social functions – in Gregory's case, representing her as facilitator of men's creativity in the role of chatelaine of Coole Park and/or of producer at the Abbey Theatre. Ironically, many of those male-authored plays at the Abbey, by Synge and Yeats in particular, dramatically foregrounded a socially marginalized woman – such as Nora Burke in Synge's *In the Shadow of the Glen* (1902). Plays like *Shadow* and Yeats's *The Land of Heart's Desire* (1894) pointed beyond the confines of the country cottage for a young woman oppressed by marriage to a zone of potential freedom. That space of possibility was frequently imbued with the trappings of folklore.

Far from being rejected as outmoded, these concepts have been taken on, refashioned and taken further by contemporary Irish women writers. This is particularly the case with women writers in the Irish language, who have a more direct and knowledgeable access to the folklore than many of the writers of the Revival. The writer who is the subject of this chapter, Éilís Ní Dhuibhne, combines the roles of a scholar of folklore in the Irish language, in which she holds a PhD and on which she has published professionally, with that of creative writer in both languages across a range of novels, short stories and plays. Her drama *Dún na mBan Trí Thine* was staged by the Irish-language theatre company Amharclann de híde [Theatre of Douglas Hyde] at the Peacock Theatre in 1994 in a production directed by Kathy McArdle. The play draws on the folklore of the Otherworld, that place of caprice and of sensual fulfilment where aging is suspended, to stage the crisis of its 40-something heroine Leiní, a wife and mother who is struggling to be an artist.

In its depiction of Leiní's lifestyle in 1990s Ireland, as she engages with her husband Eoin and children Sinéad and Timí or discusses contraceptives ('coiscín') with her best friend Áine, the play is resolutely contemporary and realistic. But that contemporary realism is only one of the several theatrical modes employed. For *Dún na mBan Trí Thine* works through juxtaposition. It disrupts chronological succession by moving between the present and the nineteenth-century past and displays a lack of spatial fixity in its fluid transitions from the modern environment to the timelessness of the dún na mban (or fort of the fairy women). Central to this feminist exploration of the social roles of women in a society caught between tradition and modernity is the changeling, the folklore belief that the ordinary mortal has been replaced by a disruptive fairy creature in their place and shape. This concept of doubling indicates profound unease on the part of a patriarchal society with aberrations from the social norm, with the behaviour of women and children who do not conform (and women and children were most often those taken 'away' by the fairies). The concept of the liminal is explored through both the language and the staging of Ní Dhuibhne's play to address such pressing contemporary issues as the treatment of children and the proper object of women's creativity.

In the early 1980s the Irish-language poet Nuala Ní Dhomhnaill published an extraordinary sequence of poems centred on the traditional Otherworldly figure of 'bean an leasa' (the woman of the fairy mound) erupting into the daily life of a contemporary woman. Nor did the 'bean an leasa' do so as a supportive member of a feminist collective; her impact was threatening and chaotic. In the poem 'An Crann' ('The Tree') the fairy woman arrives armed with a chain-saw:

> Do tháinig bean an leasa
> Le Black + Decker,
> Do ghearr sí anuas mo crann.
>
> (The woman of the fairy mound came
> With a Black and Decker
> She cut down my tree.)[1]

Part of the poem's shock effect is the placement of a modern English brand name for a technological device in the traditional and rural context of an Irish fairy narrative. Ní Dhuibhne has some of the same fun placing such English brand names as 'Hoover' in an Irish linguistic setting. But the most extended run of English in the play comes from a self-help manual which her friend Áine gives her and which contains the following mantra, which Leiní is encouraged to recite: 'I am thin. I am beautiful./ I am really happy.'[2] The initially ironic tone in which these lines are spoken by Leiní itself undergoes a change. The linguistic poverty of what is on offer is indicated by the English. But as she takes on the recitation and Áine leaves, Leiní translates the lines into Irish, 'Táim tanaí, táim go hálainn, táim sona sásta' (p. 88) and moves across the stage away from the restrictions of the home. The self-help manual may bespeak a contemporary cultural and spiritual dearth, a need which is tied up with the issue of female self-empowerment and which leads Leiní in the direction of the Otherworld.

Ní Dhomhnaill makes an important cultural point about the difficulties inherent in representing the Otherworld in relation to the two languages of Ireland: 'it is a concept of such impeccable rigour and credibility that it is virtually impossible to translate it into English, where it all too quickly becomes fey and twee and "fairies-at-the-bottom-of-the-garden".'[3] These difficulties were encountered by the English language dramatists of the Revival. In Yeats's *Land of Heart's Desire*, the arrival of a Fairy Child to take the heroine away to a place where 'nobody gets old and godly and grave' has just those qualities Ní Dhomhnaill describes.[4] The play does not follow Mary Bruin to that place; instead, she dies and her aspiration is as likely to seem delusional. When he sought to stage the direct encounter between the living and the dead in the Otherworld, Yeats lacked any precedent in the English theatrical tradition and instead turned to the Japanese Noh. Synge, when he visited the Aran Islands, heard many narratives hinging on the return of the dead or disappeared to visit those they had left behind. He draws on these stories for the mother Maurya's account in his play *Riders to the Sea* (1902) of the vision she has had at the well of her dead son Michael, resplendently arrayed and riding a horse. But Michael's ghost does not stalk the stage, and neither of her daughters credits Maurya's vision.

The play of Synge's most relevant to Ní Dhuibhne's is *In the Shadow of the Glen*, since both centre on a woman trapped in an unsatisfactory marriage and both dramatically hinge on an exotic outsider who appears to offer an Otherworldly prospect, of escape and heightened sensual awareness. As the playwright Denis Johnston once astutely remarked, in Synge's plays as distinct from Yeats's the tramp has replaced the fairies.[5] Ironically, Synge's tramp fears the fairies and wears a needle to keep them at bay. The play builds and develops sympathy for the plight of Nora Burke: married as a young woman to an old man out of economic necessity, she has had to endure not only her husband's rough treatment but a life of loneliness and frustration. The key moment is when Nora pauses in the doorway, to look back on the life she is leaving and turn to a more open prospect. As I have written elsewhere, the moment is a key one in Irish theatre, as 'the woman is poised on the threshold between the security of "in here" and the potential of "out there".'[6] The scene is liminal in two senses: with the woman who is the traditionally marginalized figure in the society moving to a position of dramatic centrality, and with the crossing of a threshold designed to symbolize her transition from one stage to another. When Nora exits both the house and the stage, Synge's play does not follow her; instead, it remains with the husband and the (former) lover, who settle down to have a quiet drink. Nor does she exit alone, as Ibsen's Nora had done, but in the company of the tramp.

Éilís Ní Dhuibhne's play is going to significantly revise all of this. What is immediately apparent is the ease with which the fairy women enter and exit the stage. This restores the comprehensive rather than bifurcated perspective of the folktales Synge heard in Irish on the Aran Islands, where the two realms exist in close and intimate connection with each other. The play's first scene stages the arrival of the fairy women at Leiní's door and their request to be given admission and some food to eat. Their appearance stresses not their likeness but their difference from the woman they are encountering: 'mná uafásacha le hadharca orthu' (terrible or horrible women with horns) (p. 75). Leiní deploys a series of delaying tactics before leaving the house to get some water for the kettle from the well. From that site she is addressed by the voice of her dead mother, warning her to beware these fairy women and telling her how to overcome them. If Leiní cries that their fairy fort is on fire, they will scatter. She does so, and they flee. Even in the course of this first scene it becomes apparent that the lines of demarcation, between a safe interior and a threatening exterior, between these demonic visitors and the protective intervention of a maternal spirit, are not so clear-cut as they appear. All of the characters on stage are female. As with Ní Dhomhnaill's poem, the fairy figures are explicitly and primarily identified as female: 'the woman of the fairy mound', 'the women of the fairy fort'. (The difference between 'mound' and 'fort' seems to be one of scale, not of kind.) The reason they will return so immediately to their fairy fort when it is threatened with fire is because 'beidh imní orthu faoina bpáistí féin' ('they will be concerned about their own children') (p. 76). These are not only women but mothers, and that biological fact will serve as their Achilles' heel, the detail which renders them vulnerable. The threatened conflagration at the fairy fort also addresses the vulnerability of children, a theme which is foregrounded throughout. If the idea of motherhood complicates the presentation of the fairy women, the voice of Leiní's own mother continues by admonishing her grown-up daughter for the chaotic condition of the house. The fact that it is 'trína chéile', 'upside down, untidy' (p. 76), she suggests, makes it particularly vulnerable to the incursions of the fairy women. When Leiní shouts the play's title, the fairy women scatter, screaming, fearing for the heads of their children with a little singsong rhyme which suggests not two separate realms, but one in-between space: 'Ó, ceann mo pháiste is ceann do pháiste-se, ceann mo pháiste is ceann do pháiste-se!' ('Your child's head and my child's head, your child's head and my child's head') (p. 76). By the scene's end certain key features which Victor Turner has identified with the liminal can be discerned: 'Liminality may involve . . . subversive and ludic (or playful) events, . . . factors or elements of culture [which] may be recombined in numerous, often grotesque ways.'[7]

The spatial configuration of the staging of *Dún na mBan Trí Thine* does much to suggest that there is a continuum rather than a stark juxtaposition between the two worlds of the play. The first scene sets up the inside/outside opposition, with Leiní secure inside her house and the fairy women knocking on the door to be admitted. But they take possession of her house, while she goes outside to fetch the water from the well, in effect exchanging places. And the well itself is the on-stage sign of the liminality of the entire stage space. Wells were associated with supernatural occurrences in pre-Christian lore in Ireland, notably with the curing of physical ailments such as blindness; and those practices remained after the arrival of Christianity, with the wells converted to a site of miracle and a place of pilgrimage. But the official Church frowned on such practices, and the wells retained their marginal status in more than the physical sense. In Ní Dhuibhne's play, she gives physical prominence to the well in her stage setting and identifies it as the locus of interchange between ordinary people and the others, between the living and the dead, by her bold decision to identify it with the voice and presence of Leiní's dead mother. As the comments pertaining to the mother in the *dramatis personae* indicate, 'tá sí marbh ach tá conaí uirthi i dtobar in aice le teach Leiní agus Eoin' ('she is dead but she is living [residing] beside Leiní and Eoin's house') (p. 74). This bald declaration conveys the readiness with which the two realms are addressed in Irish, and are in a certain sense untranslateable. In the remainder of the play, the door of the house ceases to be an issue or an obstacle. Leiní moves readily from one space to the other. The Irish term the play uses to describe Leiní's physical movement around the stage is 'ag gluaiseacht' (p. 89). The word literally means 'movement', but it combines a sense of freedom, of impulse, of wandering hither and thither, along with a determination, a drive, of psychological impetus.

The play also moves in time, between the present-ness of Leiní's house, with its Nintendo computers and domestic appliances, and the past-ness of the nineteenth-century cottage with the hearth. The actors playing Leiní and Eoin represent their nineteenth-century counter-parts by openly changing from their contemporary garb into peasant costume. The present-day mother gives way to a nineteenth-century grandmother. The two contemporary adolescent children are replaced by a baby in a cradle. The scenes set in the past centre round the illness of the child. Where the mother is seeking a rational explanation of her baby's protracted and serious illness, the grandmother is determined to prove the child a changeling. She attempts to do so by adducing a series of ever more bizarre evidence: it's not milk the baby wants but tobacco; the child was seen in the middle of the night playing fairy music with other companions. The grandmother concludes at the close of the scene that 'ní haon pháiste ceart é' ('this/he is not a right child') p. 81), but one that has come from the fairy mound. This is taken further in Scene 5 when the 'cure' is proposed. In order to drive out the fairy usurper and restore the human original, the grandmother exhorts that the baby be thrown in the fire, which Eoin undertakes against Leiní's violent protest. The scene is a shocking one and, although the stage direction 'caitheann sé an páiste isteach sa tine' ('he throws the baby into the fire') (p. 85) was modified to a mime of Eoin stooping and placing the child on the fire, no less horrifying to behold.

The scene and incident have been contextualized by the appearance of Angela Bourke's *The Burning of Bridget Cleary* in 1999. The incident on which this study is based took place in the waning years of the nineteenth-century in rural Ireland, and centres on the disappearance of the young married woman of the title. The word was that Bridget Cleary had been taken away by the others to the fairy-fort of Kylenagranagh, but then her badly charred body was discovered. It emerged that her husband, Michael Cleary, had become persuaded that the psycholo-gical changes afflicting his wife were due to the fact that she had been replaced by a changeling and that only by burning the body could the original be restored. In her study, Bourke cites Oscar's father, Sir William Wilde, a writer on folklore, on the case of a 'man in the county of Kerry

[who] roasted his child to death, under the impression that it was a fairy. He was not brought to trial, as the Crown prosecutor mercifully looked upon him as insane.'[8] Given the high incidence of infant mortality, particularly in times of dearth, many more incidents may have occurred which went unrecorded. Sir William Wilde conjoined his two interests in his studies because, as a medical man, he noted in his analysis of the 1841 census the high incidence of infantile deaths returned as consumption and surmised: 'It is this affection which has given rise to the popular ideas respecting the "changeling".'[9] Although changelings would initially be protected by fear of their supernatural origin, this taboo could be overcome by the extremity of their behaviour (whether woman or child), which could then be taken as proof of their altered condition. As Bourke puts it: 'Changelings' behaviour is often intolerable, ... since they take the form of sickly babies who never stop crying, or adults who take to their beds, refuse to speak when spoken to, or otherwise conduct themselves in anti-social ways. A last resort is to threaten a changeling with fire.'[10] There is more than one changeling in Ní Dhuibhne's play, since it is clear from the start that Leiní is destined to go to the fort of the fairy women.

The parallel that is drawn between the nineteenth and twentieth centuries in the play is in the danger to children, their vulnerability. The nineteenth-century scenes centred on the child as changeling are interwoven with scenes in the present having to do with Leiní and Eoin's eight-year-old son. Timí says he cannot go to school because he is sick and, when pressed, claims to have swallowed a piece of glass. The troubled relations between husband and wife are articulated by the exchange. Eoin is the sceptical father, questioning his son's assertion as a way of dodging school, and also saying that he cannot take the child to the hospital as he has go to the office, Leiní has her own doubts about Timí's claim to have swallowed glass but knows they cannot afford to take the risk. She too has work to attend to, but as Eoin points out, it is not real work, only an artwork class she is teaching. The next present-day scene is set in the hospital. They have been there for hours waiting to be seen and both children are extremely fractious. When Leiní objects to their treatment, and in particular to the conditions not being child-friendly, she is pointed in the direction of a stuffed dinosaur and a copy of *The Beano*. The scene concludes with Leiní withdrawing Timí and Sinéad from a waiting room where her eight-year-old has been told that if he does not behave, he will be visited by the 'bata mór' (the 'big stick'), the traditional instrument of chastisement in Irish education. In the midst of technological progress and an avowedly more caring atmosphere, the same conditions persist. The hospital scene moves Leiní to remark: 'Is fuath leis na daoine seo páistí' ('These people hate children') (p. 83).

If these interrelated scenes suggest more continuity than change between the past and the present, they also suggest increasingly that what we are witnessing is a psychological drama. As the play progresses, it establishes through the staging that the Otherworld is functioning as psychic space. This explains a great part of its appeal for contemporary women writers like Ní Dhomhnaill and Ní Dhuibhne. The former describes the figure of the cailleach (or 'hag') from Irish tradition as representing for her 'the despised, left-out, repressed female energy'[11]; and this interpretation of the cailleach lines up with the representation of the fairy women in Ní Dhuibhne's play as horrible and horned. The psychological dimensions of the Otherworld are brilliantly conveyed by Leiní's suspicion that her husband Eoin is engaged in an adulterous affair with a co-worker. The issue arises in a dialogue between the couple about a fashionable French restaurant in Grafton Street which they have visited separately, Leiní with a female friend. When Eoin says he was there too, and his wife asks him if he was on his own, the reply that he was with a friend has to be modified in terms of gender, Leiní's é' ('he') corrected to an 'í' ('she') (p. 98). The questioning and the suspicion mount about this glamorous female co-worker, and centre on the question of what they ate. When Eoin mentions 'broccoli' (p. 99), his wife retorts that he hates broccoli. The woman, apparently, ate his broccoli too. Leiní recognizes this intimate behaviour from their own dinners out, and is both shocked and worried. In a translation into English made by Ní Dhuibhne herself, the restaurant scene between the husband and the woman is directly shown and confirms Leiní's suspicions of her husband's adultery. In the Irish original, we never see the lovers meet directly. Rather, their meeting is represented through the prism of Leiní's imagination ('samhlaíocht') (p. 112) as an encounter between the Otherworld and the human. After the accusatory exchange between Leiní and Eoin, husband and wife are now asleep when the fairy women come knocking yet again to be admitted. Eoin gets up to let them in while Leiní sleeps on. To the fore of the Otherworldly intruders is his office colleague 'Máire Ní Bhrógáin atá mar dhuine de mhná an leasa' ('as one of the women of the fairy mound') (p. 100). She is beautiful, sexy, stereotypical ('steiréitipiciúil'). The 'other' woman enters the house, lies with Eoin and they simulate sex when 'cuireann siad broccoli i mbéal a chéile' ('they place broccoli in each other's mouths') (p. 100). Máire argues that Eoin should leave Leiní, urging the truism that it would be better for the children. The fairy woman departs, Eoin returns to the bed, and their ten-year-old daughter Sinéad comes in to report a bad dream. In the child's nightmare their own house was on fire, she was calling out and there was no one there to save her. At this point, there is an extraordinary fusion between Ní Dhuibhne's treatment of fairy legend and the contemporary world of gender politics, in scenes that resemble more those of Caryl Churchill in a play like *Top Girls* (1980) than anything on the contemporary Irish stage.

Leiní's imaginings extend to the past and focus on the issue of women's creativity. In her present life, she is torn between the demands of the household, her two young children and husband, and her struggle to be a painter. The question she persistently raises is: what was it like for her female forebears? There has been word of one relative who excelled in crocheting and embroidery and whose work was once exhibited at an Irish Exhibition in Chicago, though the voice of Leiní's dead mother is quick to dismiss Sally and her artistic notions as 'ráiméis' ('rubbish') (p. 111). In a classroom scene set in the past, that important precursor is being encouraged not to follow her own instincts but to manufacture the shamrocks, harps and round towers that are guaranteed to sell, especially to a foreign market. But the young artist is determined that what she wants to represent is a hare ('giorria'). The teacher is intrigued and asks why. Sally's reply is at one level completely straightforward: 'Chonaic mé giorria ag rith i measc na mbó maidin inné' ('I saw a hare running amongst the cows yesterday morning') (p. 114) and she accompanies her account with a physical mime of a leaping hare. But a folktale about a woman who is in touch with the Others and who metamorphoses into a hare has threaded its way through the play; and when Leiní approaches the fort of the fairy women and recites her mantra, she has taken on the movements of a hare. The teacher encourages Sally to follow her own suggestion and the scene segues from the past to the present where Leiní is depicted painting a hare on the wall. Eoin remarks derisively that this portrait of 'Bugs Bunny' hardly makes her Michelangelo; and that the children need looking to. When she resists his imprecations and he goes to bed, Leiní keeps painting, having insisted that the picture will remain on the wall and that it does not need to be confined or circumscribed by being put in a frame.

The scene has now been set, in the closing movement of the play, for Leiní to go to the fort of the fairy women. This time, when they come knocking, she lets them in and accompanies them off-stage. The Otherworld becomes and has come to represent a crucial dimension of her creativity, and when she enters the fairy mound what she encounters there is highly theatricalized. In the 1994 production the cluttered modern set split in two and disappeared to leave an open stage. In order further to suggest that the Otherworld setting was more organic than the house, strands of seaweed and other natural growth were suspended from overhead. Also on hangers were the clothes into which the actors walked, seamlessly becoming the part. In the mound the fairy women are there to greet Leiní but now dressed in up-to-date clothes and without the horns. Other women are familiar from folktales and stories, many of them young but some of them old. Some of the women are dressed as animals and wear masks. The fort also contains children; and all present are eating and drinking – the abundance that fairy legend always promised and which was always the clearest compensation for a historical great hunger. Leiní of course encounters the hare of her artistic imaginings, identified as her grandmother, as much an artistic as a biological precursor. But the actress who plays the mother takes this role and thereby suggests the extent to which Leiní's chiding mother suppressed her own artistic instincts in deference to marriage and child-rearing. Leiní is invited to eat, but declines. The fairy fort remains seductive, and in an even more threatening way than as the embodiment of her sexual jealousy. Here is the promise of unmediated creativity, but it is a resource on which to be drawn, a subconscious realm to be accessed, rather than a place in which to stay forever. The last scene is set, not in the fairy mound, but back in the house. Leiní returns, not by waking from a sleep, but by walking through the door. Ní Dhuibne's play by its conclusion has staged the dynamic interaction between this world and the other which has proved so difficult to achieve in English-language Irish theatre. Her children welcome her back; even Eoin seems pleased and relieved to see her. Where has she been? There is a well-known phrase from the Irish which answers it: she has been 'away with the fairies'. The play ends with Eoin taking the children to the cinema while Leiní (singing) resumes her painting on the wall.

Amharclann de híde ran for seven years, from 1993 to 2000. Its then Artistic Director Clíodhna Ní Anluain commissioned two plays from Éilís Ní Dhuibhne: *Dún na mBan Trí Thine* and *Milseog an tSamhraidh* ('Summer Pudding'). The first was staged at the Peacock in 1994, the second in the Samuel Beckett Centre in Trinity College, Dublin, in 1997. After a reading at the conclusion of her year as Writer-in-Residence in the School of English in Trinity College in 2005, Ní Dhuibhne was asked whether she had or would write other Irish-language plays. She said that if she were commissioned to do so, she would. In its commitment to new writing, to the Irish language and (it claims whenever asked) to the writing of women playwrights, the Abbey Theatre might well find example in such challenging and powerful works as the play I have just examined to commission another.

Acknowledgements

I would like to thank Éilís Ní Dhuibhne and Clíodhna Ní Anluain for invaluable help in the preparation of this chapter.

Notes

1. Nuala Ní Dhomhnaill, 'An Crann', *Féar Suaithinseach* (Magh Nuad: An Crann, 1984), p. 75. The translation is mine.
2. Éilís Ní Dhuibhne, *Milseog an tSamhraidh agus Dún na mBan Trí Thine* (Baile Átha Cliath: Cois Life Teoranta, 1997), p. 88. All future references to the play are to this edition and will be incorporated in the text. The translation is mine.
3. Nuala Ní Dhomhnaill, 'Why I Choose to Write in Irish: The Corpse that Sits Up and Talks Back', *New York Times Book Review*, 8 January 1995, pp. 26–8. Cited in Michaela Schrage-Fruh, 'The Otherworld as Psychic Space in Nuala Ní Dhomhnaill's Poetry', conference paper, 'Liminal Borderlands: Ireland Past, Present, Future', Fourth Biennial Conference of Nordic Irish Studies Network, Dalarna University College, Falun, Sweden, 22–24 April 2004.
4. W. B. Yeats, *The Land of Heart's Desire*, *Collected Plays* (London: Macmillan, 1969), p. 70.
5. Denis Johnston, *John Millington Synge* (New York and London: Columbia University Press, 1965), p. 14.
6. Anthony Roche, 'Woman on the Threshold; J. M. Synge's *In The Shadow of the Glen*, Teresa Deevy's *Katie Roche* and Marina Carr's *The Mai*', *Irish University Review*, Vol. 25, No. 1, Spring/Summer 1995, p. 145. Reprinted in Cathy Leeney and Anna McMullan (eds), *The Theatre of Marina Carr: 'before rules was made'* (Dublin: Carysfort Press, 2003), pp. 17–42.
7. Victor Turner, *From Ritual to Theatre: The Human Seriousness of Play* (New York: Performing Arts Journal Publications, 1982), p. 27.
8. Angela Bourke, *The Burning of Bridget Cleary: A True Story* (London: Pimlico, 1999), p. 33.
9. Bourke, *The Burning of Bridget Cleary: A True Story*, p. 33.
10. Bourke, *The Burning of Bridget Cleary: A True Story*, p. 30.
11. Medbh McGuckian and Nuala Ní Dhomhnaill, 'Comhrá, with a Foreword and Afterword by Laura O'Connor', *The Southern Review*, Vol. 31, No. 3, July 1995, p. 598.

11

Sick, Dying, Dead, Dispersed: The Evanescence of Patriarchy in Contemporary Irish Women's Theatre

Brian Singleton

The patriarchal essentialization and 'subjective disavowal'[1] of Irish woman as the *Áisling*, Róisín Dubh and Mother Ireland figures, as part of both theatrical canon and nation-formation in the popular imagination in the early twentieth century, is being contested by the emergence of new Irish women playwrights in the early twenty-first century. Their work, configured in a climate of first-time economic prosperity and social change that brought about the crumbling of the last vestiges of a theocratic state, seeks no longer to represent or metaphorically embody the nation on stage. The essentialized iconic and mythical women of the early nation's male imagination have been replaced by women who reject male authority, seek new lives beyond the strictures of the family unit, and refuse to be haunted by the sick, dying and dead patriarchs in their lives who left traumatized the women of the previous generation. Most of these new writers also challenge the myth-making of the realist form as a dramaturgical strategy to disrupt the time-space continuum and thereby open up new vistas and possibilities for change. All the plays, by Ioanna Anderson, Hilary Fannin, Stella Feehily and Elizabeth Kuti, focus on the contemporary experience of women in Ireland. All of the authors are in their thirties and forties who emerged into the world of theatre at a time when Irish society legalized divorce and homosexuality and contested laws on abortion. Most have experienced theatre primarily as actors and have therefore directly experienced the male formation of women on the Irish stage. Analysis of the performance texts reveals choices and strategies that work towards the de-essentialization of gender, and the new Irish woman in particular; she is taken out of the mythical country kitchen and is reconfigured on the street, the beach and in the garden. Further, and most importantly, her race and ethnicity are uncoupled from nation and contest the closure inherent in the hegemonic concept of 'Irishness'.

Hilary Fannin's 2003 play *Doldrum Bay*, produced at the Peacock Theatre,[2] and directed by Mark Lambert, presents contemporary middle-class Irish society as being at a point of crisis. Relationships are at a troubled stage, families are torn apart, and a new surreal set of conceptual values borne out of consumerism has replaced the authority of the Catholic Church. The characters drift, the men in lament for the collapse of authority, and the women in search of new configurations. And to provide a space for those new configurations Fannin sets her play on a beach that serves as a loose metaphor for the collapse of home as place of authority, though in its first production, designer Jamie Vartan created various locations that required inordinate scene shifting. Vartan's emphasis was on a reproduction of the real and he thus attenuated the imaginative possibilities that Fannin's writing suggests. Lurking in the background of the play is an actual and imminent death of a patriarch, and successful artist, Jakey (a character always absent from the stage). He is in hospital in his final hours. Magda, his art-dealer daughter (Ali White, see Figure 8) struggles to come to terms with her father's perennial infidelity and her unwitting involvement during her childhood in the conspiracy to keep the indiscretions from her mother. She is married to Francis, an advertising executive turned novelist who seduces a young barmaid. Their friends fare little better; Francis's friend Chick is also an advertising executive but is already at the point of being usurped by younger talent more in touch with demand than he. We first see Chick in the middle of a family crisis when he learns that his brother Dessie (a Christian Brother) has walked out of his parish and into a new job as a demonstration bunny in a Wal-Mart store in Iowa. As the play progresses Chick receives a telephone call that informs him of Dessie's suicide. The initial comic collapse of the once-powerful Church patriarch into a fluffy animal is a metaphor for the condition of the Catholic Church in contemporary Ireland, all the while his brother Chick is trying to compose an advertising campaign for recruitment to the Christian Brothers.

Further compounding Chick's misery is the revelation, through monologue, of his mother's disappearance when he was still a child, and later his discovery of his magician father's paedophilic tendencies, those being the drive behind his father's choice of profession. The details of Chick's background are interesting because they completely undercut his rabid sexism and selfishness. His revelation of suffering, through a confessional monologue, serves perhaps as a first step on the road to

Figure 8   Ali White as Magda in the 2003 Abbey Theatre production of *Doldrum Bay* by Hilary Fannin. Peacock Stage. Photo: Courtesy of Tom Lawlor.

healing: 'I am depressed. It's nothing I can't handle. It manifests... It is physical. It is a physical depression.... My heart. I have neglected my heart.'[3] Fannin, here, presents a world in which male authority is at the point of collapse. And she permits it to collapse, but not as a spectacle that might further embolden and resurrect its authority. This authority simply disappears; Dessie's rejection of religion and his eventual suicide are reported events, not presented in real time; similarly Chick learned of his own father's death by a third party. Again in monologue form Chick reveals how he heard about that particular collapse of authority: 'Then a readdressed letter told me he was dead. Peacefully, the letter writer, some mildewed relation said.... A great man for the tricks. ... He disappeared; the greatest trick of them all.'[4]

The central figure of male authority, and the reason behind Magda's difficulty with relationships and her general disillusionment, is her father Jakey. He, too, is at the moment of his departure from the world. Although we never see him, his presence permeates the space. In the Peacock production his presence was marked by simple indices, namely a hospital bedside screen, plastic moulded chairs, and the sound of a heart monitor. But it is through dialogue that we learn not only of his despicable treatment of his mother but also of his disturbing relationship with Magda as a child; he would take her on his secret rendezvous with his mistress forcing her to keep the affair secret. Clearly the man was selfish, and indeed abusive. But just as Fannin does not permit us to actually see him, she conjures up for us his physical decline through dialogue. Magda first reports that she is not sure if her father can hear, and signals the beginning of his loss of senses. She goes on to fill out the details of his corporeal collapse: 'His tongue is black...The last time I picked him up I thought his skin would come off in my hands.'[5] Later we learn that his fingers have turned black and that his body is cold. By the second act Jakey is simply represented by a heart monitor. In the production we did not even see the monitor but heard the interrupted bleeping sound that signifies life, and then the continuous sound of death. An incomplete sound for life; a piercing, constant sound for death. And Magda charts his recrudescence: 'I didn't think he would die like this – nappies and tubes.'[6] At the moment of death she re-infantilizes him in a final reconfiguring of the principal source of her pain. In the final scene they all gather at the beach to 'disperse' his ashes in the water. Her friend Louise is concerned about that dispersal: 'You don't want bits of him washing up in rock pools, frightening small children.'[7] It is important for the women to know that he will not be able to rematerialize. His body has already been reduced to ashes, and by dispersal in the sea that body can dissolve still further until there is nothing left of it. This is the complete and utter evanescence of the patriarch with no visible residue to signify a lost authority, or to haunt the recovery of Magda from that authority.

The two women in the play, Magda and Chick's wife Louise, are two sides of one coin; Magda has the wisdom and insight to comment not only on her relationships with men, but also about the current condition and representation of men, religion and sex in contemporary Ireland. Gender binaries are being blurred by a rampant consumerism, according to her: 'There are no men and women any more, there is just population. A technological population...'[8] Magda presents for us an Ireland that is simply dissolving its hierarchies and boundaries. Her analysis permits her a space in which to discover that her identity is not constructed by or in relation to a man (her father Jakey and her equally unfaithful husband Francis). She sees the world, and the relationships that form the world, as fluid and as changing as the sea. Louise, on the other hand, is a woman of action who fills her days with part-time courses as a retreat from the real world. She sees the world in binaries; the world of work (the workplace) and the world of non-work (the home). Her view underlines the agenda of male authority as the courses with which she fills her day underscore her absence from the workplace, and thus her imagined 'uselessness' in the male-constructed binary. This lack of rejection of the binarized male world of work leads to her psychological endangerment. On stage, she undergoes a spectacular collapse into severe depression after some manic scenes during which she feeds her tranquillizers to her dog. The sexist patriarchy that surrounds her, and her inability to challenge and reject it, makes her literally 'sick'. In between the two is the youthful barmaid/student Java. At the beginning of her adult life, she has no complicated patriarch. She works in a bar selling drinks, and also oxygen, to its customers. She is fascinated by the attentions of the older Francis, but does not permit the relationship to materialize, as she is in an emergent state of the discovery of her desires. In the Peacock production she was played by Ethiopian-Irish actress Ruth Negga, who, by her very presence, disrupted the white spectacle of middle-class Dublin. Her race and exotic character name marked the presence of a new Irish woman, one at the beginning of her voyage of discovery, one tempted by a predatory patriarch, but one ultimately and indefatigably independent. Java's refusal of Francis acts as a model for Magda who decides undemonstratively to finish her relationship with Francis. She needs him around her, but will not have a relationship with him. His own comment on the situation is interesting: 'I'm being left.'[9] She is not leaving him and he is not leaving her; he is being left. Like Jakey's ashes being scattered in the sea, Francis too is slowly undergoing his own dispersal, as a soundtrack of waves (composed by Ivan Birthistle) paints the aural picture of a patriarchy being washed away.[10]

Another play similarly begins with the evanescence of a patriarch, but one who has re-materialized to give impetus to the play. Dublin-based Rough Magic, which has been engaged in a mentoring/training programme for theatre artists entitled SEEDS since it established a Literary Department in 2001, produced in February 2004 Ioanna Anderson's *Words of Advice for Young People* – directed by Philip Howard at Project. The central premise of the play is the attempted reconciliation of a family torn apart after the disappearance of children's author Harry Golden in a remote area of County Leitrim. The discovery of the body and the subsequent funeral are opportunities for his two daughters Nora (in a marriage wracked by violence) and Clara (struggling with a cocaine addiction) to come to terms with each other, their own failed relationships, and to put to bed the ghost of the father. Harry

Golden is instituted as an arch-patriarch. His job, writing for children, and reading his stories for the taped versions, constructs him as the benevolent patriarch, the ur-father of all children. He was famous for his stories of Colin the Rabbit, and that in itself is indicative of how for a generation of children their worlds were gendered. Colin the male rabbit is the rabbit of action, the rabbit of adventure and the eyes to the world for all children. Harry's death brings together the siblings and their (ex-) partners who attempt to come to terms with their past and try to find ways of processing it and moving on. The play's impetus is perhaps the HBO television series *Six Feet Under*, which is motivated by the death of a patriarch, leaving exposed an already dysfunctional family.[11] The arch-patriarch, though absent in stage time, 'embodies' the hegemonically masculine, that is the male who has attained primordial social status, who has fathered children and who dominates and controls all around him. Immediately Anderson disavows that status by refusing to permit his presence, even as a ghost. He is only present in the form of a voice recording of one of his children's stories. The cassette recorder is a permanent fixture on the stage throughout the play, but it is only in the final moments of the drama that we are permitted to hear that voice. Even when we do hear him, Harry is narrating a story. Though clearly using his own voice, he is speaking as a narrator and not as himself. This tape is a residue of the masculine. Although a fragment of a whole character, and a small object in the vast expanse of the stage, that voice occupies the space of the theatre and the world of his two grieving daughters. But now the tape hisses and crackles and the sound is weak. Though not embodied, the weak-sounding tape of Harry represents an evanescence even of his own residue. In the third act we learn through a monologue by Nora of the status of Harry as a hegemonic male. She insists her parents had a good marriage but after the death of her mother through illness, Harry her father went into rapid decline:

> After that I talked to him every day on the phone and I thought it was a bad line, his voice had gone so soft, like he was always talking from the next room. He spent a lot of time sleeping... This was my dad who was a fixer, who could mend anything, who always knew what to do. If you held his hand you felt safe in a strange city, in a bad neighbourhood, on a dark country road without a map.[12]

The physical and mental collapse of this patriarch is far from comic. It is constructed as a result of the loss of his wife. Without his wife he could not exist; he drove to a cliff and presumably took his own life. The patriarch here does not take action. His action (suicide) is questionable. The slow collapse was never allowed completion as his body was not found for five years. The patriarch simply disappeared.

Despite the centrality of Harry's taped presence and physical absence, the dead are embodied by the presence of the ghost of the wife of the local undertaker, Jack. Anderson's play, like in the HBO series, employs an imagined dead character to confront the fears of the living. Whereas in the television series the ghosts appear to the central characters in the drama, Anderson's ghost only appears to the undertaker. Her voice, immaculate hair as if dressed by an undertaker for a viewing, and red evening dress propel her instantly out of the stage reality all the while she moves within it. This ghost, Ruby, is not a troubling, haunting instigator of action and pricking of conscience, she is very much a soothing and healing presence. Her death robbed Jack of his hegemonic status. He cannot be the patriarch over no one and the absence of children further reinforces his crushed status. But Ruby does not punish him, for there is nothing to punish him for. She comes back to move him on through the grieving process. This stoic male is not heroic as he has no project. We find him trapped in grief and barely functioning. Through the agency of Ruby, and by taking charge of the Golden household in various ways, we begin to see that a heroic project for Jack just might be possible. However, Anderson does not permit it to form fully, stopping it just at the point of its possible appearance.

The main action of the drama is set in the garden of the Golden household in Co. Leitrim with its collection of comical gnomes. Nora runs the family home as a Bed and Breakfast establishment patronized mostly by fans of her father's work. With the stage picture of the gnomes and the lack of clear grieving of the daughters for their father, no dominant formation of the patriarchal is allowed to emerge. Of course, the lack of visible grieving is the result of the five-year delay between Harry's disappearance and the discovery of his remains. Furthermore, they do not have a whole body to mourn; again, like his tape, Harry is only a distancing residue in the drama. Nora is the one with centrality in the household. Her abusive, though now estranged, husband Danny has returned to lend support. He has curiously found God in the intervening period. While this is mocked by Nora, and almost dismissed, his conversion to religion could also be read as a retreat further into the hegemonically patriarchal. How more hegemonic can one get than the male Creator? We hear tales of Danny's previous potential for violence but Anderson does not permit it to emerge on the stage. His status has been eroded and he has embarked on his new project with a trusty male god, leaving Nora to occupy the social and economic position he once held. This patriarch, though still frightening for his past misdemeanours, has suffered an almost comic collapse into religion. His horrific past haunts the stage despite his present real-time 'grudgingly ethical behaviour', but it is again a residue that is tolerated but not allowed to re-materialize.[13]

The setting for Anderson's play is crucial to an understanding of her representation of the patriarchal. Nora, though the owner and manager of the bed and breakfast is never seen inside the house. The entire action takes place outside in the garden. Anderson's Irish woman has been displaced from the hearth. Here she is seen to control the exterior space. She emerges on several occasions from the house but chooses to entertain in the garden. It is a clear rejection of the association of the house with her role as wife. She has rejected her husband, but also by implication she is rejecting her father and his status by not occupying his house. The garden permits her a space in which to discover a new function in the family drama, and emerge from the constrictions of a gendered space. The gnomes that are dotted all around the garden are ironic pointers to the tragedy within. When they light up, they render the masculinity they represent as comic, with a hint of the grotesque. To further reinforce the symbolic function of the absent house, we learn that its roof is at the point of potential collapse. All around the garden Jack and Ruby appear as a counterpoint to the lack of healing being experienced in the garden, until the third act when Jack is permitted to enter the garden and suggest a slight hint of a moving on for Nora. But moving on with another man is not permitted to materialize.

Moving on as a next step is also the challenge facing the protagonist of *Duck*, a play by actor turned author Stella Feehily. *Duck* was produced by English company Out of Joint together with the Royal Court Theatre (directed by Max Stafford-Clark) and toured Britain and Ireland in 2003. It was also presented in association with the Abbey Theatre and ran for a month at its studio space, The Peacock, in October of that year.[14] The play begins explosively with an arson attack by one of the young women protagonists, Cat (played by Ruth Negga). Cat has pushed an item of clothing into the fuel tank of her boyfriend's car and set fire to it. She does this in response to his forgetful treatment of her, his controlling urges and for her dislike of the nickname he has adopted for her (Duck) because he thinks she has large feet. The boyfriend, Mark (played by Karl Shiels), is a large man with an overbearing personality. He has all the trappings of a hegemonic masculinity at such a young age (mid to late-twenties); he owns a night-club/bar and is reputed to use it as a front for his drug dealing; he has his own apartment and a seemingly endless supply of cash. He appears in the play with just one other male, Eddie (Aidan O'Hare), who has just been released from prison for robbery. The two men together present a masculinity beyond redemption. Mark pulls Cat on to his knee in an attempt at infantilization. He then tries to coerce her into telling him she loves him. He simply cannot relate to a woman on equal terms, but uses his large physical and vocal presence to objectify Cat on his terms alone. The two men talk of Cat simply according to her use-value as an object of their various bodily urges (to provide food and sex):

Mark: You can have her.
Eddie: Wha? You're on.
Mark: What are friends for?[15]

Interestingly, though, Mark is never seen to consume either. The two men ask for sandwiches in Scene 3 but then leave on their masculine project of football and beer in the pub without telling her they are leaving. Woman, for these two men, is clearly disposable. Man, for Cat and her Benylin/laxative/alcohol-addict friend Sophie (played by Elaine Symons), is irredeemable.

Cat's subsequent rejection of Mark comes after a violent scene in a bath during which he attempts to drown her as punishment for setting fire to his car. This prompts her to leave and fall into the arms of a 60-year-old author, Jack Mullen (played by Tony Rohr). The age difference is so great that it skips a generation, and the difference in education and experience is also remarked upon by both of them. Jack, it transpires, is a serial adulterer who fails to protect Cat, or to commit to her. Cat discovers that despite his apparently caring charm and the comfort and safety he provides for her in her time of need, these are simply surface-deep characteristics employed to secure another sexual conquest. The only other man on the stage is Cat's father, Frankie. In the first production this character was also played by Tony Rohr, a fact that added an extra dimension to the father-figure role of Jack. In Scene 14 Frankie sits with his back to the audience for the entire scene, watching television up-stage. This was an interesting refusal of the full materialization of the patriarch, as the words he speaks are not his own. He chants a mantra about Cat's presence back in the home: 'We cut the umbilical cord you know...Are you gay...Keep the living room doors shut. Keep in the heat...Wipe your feet on the mat. Don't ask me for money.'[16] These statements and questions are rhetorical and are copies of his wife Marion's (Gina Moxley) similar admonitions and instructions that are not permitted a reply. Thus we can infer that Frankie is simply chanting orders to Cat, but the words and sentiments are not his at all. Instead, Frankie has retreated into an inferior position, facing up-stage. We learn of his fondness for alcohol and his predilection for spending a lot of time in Cat's vacated bedroom. It is almost as if he has renounced the practice of masculinity in terms of the traditional/conventional performance of gender (he is virtually invisible, and almost laconic). This retreat of the patriarch is not total as he has a continued visual presence. Instead, Feehily writes Marion as a product of gender integration as she embodies aspects of what R. W. Connell describes as 'true masculinity'; in other words, an idealized and wished-for masculinity that she perceives as being 'true'.[17] Marion has become 'masculinized' within the family home. She takes on the role of patriarch, setting boundaries and limits to the family's action, while he stares vacantly into the infinity of an up-stage space.

Cat and Sophie, however, drive the action. They are a young Thelma and Louise, beating off potential rapists in their adventurous journey through their discovery of the aggressive sexuality, and the arrogant self-belief (and selfishness) of hegemonic masculinity. There is a hint of there being some kind of sexual attraction between Sophie and Cat but it 'stops just short of physical desire'.[18] They have no role models for parents as neither set communicates in real time with each other. Sophie's addictions are a counterpoint to her university education. That education is not presented as an escape route from their feelings of rejection. However, it does provide her with an insight to their condition, as she recites an essay on the subject of their recent actions and their historical antecedents: 'Arson and scolding appeared to offer a dramatic form of protest to the poor and rejected/ Enabling them to vent an inarticulate rage against the hopelessness of their condition.'[19] They have become women of action in an attempt to take charge of that condition through the rejection of men. Cat's complete rejection of Mark (and ultimately Jack) only comes towards the end of the play:

> You don't own me
> You don't know me
> I'm not Duck or love or
> Whatever the fucking hell spews out of your mouth
> I don't need you
> I don't need any fucking one of you
> I choose to be here.[20]

But these are unlikely heroines as their new project (to take control of their lives) is interrupted by comic challenges to it. In the final scene they are on the street with their belongings, including a space-hopper from their childhood. This is a ridiculous visual sign that they have not fully accepted the loss of childhood. Then we learn that Sophie accidentally fell out of the bedroom window while having a secret cigarette. And all the while the expected taxi fails to appear, mobile phones are out of credit and landline phones are vandalized. And they are too embarrassed to go to the neighbours for help. Yet despite these problems, the two remain on the stage at the end, sharing a joke and a determination that their educational journey as women in a world of abusive masculinity is at the point of departure. Cat can now also shake off the nicknames given to her by her mother (Gull) and by her ex-boyfriend (Duck) and begin to form an identity based on her own name.

The death of the father again gives impetus to the earliest play I wish to treat. *Treehouses*, by author/actress Elizabeth Kuti, was first performed at the Peacock Theatre in 2000, directed by Jason Byrne.[21] Of all the plays I have examined, *Treehouses* is the only one to feature multiple locations and times operating simultaneously on-stage. This travelling across time and space permits interesting resonances on the performance of gender. The three locations consist of a nursing home (presumably in Ireland although there are few markers as to the location), an Eastern European country during World War Two, and a family home (again presumably in Ireland). The characters who occupy each space respectively are Old Magda (who has obviously travelled West and settled in Ireland), a younger version of herself over 50 years prior, and Eva, who it turns out is connected to Old Magda's story, although they are never permitted to realize this or to interact in real time or space. Magda has a key for a jewellery box but no box. Eva has a box but no key and thus the two are linked in the final moments of the play. What links them is Eva's father to whom, as a boy, Eva's family attempted to give refuge from Nazi persecution, but who ultimately they had to let go to an uncertain fate. Eva's reason for being on the stage is to shed the burden of her father's remarriage and to recount her own violent reaction to that. The play focuses on the theme of betrayal; Magda betrayed Eva's father as a Jew in Nazi-occupied Eastern Europe, for the sake of her own family's survival. Eva's father betrayed his daughter in the sense that he married twice and thus broke the special bond that had developed between a single father and his daughter. Old Magda imagines how the betrayed can also be the betrayer: 'And perhaps somewhere too a child of his loves him and forgives him for some betrayal of the heart.'[22] Both women have to come to terms with their own reactions to acts of betrayal and find the courage to accept that betrayal, at times, is committed out of acts of love and a desire for happiness.

Eva as a child configured her father in terms of his material constructions. The treehouse he built for her was a space in which she could retreat from the harsh realities of the world (and from the reality of her mother's betrayal of her father and her subsequent disappearance), and a space in which she can fantasize and look down upon her father from a position of dominant specularity. However, a new neighbour and single woman, Miriam, attracts her father's attention and thus causes Eva to suffer a breakdown of her sense of self and her construction of the world:

> No matter how much I have tried to forgive I can only think of that summer everything changed, the summer that all I surveyed from the treehouse was no longer wholly mine, the summer I was twelve, the summer I wasn't enough, the summer he chose another woman. The summer he betrayed me.[23]

Eva's response to the perceived betrayal was to set fire to the treehouse that had come to represent the safety her father had constructed for her after the departure of her mother, on the very day of her father's remarriage, in front of the wedding party. This spectacular reaction was an act of expressive violence (similar to Cat's torching of her boyfriend's jeep in *Duck*), a scream for attention, but also at the same time it is an act of destruction of a relationship.

What is interesting is the fact that for most of the play Eva is dressed in black as she has just attended her father's funeral, his own conflagration in a sense, and thus all she can do now is vent her anger and berate herself through a confessional monologue. Northern Irish actress Morna Regan, as Eva, provided a vocal location with her suffering that provided perhaps a metaphor for the betrayal and death of something much greater. Critic Mic Moroney picked up on Regan's 'chilling Northern tones' that gave added resonance to expressions such as 'our territory' and 'recovering the clarity of my hatred'.[24] In her nursing home Old Magda (played by another Northern actress Stella McCusker) essentially does the same as she looks back, although McCusker played her with a vague East European accent. Young Magda (Gertrude Montgomery) spoke with a southern Irish accent, however. And thus the three women, despite their split subjectivity and the grandmother/daughter relationship between Magda and Eva, had a range of accents that pointed to a destabilizing of the fixity of Irishness in terms of nation.

The characters Young Magda encounters (her boyfriend teacher Stephen – played by Robert Price – and a young and presumably Jewish boy to whom she is giving refuge – played by Sean McDonough) talk in real time and in the present tense. The older generations of women talk in the past tense in an attempt to come to terms with that past. Towards the end of the play the writing shifts gear to give interweaving monologues to all the characters and thus linking them inextricably as an extended family. This family is not necessarily an Irish one. It has roots in Europe's fascist past that stretches beyond the boundaries of nation. The new Irish woman, in the form of Eva, is one deeply troubled and full of regret. Her childhood construction of the patriarch was betrayed; she herself was not. But the play gently reveals that once one has accepted the desire to love and be loved as necessary, then the paths to forgiveness can be opened up for discovery.

Each of these four plays by contemporary Irish women playwrights questions patriarchy to some degree and presents it as sick or recently departed. In its literal and metaphorical wake, the women who remain behind are struggling to come to terms with the new re-gendered space they find themselves in, and have to construct new possibilities for themselves beyond the gender divide. But these women are to some degree post-feminist. They have had no moment of liberation through contestation. They do not attempt to occupy the space left by dead or departed men. They refuse to occupy that space and instead remain in the street, in the garden, or on the ambivalent, shifting site of the beach. The need to replace the men simply is not there as the men have all disappeared, or to be more accurate, 'dematerialized'. The women have had no fight with, or protest against, the men. Instead they 're-imagine a habitable world, rather than remaining in a repressed alternative'.[25] And further, the various directors of the first productions offered no iconic women with a subjectivized 'to-be-looked-at-ness'. The spectator's gaze on the sexual was invariably disavowed. Each of the women protagonists refuses to be subjected to the gaze and offers no hint that she might do so in the future. As for the men, there is no 'hard-body' character (someone who is primarily constituted as a phallic spectacle) that can be objectified either.[26] Men do not delight, as we see them either at the point of collapse, or at the moment of their dematerialization. Instead, man's evanescence marks a slow, though precarious and transitional dawn for the new Irish woman (and her project outside the family and the patriarchal) to be imagined.

Notes

1. See Melissa Sihra, 'Renegotiating Landscapes of the Female: Voices, Topographies and Corporealities of Alterity in Marina Carr's *Portia Coughlan*', in Brian Singleton and Anna McMullan (eds), 'Performing Ireland: New Perspectives on Contemporary Irish Theatre', *Australasian Drama Studies*, Vol. 43, October 2003, pp. 16–31 (p. 19).
2. First performed 7 May 2003.
3. Hilary Fannin, *Doldrum Bay* (London: Methuen Drama, 2003), p. 48.
4. Fannin, *Doldrum Bay*, p. 89.
5. Fannin, *Doldrum Bay*, p. 8.
6. Fannin, *Doldrum Bay*, p. 82
7. Fannin, *Doldrum Bay*, p. 102.
8. Fannin, *Doldrum Bay*, p. 76.
9. Fannin, *Doldrum Bay*, p. 104.
10. Mark Lambert's production was heavily mired in realism due to its use of mostly interior locations. Fannin's text specifically calls for a beach on which to play out the scenes, thus for the most part this production lost the metaphorical and performative resonances of the beach. See the review by Karen Fricker in *The Guardian*, 15 May 2003: http://www.guardian.co.uk/arts/reviews/story/0„956131,00.html (accessed 6.12.05). In 2005 the play was produced at La Licorne, Montréal, in a translation by François Letourneau, on a stage covered in sand in which were embedded a few metonymic props and sets. For a description, see Amy Barratt, 'God, Sex and States', *Montreal Mirror*, Archives, 28 October – 3 November 2004: http://www.montrealmirror.com/2004/102804/theatre.html (accessed 16.12.05).
11. First aired in late 2002 in Ireland on RTÉ2 (or Network 2 as it was then known). For an example of the use of the ghost figure and how it operates in the series, see Brian Singleton, 'Queering the Church: Sexual and Spiritual Neo-Orthodoxies in *Six Feet Under*', in Kim Akass and Janet McCabe (eds), *Reading Six Feet Under: TV to Die For* (London and New York: I. B. Tauris, 2005), pp. 161–73 (p. 166).
12. Fannin, *Doldrum Bay*, p. 58.
13. Amy Aronson, 'The Saviours and the Saved: Masculine Redemption in Contemporary Films', in Peter Lehman (ed.), *Masculinity: Bodies, Movies, Culture* (London and New York: Routledge, 2001), pp. 43–50 (p. 44).
14. First performance: 24 July 2003 at the Theatre Royal, Bury St Edmunds. It ran in the Peacock Theatre, Dublin, from 30 September to 1 November 2003. The final performance was at the Royal Court Theatre on 10 January 2004.
15. Stella Feehily, *Duck* (London: Nick Hern Books, 2003), p. 19.
16. Feehily, *Duck*, p. 81.
17. R. W. Connell, *Masculinities*, 2nd edn (Cambridge: Polity Press, 2005), p. 45.
18. Review by Michael Billington, *The Guardian*, 4 August 2003: http://www.guardian.co.uk/arts/reviews/story/0„1011837,00.html (accessed 6.12.05).
19. Feehily, *Duck*, pp. 58–9.
20. Feehily, *Duck*, p. 105

21. First performed 5 April 2000.
22. Elizabeth Kuti, *Treehouses* (London: Methuen Drama, 2000), p. 81.
23. Kuti, *Treehouses*, p. 31.
24. Reviewed in *The Guardian*, 21 April 2000:
    http://www.guardian.co.uk/arts/reviews/story/0, 699919,00.html (accessed 6.12.05).
25. 'Performing Ireland': *Australasian Drama Studies*, pp. 3–15 (p. 8).
26. Kenneth MacKinnon, *Representing Men: Maleness and Masculinity in the Media* (London: Arnold, 2003), p. 55.

12
The House of Woman and the Plays of Marina Carr

Melissa Sihra

Laying foundations

Marina Carr's early dramas explore themes of love, sex, life and death in surreal, absurdist and comic ways while her more recent works focus on the fraught relationship between woman, family and home in rural Irish settings. The theatricality and irreverence of her early plays were attractive to young independent theatre companies as well as to the National Theatre in the late 1980s and early 1990s. In the programme note of Carr's first play, *Ullaloo* (not the first to be performed), at the Peacock Theatre in March 1991, Tom Mac Intyre observes the significance of her nascent voice:

> Marina Carr is at the beginning of her career as a playwright.... It makes perfect sense that – with female energy at last being given room to move in this society – a young female playwright should unhesitatingly set about banishing the taboo successfully imposed by male playwrights (with the connivance of critics, and it must be said, audiences) over a period of up on a hundred years. Cometh the hour, cometh the writer. And – consider – Ms Carr is, as yet, merely limbering up.[1]

Ullaloo, an old Gaelic word meaning 'funeral lament', was given a rehearsed reading with Olwen Fouéré and Tom Hickey at the Peacock Theatre during the 1989 Dublin Theatre Festival. The play subsequently received a full production in 1991 with Fouéré and Mark Lambert, directed by David Byrne. Mac Intyre places Carr's early work into context: 'A large part of the fun in her two recent plays – *Low in the Dark* and *This Love Thing* had to do with her healthy willingness to discard traditional forms. *Low in the Dark* in particular, realized a zany equilibrium from a melange which included slapstick, cartoon, gender-bending, song, dance, story-telling, interlude and ebullient dialogue.'[2] Carr reflects:

> The first four plays are about stretching my limbs. That is all they were, exercises....There was no focus, no central opinion or back-ground knowledge in them, they were meant to be understandings of living and dying, all the big themes. Something instinctive was calling me along, a love of words and sounds, having no idea what I was doing. There was nothing underlying the first four plays; I am not saying it is a bad thing, maybe that is the best way to write.[3]

While Carr's later works move away from consciously experi-mental forms towards character and plot-driven drama, they remain 'instinctive', displaying and developing that same energizing love of words and sounds and encompassing non-realist theatrical strategies such as multiple playing-spaces and storytelling, often with light humorous touches of absurd detail.

In *Ullaloo*, Carr 'applies herself to her persistent theme – A man, a woman; a woman, a man.'[4] There are two characters in the play, Tilly and Tomred. Tilly, the woman, is, for the most part, immobilized in bed while Tomred, at the other side of the room, is intent on cajoling his toe-nails to grow longer. While the situation is consciously absurd, the themes which emerge in Carr's later works are established. Throughout the play the couple attempts to define the nature of their relationship and to ascertain some sense of meaning in their ongoing lives. The private, inner world of the bedroom is opened up, as both characters speak to each other without being able to connect. The piece is an early study in co-dependency, intimacy and isolation, where the split-stage space of the woman and man becomes increasingly claustrophobic. Loneliness, alien-ation, the inevitability of death and the need for solace are at the heart of the piece, where Tilly's confinement to bed, and subsequent death, anti-cipates the dying bed bound Woman in Carr's most recent play, *Woman and Scarecrow* (2006). Just as the characters in *Ullaloo* reflect upon their unfulfilled ambitions and desires as they journey towards death, Woman, in the later play, contemplates her life: 'I look over the years and all I see is one wrong turn leading to another wrong turn. I cannot remember a moment when it was right.'[5] In *Ullaloo* the pair meditates upon the passing of their days together, and the approach of death: '*Tomred*: How long are we going to do nothing for?/ *Tilly*: You're only here for a little while, you'll be dead forever.'[6] In *Woman and Scarecrow*, Woman asks her soul or inner self, Scarecrow: 'Why didn't I have more sex when I could have?'/ *Scarecrow*: 'You were too busy hoovering. ... I was trying to prod you on, hoick you from this half existence.'[7] Similarly, *Ullaloo* portrays, at times, a suffocating immobility resonant of Beckett's theatre, where the present is arrested and it seems that the future will never appear. In Act One, Tomred asks the essential questions: 'Who am I? Why am I here? Where am I going? Will it ever end, and if so, When?' With his stunted toenails comes a desperate cry for action and renewal: 'Grow, grow!' he pleads.

Low in the Dark was produced by Crooked Sixpence Theatre Company at the Project Arts Centre in 1989, directed by Philip Hardy. Carr says 'This is a play with gender. I was trying to take stereotypes and clichés and have a romp with them.'[8] In this 'homage to Beckett', Carr replaces the traditional matriarchal space of the kitchen with the intimate, bodily bathroom and humorously undermines the traditionally sanctified role of motherhood in Irish culture.[9] The female characters, Bender and Binder, give birth continuously and indifferently. In Scene 5, *'Binder goes to the shower, throws three babies on Bender and sits with two, both breast-feeding. Curtains gets up and goes over to the shower. She grabs an armful of babies, and orchestrates the feeding of the babies. Soundtrack of babies gurgling and crying comes over.'*[10] In a later interview, the playwright says: 'I was tired of the sentimental portrayal of mothers.... We have this blessed Virgin myth imbedded in us, and there is some huge arrogance about carrying life and all the importance of it. They like to talk about childbirth, which is beautiful, but there is another side of it where it is mystery.'[11] In *Low in the Dark*, Carr hilariously parodies the rigidity of gender roles and the Roman Catholic hierarchy through absurdist strategies of carnivalesque excess, hyperbole, subversive humour, cross-dressing and role-play. The 'male' characters, Baxter and Bone, innanely build and rebuild the same wall while the 'women' knit a twenty foot scarf and back trayloads of buns. In Scene 5 of Act One, Bender looks for her baby 'the Pope':

> I'll feed him again. I want him fat and shiny. Holy Father, (*bows to the baby*) you'll pull your auld mother up by the hair of her chinny chin chin, won't you? We'll have tea in the palace and I'll learn Italian and the pair of us side by side, launching crusades, banning divorce, denying evolution, destroying the pill, canonizing witches.[12]

'Curtains' is the central storyteller in *Low in the Dark*, whose ongoing tale of an unnamed woman and man 'walking low in the dark through a dead universe' resonates with the disillusioned characters in *Ullaloo*.[13] In the earlier play, Tilly says: 'Maybe we should pretend to be dead for a while, we might get on better.' In Act Two she states: 'I wish we were dead', to which Tomred replies, 'I wish we were alive.' Throughout *Ullaloo*, the woman and man attempt to reconnect and rekindle the spark of their relationship as Carr acutely observes the painful emotional stasis of their long-term intimacy. This is echoed in *Woman and Scarecrow* when the unnamed man asks: 'So what were the last three decades about?' Woman replies: 'You and I? They were exile of course. Exile from the best of ourselves ... beasts in a cave with night coming on ... no way to live at all.'[14] *In Low in the Dark*, Curtains relates similarly how far apart the woman and man have grown on their journey:

> When we spoke, and it wasn't often, we spoke mostly of the landscape or of food. ... He no longer had words to describe that landscape and I had not the courage. So we lay there, side by side, like two corpses, horrified at our immobility. And if we merged, must've been by some accident. No passion there for a long time now. My eyes sought the ceiling above him, while his moved towards the back door.[15]

Both *Ullaloo* and *Low in the Dark* end on hopeful notes of possibility. In the final moments of the former play, Tomred says: 'I wouldn't have missed this.' While in *Low in the Dark*, the woman entreats the man to stay with her: ' "You", she said, "if you have courage get off your bicycle and come with me".'[16]

Carr's emergence in the late 1980s and early 1990s coincided with a major moment of visibility and presence for women in Irish culture and it is no accident that newly appointed President Mary Robinson attended the press reception of *This Love Thing* at the Project Arts Centre in Dublin in 1991. Sarahjane Scaife, who played Binder in the first production of *Low in the Dark* in 1989, reflects:

> I don't think I was conscious of it at the time, but retrospectively, the facts of Marina's sex and youth removed her from the traditional male hierarchy that had been predominant in theatre in Ireland. There were few prominent female playwrights in Ireland at the time. Theatre was run by men for the most part. Plays were directed by men and written by men.[17]

This Love Thing was co-produced in 'an unprecedented North/South collaboration with Dublin's Pigsback company' and Belfast's Tinderbox

Theatre Company in 1991, and was directed by Jim Culleton.[18] Derek West reports on this cross-border initiative in *Theatre Ireland*:

> From a meeting with the author came mutual agreement on the areas they wished to explore together. The process of evolution, which has been going on since the early summer of 1990, has consisted of workshops, improvisation, looking at paintings, playing games – every and any ploy to enable them to find the dramatic direction they seek. Jim [Culleton] is adamant that, after the work and several drafts, there will be a play and it will be Marina Carr's.[19]

In her speech at the Dublin premiere of the play on 27 February 1991, President Robinson celebrated the fact that this was a new play by a young woman. Unusually, the piece was reviewed mainly by women, all of whom enjoyed its energy and anarchic sense of fun. In *The Sunday Tribune*, Helen Lucy Burke picked up on Carr's instinct for language – 'there are signs of a gift for words, combined with bounce and confidence.'[20] A male critic for *The Irish Times* commented that the event surrounding the opening overshadowed the play itself and while holding off on fully praising the work, nonetheless conceded: 'Ms Carr demonstrates a fine sense of comic irreverence and anachronistic irony in her satire on contemporary relationships between the sexes.'[21] In *This Love Thing* historical figures such as Michelangelo, Leonardo Da Vinci, Eve, Mona Lisa, Jesus Christ and Mary Magdalene are coupled in a 'bitingly witty, at times hilarious' series of fast-paced scenes, where splendid Renaissance costumes and a set by Japanese designer Chisato Yoshimi added to the theatricality of the production.[22] Eve is a strong independent woman, who tolerates men purely for her own satisfaction. She dismisses them: 'I created God.... He was jealous of me.... You're all jealous of me as well! Of my power to create.'[23] The story of the Princess and the Gypsy King is reminiscent of the couples in Carr's earlier plays, and also anticipates the lyrical qualities of her later works: 'He rarely spoke, no longer sang and when she tried to teach him the songs and dances of the cage he had no desire to learn. "It's no use", he said, "You know I was born for the air, and the high wind, and the raven on my ear."'[24]

Tim Loane, co-founder of Tinderbox, commented of the process: 'The final script will evolve through rehearsals and exchange of ideas. But when it comes to putting pen to paper, it is the writer who has the monopoly. Nobody except Marina will actually write a single word.'[25] In terms of authorship, Carr has instinctively protected her position as playwright since the beginning of her career, at a time when very few women were seen to be writing for the theatre. Carr comments on Lady Gregory's lack of acknowledgement as co-author of *Kathleen ni Houlihan*:

> [It was] actually her play, which Yeats revised and then added the last scene.... she wrote the play and Yeats gave his name to it, and then took it over. Yeats called himself the author of *Kathleen ni Houlihan* in front of the public... Lady Gregory says it was particularly hard for her, but she let it go. I do not understand why she let it go, but that was another generation.[26]

Scaife recalls from rehearsals of *Low in the Dark* how 'even at that early stage in her career, Marina was absolutely sure of her theatrical voice.'[27] When *Ullaloo* closed early at the Peacock Theatre, Carr says: 'I went straight in to the Abbey. Garry Hynes was the artistic director at the time and I asked her for money [and] she said, "No, I can't give you money." I said, "Well, will you give me a commission or something," and she did.'[28] Carr then moved to the west of Ireland and wrote her break-through drama *The Mai*.

The house of woman

The second period of Carr's writing begins with *The Mai*, which premiered at the Peacock Theatre in 1994, in a production directed by Brian Brady with Olwen Fouéré playing The Mai and Derbhle Crotty playing Millie. While there is a significant shift in style and form from the early works, Carr's thematic explorations display a strongly organic development from play to play. In *Low in the Dark*, Curtains's story of the unnamed man and woman, and Tilly and Tomred in *Ullaloo*, now reappear in the tragic figures of Robert and The Mai, who move 'like sleepwalkers along a precipice' into further realms of alienation and emotional aporia.[29] In this lyrical memory-play, Carr excavates deeply embedded characters from the landscape of rural Ireland. *The Mai* is set in 1979 and presents the histories of seven Irish women (and a number of absent, dead women) spanning four generations, from 100-year-old Grandma Fraochlán, who was born post-Famine in 1879, to 30-year-old Millie. Carr says: 'The best writing is layer upon layer of detail.'[30] Here, traces of Hiberno-English, the Irish language and west of Ireland idiom and dialect delicately interweave with contemporary dialogue to reveal a linguistic palimpsest of folk memory, expressing the transition to modernity for women over the last century. Millie, the central storyteller, weaves the action through the filter of her memory, intro-ducing her mother and the house she built: 'The Mai set about looking for that magic thread that would stitch us together again and she found it at Owl Lake, the most coveted site in the county....And so the new house was built and, once she had it the way she wanted, The Mai sat in front of this big window here, her chin moonwards...'[31] Gaston Bachelard writes of the centrality of storytelling to the intimate process of remembering and spiritual refuge: 'If we have retained an element of dream in our memories, if we have gone beyond merely assembling exact recollections, bit by bit the house that was lost in the mists of time will appear from the shadow.'[32]

Carr's play shows the process of woman 'rehousing' herself through the act of creation and storytelling. The Mai, a 40-year-old abandoned wife, attempts to provide sanctuary and a space of artistic and imagin-ative possibility for her and her children, with music, books and 'a huge bay window' looking over the watery expanse of Owl Lake. *The Mai* has its origins in a short story, *Grow a Mermaid*, which earned Carr the prestigious Hennessy Literary Award for Best First Story in 1994. Here, a young child tells of when she saw an advertisement to send away to America for 'mermaid and sea-horse seeds. You put them into water and they grow and can even talk to you.'[33] In this tale of the child, her mother and 'Grandma Blaize', the imaginative seeds of Carr's theatrical voice are vividly evoked:

> The child's mother was building a house on the lake of the palaces. From the end of the field of their own house they could look across and see the new house. It was half way there now. The child wasn't to tell any of the Connemara click because they'd wonder where the money came from. The money was borrowed from four banks, the child's mother whispered, and when your daddy sees this house he'll fall in love with it, especially the music room, and he'll come back, for good this time. Some nights they'd talk for hours about how they'd decorate the house. 'Windows, windows everywhere,' the child's mother whispered in the dark.[34]

Grandma Blaize in *Grow a Mermaid* becomes Grandma Fraochlán in *The Mai*, and the child and woman become Millie and The Mai. In the story, Grandma Blaize talks to her ghost, just as the child talks to 'Pollonio', her fairy who lives down Mohia Lane: 'Grandma Blaize lay in bed fighting with the ghost of Syracuse. Propped by pillows, pulling on an opium pipe, she snarled at the ghost of Syracuse. "Gorgin' ya'ar gut was all y'ever done, ya *stroinseach* ya!" She takes another puff to calm herself down after this exertion. The ghost of Syracuse was the husband who stepped out the door one day "to get a breath of fresh air" and never came back.'[35] Carr's evocative mingling of everyday details – a blue formica table – with the otherworld, of mermaids, ghosts and fairies, emerges here with assurance, becoming one of the defining features of her dramaturgy. In the first edition of *The Mai* (Gallery Press, 1995), Grandma Fraochlán's speech is filled with the relics and spice of a bygone era, with expressive words such as *seafoíd* (rubbish) and *straois* (grimace), and where the *Inis Fraochlán* (island of 'heather' or 'fury') dialect and Irish language echo-chambers evoke Synge's abandoned women in *Riders to the Sea* (1904). Grandma Fraochlán remembers her fisherman husband who was drowned off the island 60 years previous: ' "*Is mise Tomás, scipéir, mac scipéara*" [I am Thomas, skipper, son of a skipper], he said. I knew where he was comin' from, wan sentence, wan glance a his blue eyes an' me heart was in his fist.'[36] Throughout the play Irish words form part of her emotional register: 'Ah Mai, great ta see ya, *a chraoí*' (love) and to her daughter 'Julie, *a stóir*?' (darling).[37]

The Mai emerged at a key juncture in Irish theatre and culture. It was four years since Friel's narrator Michael conjured up the '*five brave Glenties women*' in his memory-play *Dancing at Lughnasa*.[38] In placing a male narrator on-stage, Friel acknowledges that, for all its emphasis on women, the play 'is authored by a man'.[39] This was also a time of referenda regarding issues relating to sexuality and the family in the Republic. Divorce was not legalized when *The Mai* was first performed, homosexuality had only been decriminalized a year before, and abortion was unavailable (and remains so). Carr's multi-generational female space highlights the transitions which women have negotiated throughout the last century. Millie (whose age is split variously between 16 and 30) reveals how her Aunts, who were brought up in the 1930s, still adhere to De Valera's confining ideologies:

Two of The Mai's aunts, bastions of the Connemara click, decided not to take the prospect of a divorcee in the family lying down. So they arrived one lovely autumn day armed with novenas, scapulars and leaflets on the horrors of premarital sex which they distributed amongst us children along with crisp twenty-pound notes. Births, marriages and deaths were their forte and by Christ, if they had anything to do with it, Beck would stay married, even if it was to a tree.[40]

With Carr's next play, *Portia Coughlan* (Peacock 1996), comes a more intense and visceral assault on language and on the ways in which femininity has been constructed and represented in Irish culture and theatrical performance. Carr says: 'The early plays were absurdist; they were Standard English. The dialect came in with *Portia Coughlan*. It is an element of the way that people in the midlands speak...it is a created world we are finally talking about. It is inspired, certainly, by where I grew up.'[41] Moving from the house of her father to the adjacent house of her husband, Portia (played by Derbhle Crotty, see Figure 9) is a woman who ultimately rejects the socially prescribed roles of wife, mother and daughter, finding solace in the Belmont River. In the play,

Figure 9 Derbhle Crotty as Portia in the 1996 Abbey Theatre production of *Portia Coughlan* by Marina Carr. Peacock Stage. Photo: by kind permission of Amelia Stein.

Carr's linguistic inventiveness refuses standard English, imagining new modes of expression, just as the Belmont River overspills its borders in the world of the play. In Act One, Portia describes life at home with her husband, evoking the immobilized male and female pairings of Carr's early works:

> These days ah looches ah Raphael sittin' opposite me i'tha armchair. He's allas tired, hees bad leg up an a stool, addin' up tha booches from tha factora, lost in heeself, an' ah thinches tha pair of us migh' as well be dead for all tha jiy we knoche ouha wan another. Tha kids is aslape, tha house crachin' liche a choffin, all thim wooden duurs an' fluurs, sometimes ah chan't brathe anamore.[42]

In her troubled relationship with home, which she likens to being buried alive, Portia displays a painful manifestation of woman's exile from the Symbolic, which Luce Irigaray identifies as *dérèliction*.[43] Una Chaudhuri observes how 'the idea of home is deeply structured into the drama of this century, where (since at least *A Doll's House*) it exists in uneasy contention with the figure of the *house*. The painful noncongruence between the literal dwelling and the feeling of being at home provides early modern drama with its fundamental motivations.'[44] This sense of *dérèliction* is also echoed in the closing moments of *Woman and Scarecrow*, when Woman considers her final thought, 'What would it be...that I have never felt at home...here.'[45]

Portia Coughlan was commissioned by the National Maternity Hospital as part of its centenary celebrations and was entirely paid for by 89 high-profile women who each donated 50 pounds. Given that *Portia Coughlan* was conceived to celebrate this centenary, it is poignant that Carr deeply questions culturally inscribed ideals of motherhood in this work. In Act Three, Portia expresses her daily battle:

> Don'nen ya understan'! Jaysus! Ya thinche ah don wish ah chould be a natural mother mindin' me children, playin' wud thim, doin' all tha things a mother is asposed ta do. Whin ah looche at my sons Raphael ah sees knives an' accidents an' terrible muhilations. Their toys is weapons for me ta hurt thim wud, givin' thim a bath is a place where ah chould drown thim.[46]

A young woman in the 1990s, Portia Coughlan contrasts radically with passive and idealized images of femininity which present woman variously as symbols of nation, the maternal and the domestic. In 1997 Carr stated: 'I don't think the world should assume that we are all natural mothers. And it does.... The relationship between parent and child is so difficult and so complex. There's every emotion there. We mostly only acknowledge the good ones. If we were allowed to talk about the other ones, maybe it would alleviate them in some way.'[47] For Portia home is a space of disillusionment and limitation. She tells her Aunt about when she was leaving school: 'And I was going to college, had me place and all, but Daddy says no, marry Raphael.'[48] The position of women in the Republic of Ireland over the last 70 years has been officially located within the home since De Valera's 1937 Constitution where the words 'woman' and 'mother' are, to this day, used interchangeably. It is only now, in the twenty-first century, that the wording of the Family Article is under review to make it gender neutral. Article 41 states:

1. In particular the State recognizes that by her life within the home, woman gives to the State a support without which the common good cannot be achieved.
2. The State shall therefore, endeavour to ensure that mothers shall not be obliged by economic necessity to engage in labour to the neglect of their duties in the home.[49]

Maryann Valiulis describes how 'the ideal Irish woman was to be:

– the self-sacrificing mother whose world was bound by the confines of her home, a woman who was pure, modest, who valued traditional culture, especially that of dress and dance, a woman who inculcated these virtues in her daughters and nationalist ideology in her sons, a woman who knew and accepted her place in society [and] served the purposes of the ruling Irish male elite.[50]

Portia Coughlan opens to reveal the central character alone, in her nightdress, drinking brandy at ten o'clock on the morning of her thirtieth birthday; '*dishevelled and barefoot, staring forward*' with the curtains drawn.[51] Carr's disintegrated domestic scene challenges the rural idyll fetishized by De Valera in his 1943 address to the nation 'whose countryside would be bright with cosy homesteads [and] the laughter of comely maidens.'[52] Portia's plea for spaces of possibility beyond the monological discourse of home is expressed in her intimate connection with nature – 'the forty green fields... the mouths of the starlin's that swoops over Belmont hill, the cows [that] bellow... from the barn on frosty winter nights'.[53] She is compelled to the river bank to watch 'the salmon goin' up the river..., strugglin' for the Shannon, on up into the mouth of the sea and from there a slow cruise home to the spawnin' grounds of the Indian Ocean'.[54] Her love of the outdoors sets her apart from the other characters, who seem to have little interest in the local folktales and natural cycles. When Portia tells her suitor, Fintan Goolan, about how the river came to be named 'Belmont', after the River God Bel, he replies: 'Load of bollix, if ya ask me, them auld stories.... There's one story as interests me, Portia Coughlan, the story of you with your knickers off. Now that's a story I'd listen to for a while.'[55]

In *By the Bog of Cats*... (1998), a loose re-working of *Medea*, Carr explores the painful poetics of exile further. The award-winning play premiered on the main stage of the Abbey in 1998, directed by Patrick Mason, with Olwen Fouéré playing the role of Hester Swane. Hester, a landless Traveller, becomes homeless through the course of the drama, negotiating *in extremis* what Chaudhuri refers to as a 'geopathic crisis', a condition of ontological anxiety in relation to the ideological processes of home and dispossession.[56] Upon being forced to leave her community, Hester burns down the house of patriarchal order in the play. The domination of nature over socially prescribed structures is imagistically evoked when Hester says, 'only an auld house, it should never have been built in the first place. Let the bog have it back. In a year or so, it'll be covered in gorse and furze, a tree'll grow out through the roof, maybe a big bog oak. I never liked that house anyway.'[57] Hester's absent mother, 'Big Josie Swane', also a Traveller, disappeared without a trace from their caravan on the edge of the bog when Hester was seven years of age, further compounding the association of woman with displacement, exile and historical erasure.

Forging new rooms

While geopathy is synonymous with the crucial lack of accommodation of female subjectivity in each of Carr's plays in the 1990s, her most recent works are also concerned with the painful politics of location and selfhood, with an emphasis on both women and men in the rural familial setting. In *On Raftery's Hill* (Gate/Druid 2000), we remain trapped, along with the characters, within the walls of the single-set country kitchen.[58] In the final year of the twentieth century, this play is a radical rewriting of Gregory's and Yeats's *Kathleen ni Houlihan* (1902). A production of *Kathleen ni Houlihan* and *On Raftery's Hill* in repertory with cross-casting would powerfully foreground the dramatic resonances of these two works from either end of the twentieth century, enabling a disarming confrontation between past and present. Carr's play depicts the same country kitchen – '*setting: table, chairs, stairs, landing. Door stage right leads to yard. Door stage left leads to the pantry*'[59] and almost the same array of characters – a young couple about to wed, a father, a mother and an old woman. There is talk of land, money, inheritance and wedding clothes. In Carr's play the old woman, Shalome, is an exile within the home, repeatedly seeking futile escape across the threshold: 'Goodbye Raftery's Hill. I shall not miss you. . . . I shall never sleep in this house again.'[60] In the final moments of the drama the old woman reappears inside the kitchen in the soiled wedding dress of the young bride-to-be, Sorrel, inverting the actions of the Poor Old Woman in the earlier drama and refusing the myth of an idealized Mother Ireland.

On Raftery's Hill powerfully critiques the performative nostalgia of De Valera's 'cosy homesteads'. In Red Raftery's household, generational cycles of sexual abuse continue without intervention by Church or State. Carr draws a complex web of collusion and delusion in this work, where each character negotiates the suffering with which they are implicated behind closed doors, whether as perpetrator, victim or complicit bystander. Ded, the son, cannot bring himself to live in the house of his father, preferring instead to remain in the cowshed. He is described as '*a man in his mid-thirties, big-shouldered, long-haired, bearded, filthy; cowdung all over his clothes.*'[61] Ded's geopathy originates from the trauma of having been forced to help his sister Dinah give birth to their father's child, Sorrel, in the outhouse:

> I was the wan had to do ud all! Daddy came to me and he says, you're to go down to the cowshed wud Dinah. And I says Daddy I won't, I want to stay wud Mother, and he says, go now and do what you're tould. And there's blood and every fuckin thing comin ouh a Dinah. And I says Daddy I don't know what to do and Daddy says she's only calvin and I says I didn't want to be left wud her and he gives me a belt and draws me up alongside a hees face and says go now and do whah I'm saying and if ya ever spake of ud after I'll cut your balls off.[62]

Shortly before Sorrel is raped, 18 years later, by her father on the kitchen table, her betrothed, Dara Mood says: 'There's times I fear for ya in this house.'[63] The kitchen hearth, presented in Gregory's and Yeats's play as the feminized core, the womb of Ireland, is now irrevocably violated. The natural world offers no consolation (unlike Carr's earlier plays), where the inescapable stench of dead sheep and cattle 'maggotin in the fields' mirrors the inexorable suffering within the home.[64] The Poor Old Woman's 'four beautiful green fields' in the 1902 play are now unrecognizable.[65] Red Raftery is accused of destroying his land: 'Ud's not the hares has the land ruined and you wud a stinkin carcass in every field. You'll turn this beauhiful farm into an abattoir.'[66] Abuse is also rife in the local community. Dara Mood reports of a local girl, Sarah Brophy, who has dug up the body of her stillborn son in Clonloon cemetery. He says she was:

> Found be her father in the small hours, sittin on the coffin tryin to fade the child, couldn't say which a them bluer. Brophy throws hees coah over her and tries to take her home buh she refuses to go wudouh the child. Eventually they geh her into bed wud the corpse a the infant and she goes into some sourt a fih and dies this afternoon.[67]

Dara later recounts that Sarah Brophy's father admitted to raping her, 'thah he only ever went near her the wance', before killing himself.[68] While some audiences found Carr's play difficult to watch, it came at a time when, as Diarmaid Ferriter states: 'Greater openness about physical abuse, sexuality and public and political morality also facilitated discussion of dark pasts, as did wide-spread reportage of contemporary events such as concealed pregnancies, rape, corporal punishment and sex abuse.'[69]

Many critics have expressed discomfort and often derision that there are no 'positive' resolutions in Carr's plays from this period. However, in a society where historical processes of female oppression have only begun to be seriously acknowledged in the social, political and academic fora of the last decade or so, painful narratives need to be addressed before transformations can occur. With the unprecedented period of economic wealth at the turn of the twentieth century, it might seem on one level more apposite to pass over less appealing histories and present a society of equality, opportunity and vibrancy. The reality remains, however, that women are still underrepresented in the political and professional sectors and are still dealing with issues of pay inequality at a time when racism, suicide, sexual assault, filicide, the illegal employment and maltreatment of refugees and immigrants, and an overriding obsession with consumerism has never been more problematic.[70] As Anna McMullan observes: 'Carr's work suggests that, for the writer, and especially the female writer, the task of tearing apart the historical fabric of our appearances, articulating our exile, our displacements and the cataclysmic forces of our desires, is as important as celebrating our achievements.'[71]

Chaudhuri's concept of the geopathic crisis can also be considered in terms of the lack of accommodation of female authorship within the traditions of Irish drama. Cathy Leeney rightly states: 'Canons are formed and we are poorer for them. We have to move on from an idea of Ireland that is requiredly nationalist and masculine.'[72] Through the privileging of sites of myth and imagination, of lyricism and ghosts, Carr's plays reject the aesthetic of 'mimesis, [which] has maintained the hegemony of realism in representation', and which, as Lynda Hart observes, 'effectively masks the *re-creational* power of mimesis'.[73] In masking the processes of its own production, the cultural politics of realism/mimesis, proposes itself as an essential, almost pre- or trans-historic reality, eliding difference and privileging the patriarchal order. Carr's conceptual spaces of otherness forge rooms where enactments of alterity are possible and female expressiveness can begin to take place. In an essay on playwriting, Carr comments on 'the wisdom and the circumspection needed when dealing with the dead or the past, with memory, knowledge... I think to write like that shows incredible bravery on the part of the writer. It's about having the courage to sit down and face the ghosts and have a conversation with them.'[74] Director Garry Hynes says: 'Marina is one of those people who confidently walks down the road where other people are saying "Don't even think of going there." And Marina says "Of course. Let's go. Of course I'm going there."'[75] As we confront the ghosts of the twentieth century, Carr's fearless vision brings us forward to face the future.

Notes

1. Tom Mac Intyre, Program Note of *Ullaloo*, Peacock Theatre, 25 March 1991.
2. Program Note of *Ullaloo*.
3. Maria Kurdi, ' "I was tired of the sentimental portrayal of mothers": A Talk with Irish Playwright Marina Carr', *Modern Filológiai Közlemények 2003.V.évfolyam, 2. szam*, p. 95.
4. Mac Intyre, Program Note of *Ullaloo*.
5. Marina Carr, *Woman and Scarecrow* (London: Faber & Faber, 2006), p. 32.
6. *Ullaloo, This Love Thing* and *The Deer's Surrender* are unpublished and performance rights are unavailable. All quotations from *Ullaloo* used here are from the Peacock production archival video-tape which has some differences to the manuscript (No. 36,099/3/8), which is held by the National Library of Ireland.
7. Carr, *Woman and Scarecrow*, p. 50.

8. Marina Carr, unpublished interview with Melissa Sihra, Trinity College Dublin, 8 February 1999.

9. Marina Carr, unpublished interview with Melissa Sihra, Trinity College Dublin, 25 February 1999.

10. Marina Carr, *Marina Carr: Plays One* (London: Faber & Faber, 1999), p. 51.

11. ' "I was tired of the sentimental portrayal of mothers": A Talk with Irish Playwright Marina Carr', p. 99.

12. Carr, *Plays One*, p. 55.

13. Carr, *Plays One*, p. 59.

14. Carr, *Woman and Scarecrow*, p. 67.

15. Carr, *Plays One*, p. 95.

16. Carr, *Plays One*, p. 99.

17. Sarahjane Scaife, 'Mutual Beginnings: Marina Carr's *Low in the Dark*', in Cathy Leeney and Anna McMullan (eds), *The Theatre of Marina Carr:* 'before rules was made' (Dublin: Carysfort Press, 2003), p. 6.

18. 'Tinderbox: Jane Coyle writes on the young Belfast Company', *Theatre Ireland*, Vol. 25, Spring 1991, p. 20.

19. Derek West, 'Pigsback', *Theatre Ireland*, Vol. 21, Winter 1990, p. 21.

20. Helen Lucy Burke, 'A Jesus who refuses to become an Irish Catholic', *Sunday Tribune*, 3 March 1991.

21. David Nowlan, *The Irish Times*, 28 February 1991.

22. Madeline Keane, *Sunday Independent*, 3 March 1991.

23. Marina Carr, *This Love Thing*, manuscript, Linen Hall Library, Belfast.

24. Carr, *This Love Thing*.

25. *Theatre Ireland*, Vol. 25, Spring 1991, p. 20.

26. ' "I was tired of the sentimental portrayal of mothers": A Talk with Irish Playwright Marina Carr', pp. 96–7.

27. Scaife, in *The Theatre of Marina Carr*, p. 6.

28. 'Marina Carr in Conversation with Mike Murphy', Clíodhna ní Anluain (ed.), *Reading the Future: Irish Writers in Conversation with Mike Murphy* (Dublin: Lilliput Press, 2000), p. 55.

29. Carr, *Plays One*, p. 59.

30. Marina Carr, Public Lecture, Department of Classics, University of Oxford, APGRD, 16 November 2005.

31. *Marina Carr: Plays One*, p. 111. Millie was played by Derbhle Crotty and the Mai by Olwen Fouéré in the premiere.

32. Gaston Bachelard, *The Poetics of Space* (Boston: Beacon Press, 1994), p. 57.

33. Marina Carr, 'Grow a Mermaid', in Ciaran Carty and Dermot Bolger (eds), *The Hennessy Book of Irish Fiction*, (Dublin: New Island Books, 1995), p. 130.

34. Carr, in *The Hennessy Book of Irish Fiction*, p. 132.

35. Carr, in *The Hennessy Book of Irish Fiction*, p. 133.

36. Marina Carr, *The Mai*, (Meath: Gallery Press, 1995), p. 20.

37. Carr, *The Mai*, pp. 15, 35.

38. Brian Friel, *Brian Friel: Plays Two* (London: Faber & Faber, 1999), p. 1.

39. Anthony Roche, 'Women on the Threshold: J. M. Synge's *The Shadow of the Glen*; Teresa Deevy's *Katie Roche*; and Marina Carr's *The Mai*', in *The Theatre of Marina Carr*, p. 40.

40. Carr, *Plays One*, p. 135.

41. Ian Kilroy, 'Greek Tragedy, Midlands Style', *The Irish Times*, 2 September 2002, p. 14.
42. Marina Carr, *Portia Coughlan* (London: Faber & Faber and Royal Court, 1996), p. 15.
43. Margaret Whitford, *Luce Irigaray: Philosophy in the Feminine* (London and New York: Routledge, 1991), p. 205.
44. Una Chaudhuri, *Staging Place: The Geography of Modern Drama* (Michigan: University of Michigan Press, 1997), p. 49.
45. Carr, *Woman and Scarecrow*, p. 75.
46. Carr, *Portia Coughlan*, p. 42.
47. 'Marina Carr', Heidi Stephenson and Natasha Langridge (eds), *Rage and Reason: Women Playwrights on Playwrighting* (London: Methuen, 1997), pp. 150–1.
48. Carr, *Plays One*, p. 199.
49. Article 41.1 and 41.2, *Bunreacht Na hÉireann: Constitution of Ireland* (Dublin: Government Publications Sales Office), pp. 158, 160.
50. Maryann Valiulis, 'Neither Feminist Nor Flapper: The Ecclesiastical Construction of the Ideal Irish Woman', in Mary O'Dowd and Sabine Wichert (eds), *Chattel Servant or Citizen? Women's Status in Church, State and Society* (Belfast: Institute of Irish Studies, Queen's University, 1995), p. 178.
51. Carr, *Plays One*, p. 193.
52. Maurice Moynihan (ed.), *Speeches and Statements by Éamon De Valera, 1917–1973* (Dublin: Gill & Macmillan, 1980), p. 466.
53. Carr, *Plays One*, pp. 213–14.
54. Carr, *Plays One*, p. 218.
55. Carr, *Plays One*, p. 219.
56. Chaudhuri, *Staging Place: The Geography of Modern Drama*, p. 60.
57. Marina Carr, *By the Bog of Cats...* (Meath: Gallery Press, 1998), p. 63. Olwen Fouéré played Hester in the premiere.
58. The premiere was directed by Garry Hynes with Mary Murray playing Sorrel, Cara Kelly playing Dinah, Valerie Lilley playing Shalome, Tom Hickey playing Red Raftery and Michael Tierney playing Ded.
59. Marina Carr, *On Raftery's Hill* (Meath: Gallery Press, 2000), p. 13.
60. Carr, *On Raftery's Hill*, pp. 15, 16.
61. Carr, *On Raftery's Hill*, p. 13.
62. Carr, *On Raftery's Hill*, p. 48.
63. Carr, *On Raftery's Hill*, p. 33.
64. Carr, *On Raftery's Hill*, p. 19.
65. Augusta Gregory, *Kathleen ni Houlihan*, in Lucy McDiarmid and Maureen Waters (eds), *Lady Gregory: Selected Writings* (London: Penguin, 1995), p. 306.
66. Carr, *On Raftery's Hill*, p. 19.
67. Carr, *On Raftery's Hill*, p. 23.
68. Carr, *On Raftery's Hill*, p. 23.
69. Diarmaid Ferriter, *The Transformation of Ireland, 1900–2000* (London: Profile Books, 2004), p. 665.
70. In a feature in *The Irish Times*, 'Beyond Reason', 18 February 2006, Shane Hegarty reported that at least 16 children have been murdered by their parents in the Irish State since 2000.

71. Anna McMullan, 'Marina Carr's Unhomely Women', *Irish Theatre Magazine*, Vol. 1, No. 1, Autumn 1998, p. 15.
72. Cathy Leeney (ed.), *Seen and Heard: Six New Plays by Irish Women* (Dublin: Carysfort Press, 2001), p. vii.
73. Lynda Hart, *Making a Spectacle: Feminist Essays on Contemporary Women's Theatre* (Michigan: University of Michigan Press, 1989), p. 4.
74. Marina Carr, 'Dealing with the Dead', *Irish University Review*, Spring/Summer 1998, p. 191.
75. 'Garry Hynes in Conversation with Cathy Leeney', Eamonn Jordan, Lilian Chambers and Ger FitzGibbon (eds), *Theatre Talk: Voices of Irish Theatre Practitioners* (Dublin: Carysfort Press, 2001), p. 205.

Afterword: The Act and the Word

Olwen Fouéré

Actors are still categorized as mere interepreters within the artistic hier-
arachies of Irish theatre. Of course, many of us have bowed to that
definition and sadly trundle along, madly interpreting. I wonder why
that is. As an actor/actress – or dare I say it – as an artist, as one who seeks,
I am conscious that theatre demands everything of the actor's human
form. It demands everything of the body who acts and receives all the
knowledge we will ever need. The body is the delta, alpha and omega
of theatre and the actor's power resides there, free from the perceived
tyranny of the word. This is the task. It is as simple as putting words on
a page and it is not easy, as any writer will tell you.

A lot of things can get in the way. For instance, the idea that as I am
woman I am therefore called an actress. An Actress might be an icon,
languorous and eternally poised somewhere dangerously close to Sunset
Boulevard. She lives alone and remains forever exotic and unattainable.
There are times when I like that idea and court it for my own wicked
amusement. The idea that as an actress I am brilliant at displaying
emotion and can move an audience to tears, not to mention the nice
writer in the back row. Even the idea that this is perhaps an actress's
job, to be so 'moving' in the role that everyone says she really must play
Nora in *A Doll's House* or later even Medea so that she can demonstrate
her remarkable histrionic range – but mind, not too much rage, there
madness lies, keep charming the audience if you can and don't be too
'strong' or it will go against you. And don't be too intelligent when
you're being funny because otherwise it's not funny. I jest.

Even though she was very famous, I think of Sarah Bernhardt and her
wooden leg as one of us, sailing up the Lee to perhaps play *Hamlet* in the
Cork Opera House, and I feel blessed by the ascendent rythmns of her
voice on a salvaged recording of Racine's *Phédre*. I think of the glorious
and dangerous alchemy which is released in the roles of Hester Swane
and the Mai in the work of Marina Carr, work that blesses as it wounds. I
think of the artistic freedom of playing the ambivalently gendered roles
in *The Diamond Body* by Aidan Matthews and in *The Gospel according to*

Judas by Frank McGuinness. I think of the icy, passionate and manipulative Salomé, murdered for murdering her love.

All of the above died for their love. The man Hamlet, the woman Phedre, Hester Swane, the Mai, the hermaphrodite and his lover in *The Diamond Body*, Salomé, and poor Judas. Did you know he was a woman? He was. So was Tiresias. He was always both things. Blind and a seer. Male and female. Depending on the climate of the time. And he/she never seems to have died for long. She/he appears in so many plays and stories that he/she must have written her/his own script. He/she must have been an artist. Contrary to popular opinion, actors don't need a play to practice the art of theatre. It is a way of life. A lot of our work is about completely subverting the script. Many writers love us for it. It was fascinating for me to have an opportunity to play *Kathleen ni Houlihan*, the archetypal woman of Yeats's and Lady Gregory's Ireland. Fascinating to subvert the long-suffering image we have inherited of her. To unleash the seductive, manipulative queen with predatory desires running through the country of her body. She is a beautiful, thirsty and compelling vampire. Not unlike Gloria Swanson in Sunset Boulevard . . .

Appendix: Irish Women Playwrights

Date and place, where given, indicate first production.

Part I   1663–1980

1. Philips, Katherine: *Pompey* (1663, Smock Alley).
2. Centlivre, Susanna (? Co. Tyrone, ? 1667–1722): *The Perjured Husband* (1700, Drury Lane), *Love's Contrivance* (1703), *The Gamester* (1705), *The Basset Table* (1705), *The Platonic Lady* (1707), *Busie Body* (1709), *Marplot* (1711), *The Wonder! A Woman Keeps a Secret* (1714), *A Wife Well Managed* (1715), *The Gotham Election* (1715), *The Cruel Gift* (1716), *A Bold Stroke for a Wife* (1718, Lincoln's Inn Fields Theatre).
3. Davys, Mary (Dublin, 1674–1732): *The Northern Heiress* or *The Humours of York* (1716), *The Self Rival* (1725).
4. Clive, Kitty (Ulster, 1711–1785): *The Rehearsal* (1753).
5. Sheridan, Frances (Dublin, 1724–1766): *The Discovery* (1762).
6. Griffith, Elizabeth (1727–1793): *The Platonic Wife* (1763), *The Times* (1780).
7. O'Brien, Mary: *The Fallen Patriot* (1790).
8. Owenson, Sydney (Lady Morgan, 1776–1859): *The First Attempt* or *Whim of a Moment* (1807).
9. Le Fanu, Alicia: *Sons of Erin* or *Modern Sentiment* (1812).
10. Leadbeater, Mary (1758–1826): *Honesty is the Best Policy* (1814).
11. Balfour, Mary (Derry, 1780–1819): *Kathleen O'Neill* (1814).
12. Owenson, Olivia (Lady Clarke, ?1785–1845): *The Irishwoman* (1819).
13. Edgeworth, Maria (1767–1849): *The Absentee* (1812), *Love and Law* (1817), *The Two Guardians* (1817), *The Rose* (1817), *Thistle and Shamrock* (1817), *The Grinding Organ* (1827), *Dumb Andy* (1827), *The Dame Holiday* (1827).
14. Hall, Anna Maria (Dublin, 1800–1881): *St Pierre, The French Refuge: A Burletta in Two Acts* (1837), *Mabel's Curse* (1837), *The Groves of Blarney* (1838), *Juniper Jack* or *My Aunt's Hobby* (1845).
15. O'Brien, Charlotte Grace (1845–1909): *A Tale of Venice* (1881).
16. Riddel, Charlotte (1832–1906): *George Geith of Fen Court* (1883).
17. Milligan, Alice (Co. Tyrone, 1866–1953): *The Green Upon the Cape* (1898), *The Last Feast of the Fianna* (1900), *Oisín and Patraic* (1899), *Oisín in Tír na nÓg* (1900), *The Harp that Once* (1901), *The Deliverance of Red Hugh* (1901), *The Daughter of Donagh: A Cromwellian Drama in Four Acts* (1902), *Brian of Banba* (1904), *The Last of the Desmonds* (1905), *The Return of Lugh*(1909).
18. Gregory, Isabella, Lady Augusta (Galway, 1852–1932) selected plays: *Kathleen ní Houlihan* (1902), *Spreading the News* (1904), *Twenty Five* (1903), *Kincora* (1905), *The White Cockade* (1905), *Hyacinth Halvey* (1906), *The Gaol Gate* (1906), *The Doctor in Spite of Himself* (1906), *The Canavans* (1906), *The Rising of the Moon* (1907), *The Jacdaw* (1907), *Dervorgilla* (1907), *The*

Rougueries of Scapin (1908), *The Miser* (1909), *The Image* (1909), *The Travelling Man* (1910), *The Full Moon* (1910), *Coats* (1910), *Grania* (1910), *The Deliverer* (1911), *The Bogie Men* (1912), *Damer's Gold* (1912), *Hanrahan's Oath* (1918), *The Dragon* (1919), *The Golden Apple* (1920), *Aristotle's Bellows* (1921), *Dave* (1927).

19. Butler, E. L. Mary: *Kittie* (1902).
20. Mitchell, L, Susan: *The Voice of One* (1903).
21. Chesson, Nora: *The Sea Swan* (1903, with Butler O'Brien).
22. Varian, Susan: *Tenement Troubles* (1904).
23. Gonne, Maud (1865–1953): *Dawn* (1904) Published.
24. O'Dwyer, Delia: *All Soul's Eve* (1905).
25. Mulholland, Rosa (Gilbert, Lady) (1841–1921): *Our Boycotting* (1905).
26. McManus, L. Miss: *The Sun God* (1902), *O'Donnell's Cross* (1907).
27. Gore-Booth, Eva (Sligo, 1870–1928): *The Triumph of Maeve* (1902), *Unseen Kings* (1912), *Death of Fionavar* (1916), *The Buried Life of Deirdre* (1916).
28. Dobbs, Margaret Emmeline (1871–1962): *Memento, Lady Cantire's Courtship, The Way to Advertise, Cormac's Adventure*.
29. Letts, M, Winifred (1882–1972): *The Eyes of the Blind* (Abbey, 1907), *The Challenge* (Abbey, 1909), *Hamilton and Jones* (Gate, 1941).
30. Fitzpatrick, Nora: *Home Sweet Home* (1908, with Casimir Markievicz).
31. Tynan, Katharine (Dublin, 1861–1931): *The Stepmother* (1909).
32. Fitzpatrick: Kathleen: *Expiation* (1910).
33. Barlow, Jane (Dublin, 1857–1917): *A Bunch of Lavender* (1911, Theatre of Ireland, Hardwicke Street Hall).
34. Redmond, Johanna: *Honor's Choice* (1911), *Falsely True, The Best of a Bad Bargain* (1911), *Pro Patria* (1911), *Leap Year* (1912).
35. Scott, F, Molly: *Charity* (1911, Grand Opera House), *Family Rights* (1912, Grand Opera House).
36. Fitzpatrick, Norah (Mrs O'Hara): *The Dangerous Age* (1912).
37. Dobbs, Margaret: *She's Going to America* (1912).
38. Costello, Mary: *The Coming of Aideen* (1910), *The Gods at Play* (1910), *A Bad Quarter of an Hour* (1913).
39. Day, R, Susanne, and Cummins, Geraldine, Dorothy (selected plays): *Out of the Deep Shadows* (1912), *Toilers* (1913), *Broken Faith* (Abbey, 1913), *Fidelity* (1914), *The Way of the World* (1914), *Fox and Geese* (1917, Abbey).
40. Robbins, Gertrude: *The Home-Coming* (1913, Abbey).
41. Eaton, Florence: *Playing with Fire* (1913).
42. Kennedy, Mrs Bart: *My Lord* (Abbey, 1913).
43. Finny, Alice Maye: *A Local Demon* (1913).
44. O'Brien, Katherine (pseud. Fand O'Grady): *Apartments* (1913, Abbey).
45. Lloyed, J. W., Annie: *A Question of Honour* (1914).
46. Waddell, Helen (Tokyo, 1889–1965): *The Spoilt Buddha* (1915, Grand Opera House), *The Abbé Prévost*.
47. Leicester, Blanche: *Her Little Bit of Heaven* (1916, with Jackson Leicester).
48. Standish-Barry, Nellie: *An Irish Lead* (1916).
49. Carrickford, J. B., Mrs: *Willy Reilly and his Dear Colleen Bawn* (1916).
50. Shane, Elizabeth (Belfast, 1877–1951): *The Warming Pan*.
51. St Albans, Blanche: *Come Back to Erin* (1917).
52. O'Neil-Foley, Anastasia: *Father O'Flynn* (1917).

53. Burke, Una: *Newspaper Nuptials* (1917).
54. McKenna: Rose: *Aliens* (Abbey, 1918).
55. Casey, Sadie (Mrs Theodore Maynard): *Brady* (Abbey, 1919).
56. Walsh, Sheila: *The Mother* (1918, Queen's Theatre).
57. Macardle, M. C. Dorothy (1889–1958): *Atonement* (1918, Abbey), *Asthara* (1918, Little Theatre), *Ann Kavanagh* (1922, Abbey), *The Old Man* (1925, Abbey), *Witch's Brew* (1928), *Dark Waters* (1932, Gate Theatre).
58. Powell-Anderson, Constance: *The Courting of the Widow Malone* (1918), *The Curate of St Chad's* (1919, Abbey).
59. Callister, Christine: *A Little Bit of Youth* (1918).
60. Chavasse, Moireen: *The Fire Bringers* (1920, Abbey).
61. Purdon, Frances Katherine: *Candle and Crib* (1920, Abbey).
62. Donn Byrne, Dorothea: *The Land of the Stranger* (1924, Gaiety Theatre).
63. Travers Smith, Hester (née Dowden), and Cummins, Geraldine: *The Extraordinary Play* (1924).
64. Markievicz, Countess Constance (née Gore-Booth, 1868–1927): *The Invincible Mother* (1925).
65. Harte, Elizabeth: *Mr Murphy's Island* (Abbey, 1926).
66. O'Brennan: Kathleen: *Full Measure* (Abbey, 1928).
67. O'Leary, Margaret: *The Woman* (Abbey, 1929), *The Coloured Balloon* (Abbey, 1944).
68. O'Brien, Kate (Limerick, 1897–1974): *Distinguished Villa* (1926), *The Bridge* (1927), *The Anteroom* (1938), *The Schoolroom Window* (1937).
69. Uí Dhiosca, Una (Dublin, 1880–1958): *Cailín na Gruaige Duinne* (1932), *An Seod do-Fhágála* (1936).
70. Hughes, Isa: *Hollywood Pirate* (with Micheál Mac Liammóir, 1938, Gate).
71. Cregan, Máirín (1891–1975): *Hunger Strike* (1933), *Old John* (1936), *Curlew's Call* (1940).
72. De Valera, Sinéad (Dublin, 1879–1975): *Buaidhirt agus Bród* (1934).
73. Molloy, Maura: *Summer's Day* (Abbey, 1935), *Who Will Remember ...?* (1937, Abbey).
74. O'Neill, Davenport, Mary (Co. Galway, 1879–1967): *Bluebeard* (1933), *War, the Monster* (1949, Abbey), *Cain* (1945).
75. O'Callaghan, Maeve: *Wind from the West* (1936, Abbey), *The Patriot* (1937, Abbey).
76. Ellis, Hazel: *Portrait in Marble* (1936, Gate), *Women Without Men* (1938, Gate).
77. Rynne, Mary: *Pilgrims* (1938, Abbey).
78. Farrell, M. J. (Molly Keane or Mary Nesta Skrine): *Spring Meeting* (1938), *Guardian Angel* (1944, Gate), *Treasure Hunt* (1949), *Dazzling Prospect* (1961, with John Perry).
79. Deevy, Teresa (Waterford, 1894–1963) selected plays: *The Reapers* (Abbey, 1930), *A Disciple* (Abbey, 1931), *Temporal Powers* (Abbey, 1932), *In Search of Valour* (1934), *The King of Spain's Daughter* (Abbey, 1935), *Katie Roche* (Abbey, 1936), *The Wild Goose* (Abbey, 1936), *Within a Marble City* (c.1940s), *Light Falling* (Abbey, 1948), *Going Beyond Alma's Glory* (1949), *Wife to James Whelan* (1956), *Supreme Dominion* (1957).

80. Manning, Mary (Dublin, 1906–1999): *Youth's the Season-?* (1931, Gate), *The Storm Over Wicklow* (1933, Gate), *The Happy Family* (1934, Gate), *Voices of Shem* (1955, Poet's Theatre, Cambridge), *The Saint and Mary Kate* (Abbey, 1968).

81. Troy, Una (Elizabeth Connor, Cork 1910–1993): *Mount Prospect* (Abbey, 1940), *Swans and Geese* (Abbey, 1941), *Apple A Day* (Abbey, 1942), *Dark Road* (Abbey, 1947).

82. Kennedy, Margaret: *Autumn* (with Gregory Ratoff, 1941, Gate).

83. Gardiner, Mary: *The Ford of Farset, No Royal Road, The Right To Be Free, A Chain of Gold, Orpheus and Eurydice* (1943).

84. Bowen, Elizabeth: *Castle Anna* (1948, with John Perry).

85. O'Connor, Patricia (Norah Ingram, Donegal, 1908–1983): *Highly Efficient* (1942, Group Theatre), *Voice Out of Rama* (1944), *Select Vestry* (1945, Group Theatre), *Canvassing Disqualifies* (1948), *Master Adams* (1949, Group Theatre), *The Farmer Wants a Wife* (1955, Group), *The Sparrow's Fall* (1959, Group), *The Master, Who Saw Her Die?* (1957, Group).

86. Ní Ghráda, Máiréad (Co. Clare, 1896–1971): *Micheál* (1933), *An Uacht* (Gate, 1935), *An Grá agus an Gárda* (1937), *Giolla an tSolais* (1945), *Lá Buí Bealtaine* (Abbey, 1953), *úll Glas Oíche Shamhna* (Abbey, 1955), *Súgán Sneachta* (Abbey, 1959), *Mac uí Rudaí* (Abbey, 1960), *Stailc Ocrais* (1966), *An Triail* (Damer Hall, 1964), *Breithiúntas* (Abbey, 1968).

87. Longford, Countess, Christine Packenham (1900–1980) selected plays at the Gate Theatre: *Anything But the Truth* (1930s), *Queens and Emperors* (1932), *Mr Jiggins of Jigginstown* (1933), *The New Girl* (1934), *Stop the Clock, Lord Edward* (1942), *The Watcher* (1942), *The United Brothers* (1942), *Patrick Sarsfield* (1943), *The Earl of Straw* (1944), *Tankardstown* or *A Lot to Be Thankful For* (1948), *Mr Supple* or *Time Will Tell* (1949), *Witch Hunt* (1952), *The Hill of Quirke* (1953).

88. MacAdam, Nora (Nora O'Hare?): *Birth of a Giant* (Abbey, 1940), *Clever Lad* (New Theatre Group, 1943).

89. MacCarthy, B. G: *The Whip Hand* (Abbey, 1942).

90. Ní Shuilleabhain, Eibhlín: *Laistiar De nÉadan* (Abbey, 1944).

91. Travers, Sally: *Trilby* (with Micheál Mac Liammóir, 1946, Gaiety Theatre).

92. Shane, Elizabeth: *Time and the Dreamers* (1946), *A Night of Wind*.

93. Laverty, Maura (Kildare, 1907–1966): *Liffey Lane* (1947, Gate), *Tolka Row* (1951, Gate), *A Tree in the Crescent* (1952, Gaiety).

94. Lowe-Porter, Helen: *Abdication* (1948, Gaiety).

95. Fielden, Olga: *Three To Go* (Abbey, 1940), *Witches in Eden* (1948).

96. McClure Warnock, Anna: *Dinsmore's Cash* (Ulster Group Theatre, 1948), *The Wee Stones, The Things That Happen, Waiting for the Bus, Mrs Templeton's Tea Party, At The Dressmaker's, The Quilt, The Name of Christie, The Pessimist, The Minister of Second Drumawhoney, The Letter Writer, The Way To A Man's Heart, The Red-Haired Girl, Mrs McAllister Reads the News, The Way of a Woman, The Strategist.*

97. McNeil, Janet (Dublin, 1907): *Signs and Wonders* (1951, Ulster Group Theatre), *Gospel Truth.*

98. Hebe, Elsna (Dorothy Phoebe Ansle): *The Season's Greetings* (1957, Ulster Group Theatre).

99. Maguire, Pauline: *The Last Move* (Abbey, 1955).

100. Sadler, Joan: *The Mustard Seed* (1957, Group).
101. Maude, Caitlín (Conamara, 1941–1982): *An Lasair Choille* (with Michael Hartnett).
102. Swift, Carolyn (1923–2002): *The Lady of the Manor* (1963, Gate), *Lady G* (Peacock), *The Civilised Way of Doing Things*.
103. Kalka Cash, Geraldine: *The Red-Haired Man* (1958, Lantern Theatre Club, Dublin).
104. Daly, Anne: *Window on the Square* (1951, Abbey), *Leave it to the Doctor* (Abbey, 1959).
105. McKenna, Siobhán (Belfast, 1923–1986): Irish translation of G. B. Shaw's *St Joan* (*c*.1950), *Here are Ladies* (*c*.1960s).
106. Le Brocquy, Sybil: *A View on Vanessa*, (1967, Lantern Theatre Club).
107. Dillon, Éilís: *A Page of History* (1964, Abbey), *The Cat's Opera* (Peacock, 1981).
108. Charlton, Maureen: *Smock Alley* (1969, Gate), *Nora Barnacle* (1980, Eblana Theatre, Dublin).
109. Cahill, Helen: *The Doll in the Gap* (Abbey, 1973).
110. Bardwell, Leland: *Thursday* (1972), *Open Ended Prescription* (1979, Peacock), *No Regrets* (1983).

Part II Contemporary Women Playwrights

111. Anderson, Ioanna: *Words of Advice for Young People* (2004, Project Arts Centre), *Describe Joe* (2000, Andrew's Lane), *Why I Hate the Circus* (2001, Civic Theatre).
112. Anderson, Linda: *Charmed Lives* (1988), *The Flight Response* (1995).
113. Aron, Geraldine: *My Brilliant Divorce* (2001, Town Hall Theatre, Galway), *Mr. McConkey's Suitcase* (1977), *Micky Kannis Caught My Eye* (1978), *Joggers* (1979), *The Stanley Parkers* (1990, Druid Lane Theatre), *The Same Old Moon* (1984, Druid Lane), *The Donahue Sisters* (1991, Druid Lane), *Bar and Ger* (1975, Space Theatre, Cape Town/1978, Druid Lane), *A Galway Girl* (1979, Space Theatre/Druid).
114. Bannister, Ivy: *The Wild Circus Show* (1990), *Radical Changes*.
115. Barnes, Rosy: *Bimbo*, (1999, Andrew's Lane).
116. Barrett, Anne: *Shadowtackle* (1990, City Arts Centre, Dublin), *Chambers* (1995, Building Theatre, Ballina).
117. Barry, Alice: *I Like Armadillos* (1998), *Pam Ella* (2002, Draíocht).
118. Bartlett, Rebecca: *Shalom Belfast!* (2000, Belfast Royal Academy).
119. Binchy, Maeve: *End of Term* (Peacock, 1976), *The Half-Promised Land* (1979, Peacock), *Deeply Regretted By*.
120. Binnie, Jean: *Colours – Jane Barry Esq* (1988, Abbey).
121. Boyd, Pom: *Down Onto Blue* (1994, Project), *Boomtown* (1999, Meeting House Square).
122. Brooks, Laurie: *A Deadly Weapon* (1998), *The Riddle Keeper* (1996), *The Tangled Web* (2000), *The Lost Ones* (2005).
123. Buffini, Fiona: *The Crock of Gold* (2006, Olympia Theatre).
124. Burke-Brogan, Patricia: *Stained Glass at Samhain* (2002, Town Hall Theatre, Galway), *Eclipsed* (1992, Punchbag, Galway), *Credo, Requiem of Love* (2005,

Town Hall), *Yours Truly, Cell* (2000), *Ladies' Day, Clarenda's Mirror, Rehearsal for a Miracle, Boats Can Fly.*

125. **Burke-Kennedy, Mary Elizabeth:** *It's Called the Sugar Plum Daughters* (1976, Focus), *The Golden Goose* (1979, Focus), *Legends* (1981, Focus), *The Shape Shifter* (1980), *The Parrot* (1983, Mansion House), *Women in Arms* (1984, Ivernia Theatre, Cork).

126. **Burnett, Judith:** *So Much Water So Close to Home* (2001, Nero's Club, Kilkenny Arts Festival).

127. **Byrne, Mairead:** *The Golden Hair* (1982), *Safe* (1985, Project).

128. **Campbell, Síofra:** *Couch* (2000, Bewley's Café Theatre, Dublin).

129. **Carr, Barbara:** *Xaviers* (with Yvonne Morgan, Martin Maguire, Darren Thornton, 1999, Droichead Arts Centre).

130. **Carr, Marina:** *Low in the Dark* (Project, 1989), *The Deer's Surrender* (Andrew's Lane, 1990), *Ullaloo* (Peacock, 1991), *This Love Thing* (Old Museum Arts Centre/Project1991), *The Mai* (Peacock, 1994), *Portia Coughlan* (Peacock, 1996), *By the Bog of Cats …* (Abbey, 1998), *On Raftery's Hill* (Gate/Town Hall Theatre, 2000), *Ariel* (Abbey, 2002), *Meat and Salt* (Peacock, 2003), *Woman and Scarecrow* (Royal Court, 2006).

131. **Cartmell, Selina:** *Here Lies* (with Olwen Fouéré, 2005, Imperial Hotel, Galway).

132. **Caldwell, Lucy:** *Leaves* (2007).

133. **Charlton, Maureen:** *Berlioz and the Girl From Ennis.*

134. **Clamp, Paula:** *Jack's Too Open* (1997, Focus Theatre).

135. **Clarke, Angela:** *All My Worldly Goods.*

136. **Cluskey, May:** *Mothers* (Peacock, 1976).

137. **Coburn, Veronica:** *Blowfish* (2002, Ark Theatre), *Moby Dan* (2001, Project).

138. **Connolly, Maria:** *Massive* (2002, Errigle Bar, Belfast), *Bathtime* (2000).

139. **Corrigan, Briona, and Seaton, Zoe:** *The Pursuit of Deirdre and Grainne* (1999), *Wigs on the Green and Ja' Blades Flyin'* (with Robert Parry).

140. **Cronin, Maggie:** *A Most Notorious Woman* (1995, Garage Theatre).

141. **Crowley, Jeananne:** *Goodnight Siobhán, Pickled* (with Drina Kinsley, 1996, Bewley's).

142. **Cruise, Leonie:** *The Last of the Hair-Oil Lovers* (with Vincent Smith, 1980, Eblana Theatre).

143. **Cullen, Carmen:** *Class Acts* (plays for schools, 1994).

144. **Cullen, Sylvia:** *The Bee Woman, Broken Ground* (1996, Magners Theatre), *Flood* (1995, Project), *The Thaw* (1999, Tinahely Court House), *Crows Calling* (Firkin Lane), *Chrysalis* (City Arts Centre, Dublin).

145. **D'Arcy, Margaretta:** *The Non-Stop Connelly Show* (with John Arden, 1975, Liberty Hall), *Vandaleur's Folly* (with John Arden, 1978), *The Little Grey Home in the West* (1982), *The Pinprick of History, Women's Voices from the West of Ireland, Prison-Voice of Countess Markievicz.*

146. **De Fréine, Celia:** *Nara Turas é in Aistear* (1999), *Anraith Neantóige* (2004).

147. **Devaney, Pauline:** *To Marie With Love* (1989).

148. **Devlin, Anne:** *After Easter* (1994, RSC, The Other Place, Stratford), *Ourselves Alone* (1985, Liverpool Playhouse).

149. **Donoghue, Emma:** *Ladies and Gentlemen* (1996, Project), *I Know My Own Heart* (1993, Andrew's Lane), *Kissing the Witch* (2000).

150. **Dowling, Clare:** *The Marlboro Man* (1994, Project), *Leapfrogging* (1993, Project), *Burns Both Ends* (1992, Project), *Small City* (1995, Peacock).

151. Downes, Bernie: *Sick, Dying, Dead and Back* (1992, Project).
152. Doyle, Jackie: *The Chance* (2002, Stranmillis College, Belfast).
153. Dukes, Bríd: *The Saga of Snozzles* (1976, Project Arts Centre).
154. Egan, Karen, et al: *Lovely Betty* (2002, Bewley's).
155. Fannin, Hilary: *Doldrum Bay* (2003, Peacock), *Mackerel Sky* (1997, Bush Theatre), *Sleeping Around* (2002).
156. Feehily, Stella: *Game, Duck* (2003, Peacock), *O Go My Man* (2006, Royal Court).
157. FitzGibbon, Emilie: *Meal Ticket* (1989), *The Changeling* (1998), *Messer* (1989, Crawford Gallery), *Strong as Horses* (1985, Ivernia Theatre, Cork).
158. FitzGibbon, Sarah: *Jackie's Day* (1998), *Little Lou Tells a Story* (2002, Old Museum Arts Centre), *Rudie Bits* (2001), *The Hospital* (2003).
159. Flitton, Sheila: *Beezie* (1983), *For Better or For Worse* (1984).
160. Ford, Lin: *The Serpent Prince* (1971, Peacock), *Snake Eye and the Diamond* (1980, Peacock).
161. Forde, Patricia (with Rod Goodall): *Rhymes from the Ancient Mariner* (1996, Black Box).
162. Fouéré, Olwen (with Roger Doyle and Operating Theatre Company): *Angel/Babel* (1999, Project), *Chair* (2001, Peacock), *Passades* (2004, Digital Hub).
163. Gallagher, Mary: *Chocolate Cake* (1983, Peacock).
164. Gallagher, Mia: *Normality* (2001, Dublin Writers' Museum).
165. Gallagher, Miriam: *Fancy Footwork* (1983), *Dreamkeeper* (1984), *Omlettes* (1985), *Carolan's Cap* (1986), *Dusty Bluebells* (1987), *The Ring of Mont de Balison* (1988), *Nocturne* (1988), *Bohemians* (1989), *Easter Eggs* (1990), *Shyllag* (1993), *The Nude Who Painted Back* (with Mia Gallagher and N. Rafal, 1999), *Midhir and the Firefly* (2000), *Kalahari Blues* (2001, Parochial Hall, Clonmel), *The Mighty Oak of Riverwood* (2001), *The Gold of Tradaree* (2004), *Labels, The Sealwoman and the Fisher: A Play for Dancers*.
166. Grimason, Andrea: *Cupboard Love* (2005).
167. Grothius, Irma: *Getting 2 Level 10* (2001, Droichead Arts Centre), *To Be Queen* (2001, Project).
168. Halpin, Mary: *Shady Ladies* (1988, Abbey), *Semi Private* (1982, Gate Theatre), *Are You Listening to Me Gaybo?* (1997, Bewley's).
169. Haslett, Rosalind: *Still* (2002, Meeting House Square), *She Was Wearing* (2005).
170. Hayes, Catherine: *Skirmishes* (1992).
171. Hayes, Katy: *Playgirl* (1995, Peacock).
172. Hayes, Trudy: *Out of My Head* (1991, City Arts Centre), *Making Love To Yorick* (1998).
173. Hegarty-Lovett, Judy: *'Tanks a lot!* (with Raymond Keane, 2005, Project).
174. Henning, Jocelyn Ann: *Baptism of Fire* (1997, Townhall Theatre, Clifden).
175. Higgins, Rita Ann: *God- of- the-Hatchman* (1993, Taibhdhearc na Gallimhe), *Face Licker Come Home* (1991, Punchbag), *Colie Laly Doesn't Live in a Bucket* (1993).
176. Hines, Deirdre: *Howling Moons, Silent Sons* (1991, Project), *Ghost Acreage at Vixen Time* (1994, Project), *A Moving Destiny* (1996, Building Theatre, Ballina), *Dreamframe* (2000, Civic Theatre).

177. Holmes, Jill, and Seaton, Zoe: *I Can See the Sea* (1992, Riverside Theatre), *Little Lucy's Magic Box* (1990), *Crumbs* (with Kate Batts), *Twice Upon a Time* (1992).
178. Hooley, Ruth: *What the Eye Doesn't See* (1994, Old Museum Arts Centre).
179. Hynes, Garry: *The Pursuit of Pleasure* (1977, Fo' Castle), *Island Protected by a Bridge of Glass* (1980, Druid Lane Theatre).
180. Ingoldsby, Maeve: *The Bus* (with Philip Hardy, 2002), *Out of Line* (1994), *Tyrannosaurus Twerp* (1993, Project), *Earwigs* (1992), *Firestone* (1991), *Scaredy Cats* (1999, Watergate Theatre), *Silly Bits of Sky* (1998, Watergate), *Bananas in the Bread Bin* (1997, Watergate), *Digger, Doc and Dee Dee* (1996, Watergate), *Earwigs* (1992), *The Monkey Puzzle Tree* (1994), *Kevin's Story* (2001).
181. Jenkinson, Biddy: *Mise, Subhó agus Maccó* (2000).
182. Jenkinson, Rosemary: *Chocolate Madonna* (2002), *Bonefire* (2006, Project).
183. Johnston, Jennifer, selected plays: *Twinkletoes* (1993, Project), *Indian Summer* (1983, Lyric Theatre, Belfast), *Triptych* (1989, Peacock), *The Nightingale and Not the Lark* (1980, Peacock), *The Invisible Man* (1988, Peacock), *The Desert Lullaby* (1996, Lyric Theatre), *Moonlight and Music* (2000, Civic Theatre), *Christine* (1989, Peacock), *Mustn't Forget High Noon* (1989).
184. Jones, Marie, selected plays: *The Girls in the Big Picture* (1986, Ardhowen Theatre), *Somewhere Over the Balcony* (1987, Drill Hall, London), *A Night in November* (1994, Rock Theatre), *Stones in His Pockets* (1996, Rock Theatre), *The Hamster Wheel* (1999, Arts Theatre), *Women on the Verge of HRT* (1995, Rock Theatre), *Gold in the Streets* (1986, Arts Theatre), *The Terrible Twins' Crazy Christmas* (1988, Riverside Theatre), *Yours, Truly* (1993), *Don't Look Down* (1992), *Hiring Days* (1992), *The Cow, the Ship and the Indian* (1991), *The Blind Fiddler of Glendauch* (1990), *Eddie Bottom's Dream* (1996, Grand Opera House), *Ruby* (2000, Group Theatre), *Christmas Eve Can Kill You* (Lyric), *New Year's Eve Can Kill You* (Lyric), *A Very Weird Manor* (2005, Lyric).
185. Kay, Frances: *Burning Dreams* (1999, Samuel Beckett Theatre), *Pass the Parcel* (2001, Ark), *Bumbógs & Bees* (2002).
186. Keane, Dillie: *Boat People* (1984, Belltable Arts Centre).
187. Kearney, Oonagh: *Calling Hilary* (1998), *Urban Angels* (2001).
188. Kelly, Rita, E: *Cradlesong* (1982), *Frau Luther* (1984).
189. Kinahan, Deirdre: *Summer Fruits* (2001, Dublin Writers' Museum), *Passage* (2001, Civic), *Melody, Knocknashee* (2002, Civic), *Bé Carna* (1999, Andrew's Lane), *Attaboy, Mr Synge!* (2002, Civic), *Rum and Raisin* (with Alice Barry, 2003).
190. Kuti, Liz: *Treehouses* (2000, Peacock), *The Country Woman* (2000, Droichead Arts Centre), *The Sugar Wife* (2005, Project), *The Whisperers* (1999, Belltable).
191. Le Marquand Hartigan, Anne: *La Corbière* (1989, Project), *Beds* (1982, Damer Hall), *Le Crapaud* (1996), *I Do Like To Be Beside the Seaside, Strings*.
192. Linehan, Rosaleen: *Mary Makebelieve* (with Fergus Linehan, 1982, Peacock).
193. Looney, Fiona: *Dandelions* (2005, Olympia).
194. Lovett, Tara Maria: *The Call* (2002, Crypt Arts Centre), *The Suck* (2001, Project).
195. Lowe, Louise: *Tumbledown* (2005), *Hitting Home* (2005), *Xspired* (2006, Project), *Mind the Gap* (2006).
196. Lynch, Martina: *Tears from a Long Time Ago* (1991, City Arts Centre).

197. Lynch-Caffrey, Una: *No Chips for Johnny* (1982).
198. Magill, Rosemary: *Swags and Tales* (1995, Old Museum Arts Centre).
199. Mahon, Isobel: *So Long, Sleeping Beauty* (2003, Bewley's).
200. Mangan, Jo: *The Seven Deadly Sins* (with Tom Swift, 2003, City Arts Centre).
201. May, Ena: *A Close Shave with the Devil* (2001, Focus), *Out of the Beehive* (1984, Focus), *She's Your Mother Too, You Know!* (1989, Focus), *The Red Sandals* (2001, Dublin Writers' Museum).
202. McArdle, Kathy, and Ainsworth, Andrea: *Sisters and Brothers* (Peacock, 1999).
203. McBride, Celia: *Choke My Heart* (1998, Garter Lane Arts Centre).
204. McCafferty, Nell: *The Worm in the Heart* (1987, Project), *Sheep, Shite and Desolation* (1994, Project), *A Really Big Bed* (1995, Old Museum Arts Centre), *Bitter Fruit.*
205. McCartney, Nicola: *The Millies* (2003), *Heritage* (1998), *All Legendary Obstacles, Lifeboat.*
206. Mc Gee, Lisa: *Girls and Dolls* (2006).
207. McGill, Bernie: *The Weather Watchers* (2006, Ballymoney Arts Centre).
208. McGrath, Niamh: *Sarah's Comfort* (2005, Linenhall Arts Centre).
209. McGuinness, Eithne: *Typhoid Mary* (1997).
210. McIntyre, Clare: *Low Level Panic* (1991).
211. McKeagney, Orla, with Emily Thomas: *The Elves and the Shoemaker* (1995), *Rumpelstiltskin* (1996, Riverside).
212. McKenna, Jill: *For God and Ulster.*
213. McManus, Maria: *His n' Hers* (2005).
214. McMenamin, Patricia: *Façade* (1988, Belltable).
215. McNally, Mary: *Flaming Fables* (2004), *Anabelle's Star* (with Raymond Keane, 2002, Ark).
216. McNamara, Barbara: *Somwhere Between Frogs and Princes* (1981).
217. Meehan, Paula: *The Wolf of Winter* (2003, Peacock), *Mrs. Sweeney* (1997, Project), *Cell* (1999, City Arts Centre), *The Voyage* (1997, Ark), *Kirkle* (1995).
218. Moxley, Gina: *Danti-Dan* (1995, Project), *Tea Set* (2000, Civic), *Toupees and Snare Drums* (1998, Peacock), *Dog House, Marrying Dad, Swan's Cross.*
219. Muldoon, Kate: *Friends and Neighbours.*
220. Munro, Rona: *Bold Girls* (Peacock, 1992).
221. Murphy, Brenda, and Poland, Christine: *Forced Upon Us* (1999, Rock Theatre), *Working Class Heroes* (2002), *Binlids: The Story of West Belfast Resistance* (1997, Rock Theatre).
222. Mythen, Sue: *Stone Ghosts* (2001, Dublin Writers' Museum).
223. Neylon, Margaret: *Home From Home.*
224. Ni Chaoimh, Bairbre, and Quinn, Yvonne: *Stolen Child* (2002, Andrew's Lane).
225. Ní Dhuibhne, Éilís: *Dún na mBan Trí Thine* (1994, Peacock), *Milseog an tSamhraidh* (1997), *The Nettle Spinner* (1999).
226. Ni Domhnaill, Nuala: *Jimín, Destination Demain, Mysteries 2000* (1999, Andrew's Lane).
227. Nic Chionnaith, Siobhán: *Cúirt an Mhean Oíche* (after Brian Merriman, 1984, Peacock).
228. O'Brien, Edna: *A Cheap Bunch of Nice Flowers* (1963), *A Pagan Place* (1972, Royal Court), *The Gathering* (1974, Abbey), *Virginia* (1981), *Flesh and Blood* (1985, Cork Opera House), *The Wedding Dress.*
229. O'Brien, Lorraine: *A Different Rhyme* (1997, Peacock).

230. O'Carroll, Harriet: *A Bottle of Smoke* (1998, Belltable), *The Image of Her Mother*.
231. O'Connor, Bridget: *The Flags* (2006, Andrew's Lane).
232. O'Connor, Gemma: *SigNora Joyce* (1991).
233. O'Donoghue, Alice: *Boat People*.
234. O'Halpin, Siobhán: *Murruglach* (1999).
235. O'Malley, Mary: *Once a Catholic* (1978, Lyric Theatre), *Look Out – Here Comes Trouble* (Lyric, 1979), *Never Shake Hands with the Devil* (1990, Lyric).
236. O'Musoy, Ann: *Façade* (1982).
237. Park, Iris: *That Look* (1999, Bewley's), *A Blue Beats a Flush* (1999).
238. Porter, Cathy: *The Last Ones* (1993, Peacock).
239. Quill, Sian: *Scorpion*, (1993, International Bar, Dublin).
240. Quinn, Elizabeth: *Fanci Free* (1963, Belltable).
241. Rani Sarma, Ursula: *Wanderings* (2000, Granary Theatre), *Touched* (1999, Hillstreet Theatre, Edinburgh), *Gift* (2001, Belltable), *Blue* (2000, Cork Opera House).
242. Read, Michelle: *The Other Side* (2003, Project), *The Lost Letters of a Victorian Lady* (1996, Bewley's), *Romantic Friction* (1997, Bewley's), *Play About My Dad* (2006, Project).
243. Regan, Morna: *Midden* (2001, Traverse Theatre).
244. Reid, Christina: *The Belle of Belfast City* (1989, Lyric), *Tea in a China Cup* (1983, Lyric), *My Name, Shall I Tell You My Name?* (1989, Andrew's Lane), *Joyriders* (1986, Tricycle), *Did You Hear the One About the Irishman?* (1987, King's Head Theatre), *Clowns* (1996, The Room, London), *The Last of a Dyin' Race, Lords, Dukes and Earls*.
245. Roper, Rebecca: *Baggage* (1997, Bewley's).
246. Ryan, Judith: *The Going Away Present* (2001, Dublin Writers' Museum).
247. Seaton, Zoe: *The Water Babies* (1998, Riverside), *To Hell with Faust* (1998, Lyric), *Cuchulainn* (1995), *The Pursuit of Diarmaid and Grainne* (1999, Riverside), *Fish* (2000, Riverside).
248. Sedgwick, Lindsay Jane: *Trade Me A Dream* (1997, Focus).
249. Sheeran, Roisín: *Lunchtimes*.
250. Smith, Laura Lundgren: *Sending Down the Sparrows* (2002).
251. Strawbridge, Jacqueline: *Cracked* (2001, Mullingar Arts Centre).
252. Sweeny, Kate: *Navy Knickers and Other Hang-Ups* (1999, Garter Lane Arts Centre).
253. Traynor, Billie: *Redser* (2001, Dublin Writers' Museum).
254. Tuomey, Nesta: *Country Banking* (1982).
255. Walsh, Barbara: *Supermarket* (1982).
256. Walshe, Dolores: *A Country in Our Heads* (1991, Andrew's Lane), *The Stranded Hours Between, In The Talking Dark, The Sins in Sally Gardens*.
257. Winter, Brenda, school tours: *The Great I Am* (1994), *The Azoo Story* (1993), *The Little Wee Martian* (1999), *The Battle for Morrigan's Mound* (1996).
258. Winters, Carmel: *Time's Up* (with Patrick McCabe, 1992, Focus).

Index